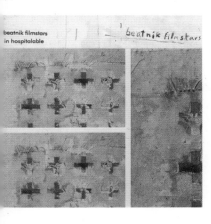

beatnik filmstars
in hospitalable

beatnik filmstars

CARIBOUandorra

WHAT EVERYONE
ELSE CALLS FUN

CAMERA
OBSCURA
UNDER
ACHIEVERS
PLEASE
TRY
HARDER

includes
SUSPENDED FROM CLASS
TEENAGER
BOOKS WRITTEN FOR GIRLS
KEEP IT CLEAN
LET ME GO HOME

THEROSEBUDSMAKEOUT

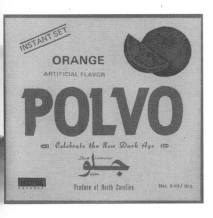

INSTANT SET

ORANGE

ARTIFICIAL FLAVOR

POLVO

Celebrate the New Dark Age

MERGE
RECORDS

Produce of North Carolina

Net. 5 oz / 142g.

THE
MAD SCENE

Chinese Honey

RADAR BROTHERS
AND THE SURROUNDING MOUNTAINS

portastatic

i hope
your heart
is not brittle

BUTTERGLORY

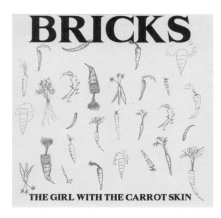

BRICKS
THE GIRL WITH THE CARROT SKIN

SPENT

ASHLEY STOVE
ALL SUMMER LONG

AMERICAN MUSIC CLUB
Love Songs for Patriots

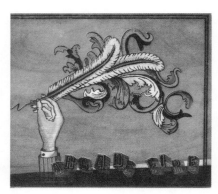

ARCADE FIRE

ANGELS
OF
EPISTEMOLOGY
Side 1
RESPONSE
THE CHARM
CARMEN MIRANDA, AT LEAST
Side 2
ANGELS DEATH SONG
TORTA DE LOS MUERTOS
VILE AND DISGUSTING
WILLIAM CAMPBELL

MERGE
RECORDS
MRG 006

GUV'NER
The Hunt

SPOON GIRLS CAN TELL

God Save The Clientele

THE
BROKEN
WEST
I CAN'T GO ON
I'LL GO ON

THE CLEAN
getaway

OUR NOISE

THE STORY OF MERGE RECORDS, THE INDIE LABEL THAT GOT BIG AND STAYED SMALL

John Cook
with
Mac McCaughan & Laura Ballance

Algonquin Books of Chapel Hill   2009

Published by
Algonquin Books of Chapel Hill
Post Office Box 2225
Chapel Hill, North Carolina 27515-2225

a division of
Workman Publishing
225 Varick Street
New York, New York 10014

Funeral review, pages 251–253, reprinted with permission from *Pitchfork*.

Frontispiece: The lyrics to "My Noise," handwritten by Mac and framed by Phil Morrison.

Library of Congress Cataloging-in-Publication Data

Cook, John, 1973–
   Our noise : the story of Merge Records, the indie label that got big and stayed small /
by John Cook with Mac McCaughan and Laura Ballance.—1st ed.
       p. cm.
   ISBN 978-1-56512-624-4
   1. Merge Records—History. 2. Alternative rock music—United States—History and criticism.
I. McCaughan, Mac. II. Ballance, Laura. III. Title.
   ML3792.M47C66 2009
   338.7'6178164—dc2

                                                2009012495

10 9 8 7 6 5 4 3 2 1
First Edition

Contents

Go to www.mergerecords.com/ournoisesampler to listen to songs from Merge artists past and present.

Your Noise—My Noise!!!

by Ryan Adams

All my favorite records and your records crackle like summertime crackles like fried eggs stove-side or accidental fireworks backyard heavy in North Carolina on the coast—mid-day it gets so hot even inside, in the cool, the blazing waves of electric orange light pant like a litter of starving dogs just outside the gate—yeah, sometimes you just need comics or records to get you through until the dust settles and the damp evening can cool your brains down enough to see past your own stupid face. That was me. Me looking at my first 7-inch record. I was all "what" and "huh," you know....

Merge 7-inch singles came packaged like candy. They also looked a little like comics, which was good because I liked both and I liked girls so much they scared me so it all seemed like the perfect distraction, at least to me, and surely to my grandmother, who would patiently listen with me on our portable record player in the wood-paneled kitchen while she baked this or that cake or whatever—she liked how much cymbal crashing was going on—somehow overlooking the melodic weirdness or angst, how forgiving and awesome those moments—in fact before I had money for records she would write the checks and mail them for each PO-boxed 7-inch I desired in exchange for however many times the lawn got mowed but I did that anyway so really she funded my habit, embarrassingly, and MY GOD at first they were so pretty I could do nothing less than just marvel at each one—SO BEAU-TIFUL—Erectus Monotone—"CATHODE GUMSHOE"—probably the best THE BEST record I own besides this super-duper warped-ass copy of Greg Sage's "Straight Ahead" but whatever, right? Exactly.

I used to think to myself, WHO ARE THESE PEOPLE? WHO ARE THEY and ARE THEY REAL? Also, CAN THEY ACTUALLY BE North Caro-linian? I loved PURE so so much too. The "Ballard" EP is insanely classic stuff. I hunted forever for these people and their stories. I wanted to be inside that dream. I was having such an awful time growing up in the coastal lurch of Onslow County. I started making plans in my mind, in school, for taking off on the weekends for shows (my brother was in Raleigh attending college and would bring me news of bands in Chapel Hill and Raleigh and FLYERS—HELL YES!!! All over my room!!!) and I got closer and closer to these people making this mysterious candy with the petroleum shiny insides. And at my best, I would try and be as engaging as the Merge music candy packages all the way down to the little notes xeroxed on colored paper inside. I loved those fucking Mac notes. It was later I realized it was the same Mac as the guy in WWAX. NO WAY—

EVERYBODY had their crushes on Laura. I mean, guys did. And ALL THOSE GIRLS they loved Mac. And you know, they were these sophisticated weirdos living in Chapel Hill, that "pretty" college town. I eventually left home (long story) and I lived in Raleigh and, well, we were supposed to be "working class" musicians or something—we were supposed to have issues with the Chapel Hill scene. It was totally unspoken but it was all right there—written on the faces of all our local musicians and I think I saw a lot of envy by the time I got to Raleigh. I mean, I came late. I crawled from the wreckage of the crystal coast— the graveyard of the Atlantic, all water-logged and salt heavy—tears in my eyes. I just wanted to SEE all this music get made. I ended up making just a little myself. Most of it as a way to understand this music

I loved and just how much went into making it. The rest happened the way night comes, the way a reed bends in the humidity and how dust gathers where you can't reach it.

Merge singles never worked like that. I mean, I still look at them and think, "what exactly is this" or I think, "God—what if everyone could have the experience of living in a place so isolated from everywhere and KNOW this came from only a few hours away." I mean, it was a dream. A hot dream.

I first heard Mac sing when I stopped by a friend's house, a guy that lived a block from me in my neighborhood nightmare 1980s mall theme-park world, to record more of his badass mail-order *FLIPSIDE* magazine–sponsored singles. I was over to get a few cassette burnoffs of a few Japanese thrash bands and the new Seaweed. Gosh I loved Seaweed. And there was this single. My pal said, "Hey man, I got this and it's a bit melodic for my taste but I think you would really love this."

It was WWAX, "Pumpkin"/ "Inntown." I took the single home and busted it out on my Barbie-themed little record player (now covered in thrasher magazine stickers)… I probably stared holes through the universe trying to understand how much I loved it. I actually CARRIED IT TO SCHOOL hahahahaha, a record, a 45-rpm single, in my backpack to ensure nothing NOTHING would ever ever ever happen to it.

When I finally made my first record, as in my first real album for a real major label (a no-no where I come from, at least the scene I had come from), I named the first song after that song—the very song that made me want to make any music at all, really.

So the bands envied Superchunk (of course) because Superchunk were effortlessly great. They weren't trying to be anyone. So ALL these bands started little 7-inch companies and "didn't try" the way Superchunk didn't have to and a whole scene of, well, just posers trying not to pose happened. All you needed was a RAT pedal and an attitude.

And all the guys, the guitar guys, the band guys, they would basically all line up at SChunk shows and pretend not to drool over themselves at how badass Laura was. I mean, I used to listen to conversations about Mac and Laura at our local AWFUL—I mean terrible—

coffee house; people saying things like, "They went to college, totally left the state" and "Really?" and "Yeah like in New York." HAHA—wtf? People were afraid of that. Strangely, an entire scene was nourished in this little GIGANTIC beautiful little time and I saw some of the most amazing bands (POLVO, SEAM, ERECTUS MONOTONE, FINGER, BREADWINNER), shows, and records come out as my whole world developed before me like a little series of Polaroids if they made sugary noise and rattled into the sparkling cloudless night sky—I was, and they all seemed to be, hovering just there—and everything felt clean and just rang for an entire four years.

When I left North Carolina Superchunk and Merge had become names muttered easily after Chapel Hill or the Triangle (three cities of colleges, three scenes, people called it that—too much breaded food, not enough coffee) and I left with a crate of records and a boxed heart bowed with electric guitar cable static and radio frequency shards.

I am really lucky to write this. I remember the day I sauntered up to Mac. I was seventeen years old. He sat on the edge of the stage at a Dinosaur Jr. / Finger concert at the Cat's Cradle. I was seriously starstruck but so young and totally naive as to how to appropriately talk to someone who represented so much to me. I walked up, introduced myself, and slowly but surely asked him a million questions. I admired his industriousness, his nobility, and his pure shining poetic heart—and he had the coolest band, the coolest girlfriend and business partner— Mac was someone I could learn from. And I got lucky. He answered them all right there as I asked. I was blown away, and just lucky.

Merge, Mac, and Laura are still out there answering all my questions about following your gut and making things new with each turn and following the muse all the way. Over the years I keep running into Merge bands in New York City, even sometimes seeing Mac here and there, hell even last year at RADIO CITY MUSIC HALL, I mean, wow, for the Arcade Fire—who more or less blew my entire mind in THE SAME WAY, man, that seeing Polvo and Seam at the older Cat's Cradle had when Mac was on drums. There he was again—that guy—and he just had nothing but nice things to say and a big hello. Hell he even answered a few more of my nagging "How did ya's."

People just never know how much that really means to you when you just love what someone does.

Merge rolls non-hostile.

I am really thankful for each new treasure they come around with. I love how unpretentious their whole scene is, how they rescued so many Homestead Records bands from obscurity—how they put out the HONOR ROLE CD even though they probably knew that record mattered only to a handful of heart-weary fans like me. Damn, man.

Also I am super lucky they didn't beat me up for stealing their album title "Come Pick Me Up."

I will always be a sucker for Merge and I will be that guy in the front row at the shows with all the questions, beaming—inspired—over the moon—with this little bee in my hat, knowing that something so great, greater than my imagination, like a perfect teenage dream shining so bright and so hard so easily, could come from my home state where everything moves at a pace slower than afternoon naps with a face full of orange ride maze hot yellow light.

Rock on, Merge! Happy 20th. Keep it coming!

Mac and Jonathan Neumann in high school, 1984.

Claire Ashby in the Angels of Epistemology.

Honor Role, circa 1988.

Left to right: Ethan Smith, Wwax's Wayne Taylor, and Brian Walsby with Reed Mullin of Corrosion of Conformity (bending over) in the summer of 1985.

Laura in her goth years.

Slushpuppies flyer from 1987.

Laura's first bass guitar, a short-scale Fender.

Angels of Epistemology promo photo, 1987.
From left: Bill Mooney and Rob Stewart (who were not in the band), Mike Carter, Sara Bell, and Jeb Bishop.

Mac and Brian Walsby in Wwax.

Flyer for a 1986 COC show with the Slushpuppies.

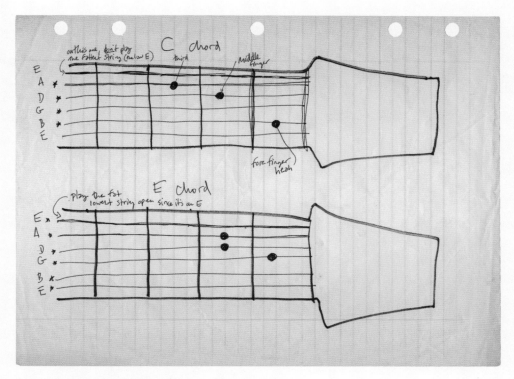

Chord chart Mac made for Amy Saaed, Laura's roommate, in the late 1980s.

Laura and Sam Mauney (Days Of…) in 1986.

Zen Frisbee, with Chuck Garrison on drums.

Typical Carrboro house party in 1992. Spott is second from left;
Garrison is fourth from left.

Bricks at a house party in Fairfield, Conn., 1989. Left to right: Laura Cantrell, Josh Phillips, Mac, Jim Wilbur (holding cup), Andrew Webster, and Mahinder Kingra.

Chunk flyer, August 1989.

Bricks and Fugazi flyer, March 1990.

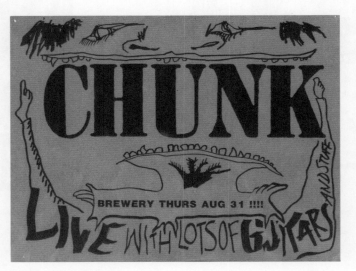

Erectus Monotone.
Left to right: Andy Freeburn, Caspar Lee, Jennifer Walker, and Kevin Collins.

Insert for the first Angels of Epistemology 7-inch on Merge.

Chunk flyer, August 1989.

AUBREY DEAR ———→

Well I trust you had a tolerably joyous Christmas season — it is now February and unseasonably warm here in the Big Apple. We haven't had shit for snow this winter, either, and I think I've contracted mid-winter's depression. My semester is easy — 13 points, 3 of which are woodcut, but I can't bring myself to do any of it; even woodcut is frustrating. I'm sure I'll come out of it, even if it's not 'til May. My vacation was awesome and the lovely Laura Ballance (included here balanced on a trash can in Nevada) and I got along famously for a change (last semester was kind of rough). Well, I had a record deal with Homestead Records, but it seems to have fallen through because Gerard (head honcho) has left the label. He's a cool guy and still wants to put out the albums (Bricks, Superchunk, Wwax, and a compilation of bands I've been in) but is not sure where, so I'm kind of in limbo at the moment, we'll see. MERGE Records is coming along fine, however, and we've sold out of about everything so far. The 'BRICKS 7" is coming out soon, if Josh hasn't already told you. Nils will get some at his store if we don't happen to send you one (we're low on promos). I was sad not to see your beautiful self more when you were here, maybe next time if you visit this spring. I'd love to come out there, as would Laura I'm sure, but
Q: when will I have money? A: never. Anyway, I gotta go to class (remember that?) so enjoy these fotos. Write back soon / I won't hold my breath...
                                Love,
                                MAC

P.S. the Christmas card was awesome

A February 1990 letter from Mac to Aubrey Summers.

Superchunk in the early 1990s.

Tourist coin that Mac, Laura, and Aubrey Summers bought at the Space Needle during their 1989 road trip to Seattle.

date sent:

date ordered:

MERGE

SHIP TO:

R E C O R D S

BILL TO:

P.O. Box 1235
Chapel Hill, NC 27514
(919)-929-0711

Qty Ord	Qty Sent	Description	Price/ Item	Qty . price
Tot Item Sent			Subtotal	
			Shipping	
			Total Due	

note:

Merge's first invoice form, made by Laura on her typewriter.

Superchunk at O'Cayz Corral, Madison, Wisc., 1990.

Mac in 1990.

Death Chick and the Caveman

1987 to 1989

It's summer. The days are soggy and long in Chapel Hill, and the University of North Carolina kids have gone home to wherever they're from, leaving Franklin St. to revert to its native torpor. At night the bars are emptier, and the insects, emboldened by the heat and still air, are louder and more insistent.

It's always summer with Merge. Aside from three crucial, bitter-cold days in the dead of a Minnesota winter, Merge's story could almost be told in summers. It was conceived in the summer and born in summer; its birthdays, when it stands up in the kitchen doorway to have its height marked off in pencil, have always been celebrated late and long on summer nights at the Cat's Cradle. So many of the songs that define Merge are hymns to summer, to staying up late and sweating and leaving the windows open. So many of the records are the kind, in the words of cofounder Laura Ballance, that you can spend a whole summer listening to.

The summer in question is the summer of 1987. Ronald Reagan has just nominated Robert Bork to the Supreme Court, and Guns 'n' Roses has released *Appetite for Destruction*. And

Mac McCaughan, a scrawny, dreadlocked nineteen-year-old, has moved to Chapel Hill after deciding to take a year off from his studies at Columbia University. Mac had been raised in a genteel neighborhood in nearby Durham; his father, an attorney for Duke University, moved the family there from Florida when Mac was twelve. Mac had always been fanatical about music. At first it was Big Rock: AC/DC, the Who, Led Zeppelin, Molly Hatchet, the sort of bands who looked like little miniature animatronic figurines from the upper deck at your friendly neighborhood amphitheater. To Mac, they were like cartoons, or characters playing themselves in a movie. Then one day in his early teens, intrigued by a flyer he saw at his high school, he caught two local hardcore bands, the Ugly Americans and A Number of Things, at a coffeehouse. That was different. There was noise, and speed, and aggression, and slamdancing. He wasn't sitting in a chair, apart from the band, admiring a lightshow. He was standing right in front of them.

He went to Schoolkids, a record store in Chapel Hill, and bought records by bands that he'd been hearing on the local college radio station and reading about in *Rolling Stone*: Hüsker Dü's *Zen Arcade*, the Minutemen's *Double Nickels on the Dime*, and Minor Threat's *Out of Step* EP. He saw the Minutemen play in the basement of a church. They carried their own gear and sold their own T-shirts after the show. AC/DC was cool, but this was real.

Mac has a way of meeting the people he wants to meet. He eventually wound up playing guitar in A Number of Things. But before that, he started his own high school band, the Slushpuppies, with his friend Jonathan Neumann playing drums. Mac and Jonathan learned that they weren't too bad at aping the sounds of all these new records that they loved.

When he went to Columbia in 1985, Mac papered his dorm-room wall with flyers and show posters. New York was great for seeing bands — Sonic Youth, the Damned, Mudhoney, Big Black, the Replacements — but lousy for being in one. There was no place to practice, no one to play with. You had to haul instruments around on the subway. He wanted to play with his friends, who'd stayed down South.

So in the summer of 1987, Mac took a year off and came home to live in a dingy rental house in Chapel Hill.

Laura Ballance lived in Chapel Hill, too. She had just finished her freshman year at UNC. Laura's parents moved her around a lot as a kid; she was born in Charlotte, and had lived in Atlanta for a few years before spending her last year of high school in Raleigh. Laura was a goth girl — dark, painfully shy, a little bit lost, and prone to crippling self-doubt. She was also beautiful and, with her severe black makeup and combat boots, cut an intimidating figure on campus. She kind of scared people.

In Raleigh, Laura had fallen in with the hardcore crowd. One of the first concerts she ever went to was Bad Brains in Atlanta. She didn't know anything about hardcore, and it was overwhelming and loud and frightening. She had to concentrate on breathing amid all the chaos and aggression. But she always felt like an outsider, and her friends were all outsiders, so she started hanging out at Atlanta's Metroplex with skinheads and catching shows.

Raleigh and Chapel Hill are just a short drive apart, but they had very different scenes. Raleigh was dark, angry, and punk — more leather jackets and houses with spray paint on the walls. Chapel Hill was collegiate and hip. Laura was a Raleigh girl. She started dating Scott Williams, the lead singer of Days Of . . . , a hot-shit Raleigh punk band that was starting to graduate from the loud-fast-hard approach and incorporate a few of the angst-ridden adolescent tricks that later would come to be known as "emo." Williams was a little bit older, and knew just about everybody in the Raleigh hardcore scene. When Black Flag came through town on tour, they crashed at Williams's house on Ashe Avenue, known as the "Ashe-hole" for its rundown appearance and frequent parties.

L.A. and Washington, D.C., are usually credited as the prime generators of the do-it-yourself hardcore movement that proved to a generation of disaffected kids that making music, and records, was within their grasp. But Raleigh had its own roiling scene in the eighties, anchored by Corrosion of Conformity, a blazingly fast, angry-sounding band of high school kids founded in 1982. COC, like their inspirations Black Flag and Minor Threat, didn't believe in waiting around for someone with money to tell them that it was okay for them to make records. And as Black Flag and Minor Threat sold their self-made EPs and 7-inches, so COC began to organize compilations of local hardcore bands, which they released on their own No Core label. They started touring on their own, just because they could.

Raleigh was home to an ever-shifting con-stellation of bands, usually sharing members, practice spaces, and even instruments, and COC served as an example to anyone who was paying attention that making noise wasn't rocket science. Though their music was violent and dark, they made a habit of being inclusive and encouraging to anyone else who wanted to join in. They played at house parties or at dives, generating plenty of chances for lesser-known local hardcore bands to open the show and gain an audience. Drummer Reed Mullin's parents had an office space in downtown Raleigh that was open to anyone who needed to use the copy machine to run off flyers for their show, or the telephone to make long-distance calls to clubs to set up a tour. Whenever a hardcore show was going on, he'd drive a circuit through Raleigh, Durham, and Chapel Hill in his van, offering a ride to anyone who needed one. They didn't just want to be in a band. They wanted to build a community.

By the mid-1980s, that community found itself growing up. Hardcore started to sound formulaic, and bands like R.E.M. and Sonic Youth demonstrated that the spirit of independence and casual rejection of mainstream tastes could be accomplished without tossing nuance and melody out the window. By 1986 or so, a legion of COC acolytes had begun to branch out. Stillborn Christians' Jeb Bishop veered toward carnivalesque retropop with Angels of Epistemology, which included Sara Bell and Claire Ashby, high school classmates of Mullin. No Labels' singer Wayne Taylor, whose hardcore credentials went all the way back to opening for the Dead Kennedys, picked up a bass guitar for the first time and started playing angular, unconventional pop in Wwax.

So it's the summer of 1987. Mac and Laura both find themselves in Chapel Hill.

Claire Ashby (Angels of Epistemology and Portastatic; Superchunk merch girl)
The music scene was so small then. Raleigh was like Mayberry. The Raleigh and Chapel Hill and Durham people all knew each other.

Barbara Herring (Cofounder of Tannis Root productions, a Raleigh indie-rock T-shirt company) If there was a show of any kind, anywhere, around Chapel Hill or Raleigh, everybody went. All fifty people that were interested in that music.

Scott Williams (Days Of..., Garbageman, and -/-) But those fifty people *wanted* to be there. And those were the people that went on to be in the early Merge bands.

Jack McCook (Superchunk) When he came back to Chapel Hill, it was like "Mac's back! Mac's back!" That kind of thing. I thought, "Who is this little fucker?" You know?

Glenn Boothe (Former music director for UNC's college station, WXYC; former A&R and radio promotion manager for Island Records, Sony, and Caroline Records; currently owns Chapel Hill club Local 506) I met Mac one night at a party at my house, when he was literally rifling through my records. And I had this Buzzcocks record, this weird import, that he hadn't seen. That was our first conversation.

Laura Cantrell (Bricks, host of WFMU's "The Radio Thrift Shop," singer/songwriter) He seemed like a creature from another universe. A super-shaggy, long-haired, straight-edge kid from North Carolina.

Kevin Collins (Subculture, Days Of . . ., and Erectus Monotone) He looked like a caveman.

Jim Wilbur (Superchunk) He had big dreadlocks. He's always been a very cheerful, kind, outgoing, and smart guy. But I've got to say, when I first met him, the hair put me off. He was always messing with his four-track, and late at night, we'd make noise tapes. We had a band called Dust Buster, in which the main instrument was a dust buster. It was, like, high concept.

Mac Jonathan Neumann's family lived on a farm on a gravel road between Chapel Hill and Durham. Since he had distant neighbors and parents that went out of town a lot, we could make lots of noise all weekend at any hour, and we did. In high school, a typical day out there would consist of playing music for a long time, drinking beer if we could find someone to buy us some, and then dancing

We had a band called Dust Buster, in which the main instrument was a dust buster. It was, like, high concept.

— Jim Wilbur

around the tiny living room to the Clash or the Violent Femmes or something like that.

Jonathan Neumann At first, we called ourselves Ranger Rick. It was silly. One of my most vivid recollections is playing "Jump" by Van Halen out in my yard. Just being ridiculous. "Smoke on the Water," things like that. And this is all in the shadow of my chicken pen. We were completely terrorizing the chickens.

Mac Jonathan was at UNC that year while I was back, so we got the Slushpuppies going a little more seriously than we had in high school. We recorded some songs on my four-track at my parents' house. We also recorded a bunch of stuff at Duck Kee in Raleigh.

Laura Duck Kee was run by a guy named Jerry Kee, and basically what Jerry did was turn his whole house into a recording studio. He's like a little monk of recording. There's still a sink and a refrigerator in the kitchen so that he can eat. But every corner of the house has recording gear and instruments in it. There's cat hair everywhere. It's not what comes to mind when you think "recording studio." When Superchunk recorded there, I was always in the bathroom with my bass amp.

Mac My friend Lydia Ely at Columbia was from D.C., and used to work at Häagen-Dazs with Ian MacKaye and Henry Rollins. She introduced me to Ian. When Fugazi started up, in 1987, Ian called me to see about setting up a show in town. I called Frank Heath, who owns the Cat's Cradle, and we figured out how to make it an all-ages show. It was Fugazi's first show outside of D.C., and the Slushpuppies were going to open, and it was all very exciting. I drew up a bunch of flyers for the show featuring a photograph of some cows that I had taken. I was a little worried about how we were going to get people to come to this show by a band that no one had heard of yet, since they didn't have a record out and had never played outside of D.C., so I put, in *tiny* letters underneath the name Fugazi: "Ex–Minor Threat."

Ian MacKaye (Minor Threat and Fugazi; cofounder, Dischord Records) I was not happy. I really was not interested in selling Fugazi as anything other than Fugazi. It was just a pretty firm rule with us.

Mac I went around town and took down every flyer, made new ones, and posted them. I felt like the dumb kid that I was.

Jenny Toomey (Geek, Tsunami; cofounder of Simple Machines Records and the Future of Music Coalition) The first time I ever saw Mac play was in the Slushpuppies at a club in D.C. called d.c. space. I think I went because Ian probably was going. They had this great song that was basically Mac singing, "Let me count the ways I love you," but in this totally punk-rock way. It was so incongruous: This very twee sentiment and this very punk sound. It's been mined quite a bit since that time, but it was fresh as a daisy for me. I bought a Slushpuppies tape from him.

Josh Phillips (Bricks) Actually, she gave Mac money for a tape, but he never sent it to her. The next year, I went to Columbia and she said, "If you see Mac ask him where my damn tape is."

Mac had also begun playing guitar in Wwax, with Wayne Taylor and drummer Brian Walsby.

Wayne Taylor (No Labels, Wwax; unsuccessful 1993 mayoral candidate in Raleigh) I had wanted to release a Wwax single. And me and Mac and Brian were going to do it by ourselves. And at one point we realized, it would be much more economical – and more *important* – to involve everyone that we were playing with. And there were all these other bands, and we just tossed the idea around a little bit, and then we were doing it.

Mac We just got this idea that we were going to put out a collection of 7-inches from all the bands we were playing with around town that year. It was kind of a gimmick, almost – this ludicrously ambitious thing. The ridiculousness of putting out a box of singles by five bands no one had ever heard

Flyer by Mac for Fugazi's first North Carolina show, and third show ever.

of was part of the charm of it. Wayne came up with the name *evil i do not to nod i live*. Which, in case you missed it, is a palindrome.

Sara Bell (Angels of Epistemology, Shark Quest)   They just said, "We're going to do this. We can make records." They just started rounding up the bands. And it was such a cool, weird collection. There was the Black Girls, which had a very unusual, folky sound. And then the Angels of Epistemology, which didn't fit into any category of anybody's. And Wwax, and Egg, and Slushpuppies. It was really an eclectic combination of things. And that's what it was like then. There would just be very different bands coming together, because there was no other place for them to be. So you didn't have to adhere to any kind of genre.

Mac   Wayne really made it happen. He found a place to press records, and he knew the people at Barefoot Press for the printing. Our slogan was, "5 bands, 13 songs, 14 people." There were five 7-inches in these little boxes, with a cool booklet of art by all the bands. And we knew it could be done, because places like SST and Dischord had done it.

Andrew Webster (Bricks, Tsunami)   It was kind of like trade secrets passed down. You know what? It's not that tricky to put out a fucking record. You've got to call the pressing plant, you've got to have the master shipped to them. They make a plate, they press some records, they ship them back to you, you have someone design the cover, and then you put them all together by hand. Put them in a plastic bag and suddenly you have a record. Growing up, that always seemed like a magical process. But people started opening the door onto that sausage-making machine.

Ian MacKaye   We set up a model at Dischord. I mean, the way we figured out how to make a 7-inch sleeve is that we took a British picture sleeve, pulled it apart, and looked at how it was constructed. And we literally just traced the outline of that on an 11 by 14 piece of paper and put our own graphics on the outline, and took it to a print shop and said can you make 1,000 of these?

And then we cut them with scissors, and folded and glued them all by hand. We did that for the first 10,000 records at Dischord.

Wayne Taylor   I just basically worked up an estimate, and figured out the budget for the pressing and the boxes and the printing. We all pitched in. I think it was like $2,000 total. The boxes were cases for quarter-inch reel-to-reel tape. I would see them in the studio, and one day I realized – you, know, that fits a 7-inch.

Mac   We bought the boxes blank and screenprinted them by hand at our house. I remember laying like six boxes down at a time and doing a pass with the squeegee. We made a thousand copies and booked release shows in February 1988 where all five bands played in Chapel Hill at the Cat's Cradle and the Brewery in Raleigh, and both shows sold out. It wasn't just our friends in the audience at those shows. People wanted to see it.

Frank Heath (Owner, Cat's Cradle)   It was so impressive. You could tell that there was a lot

Flyer for *evil i do not...* release show at the Brewery in Raleigh, February 1988.

Front cover of the *evil i do not…* box.

Back cover of the *evil i do not…* box.

of thought put into it, and that they grasped the concept of generating excitement by having a crowd.

Mac   It got local press. It was a big deal that strange-sounding local bands — Slushpuppies were probably the most "normal" of the bunch — could get people's attention like that. Today, the writers for the *Independent Weekly* in Chapel Hill are young, they're bloggers, they're looking for cool stuff to write about. Back then, the music coverage was likely to be a review of a Bruce Hornsby concert or something. I think the "adults" were surprised that something like this could be put together basically under everyone's radar.

Glenn Boothe   It kind of showed, like fuck, anybody could do this. You don't have to have a label, you don't have to have a lot of money, you just get your friends together and record some songs and make it.

Wayne Taylor   **It was a bunch of creative people hanging around together who got some shit done.**

Mac and Laura had seen each other around at shows, but they first got to know each other when they both got jobs at Pepper's Pizza on Franklin St. in Chapel Hill.

Norwood Cheek (Filmmaker and video director for Superchunk, Squirrel Nut Zippers, Ben Folds)   My friends and I called Laura "Death Chick." She looked like a classic goth chick. But she was beautiful, and just so *cool*. I grew up in a small town in North Carolina, and that's the kind of girl you dream of going to school with. It's straight out of the movies. Oh man.

Jim Wilbur   **Everybody was in love with her. And she could give you the 500-yard stare and look right through you. But she also liked horses. The black hair and the clothes, that's sort of a barricade between who you are and the rest of the world. And it's indicative of a personality that's vulnerable and sweet.**

Lane Wurster (Former creative director for Mammoth Records; brother of Superchunk

Laura at Pepper's Pizza, 1987.

drummer Jon Wurster)   Laura's laundry day was like, "Is today a gray load or a black load?" You know, not a lot of color. Not really much for small talk.

Mac   Pepper's was basically selling pizza to the drunk frat boys. Laura was pretty good at projecting an air of, like, Don't try to talk to me, punk. Which I think some of the drunk frat boys took as more of a challenge.

Laura   Mac and this other guy that worked there, Matthew, made me cry because they were talking trash about Scott.

Mac   It was just because I wanted to go out with her.

Amy Saaed (Former roommate of Laura's)   I liked Scott Williams. I thought he was hilarious. Also I knew how hard Mac was trying and scheming.

Scott Williams   This is going to sound really stupid, and I know I sound stupid saying it. But I was the king of the scene at the time.

Amy Saaed I always made the joke that Scott was king of the Raleigh scene, and then Mac became king of the Chapel Hill scene. That was my little joke.

Scott Williams That was it. Feuding kingdoms. A feudal war.

Kevin Collins Raleigh was the other side of the tracks. The kids who couldn't get it together. Around that time, like 1986 and '87, in the hardcore scene, people were starting to get into this other, Sonic Youth–type stuff, and all the punks were growing out their hair. And I think Mac kind of came from that.

Ian MacKaye Chapel Hill is such a college town. It was like a slightly defanged hardcore. It was still unique, but it was coming from a less angry place.

Scott Williams Raleigh was this blue-collar, or no-collar, rock scene. We were all about partying, and rock, and fuck tomorrow. And in Chapel Hill, they had come from a wealthier background, gone to great colleges, and knew there was a tomorrow. And knew where to invest in that tomorrow. We didn't see tomorrow.

Mac So with the Slushpuppies, every bass player that we'd ever played with was insane. They were all over the place and just really into overplaying. So I thought, Great! We'll get someone who doesn't know how to play bass, and there's no way she could be doing bass solos the whole time. So I asked Laura to learn how to play bass.

Laura I felt like I was pushed into it. Music was important to me, but I had never wanted to actually play music or be on a stage. The idea petrified me. I was mystified by Mac and his friends' knowledge of all these obscure punk-rock bands. They were punk-rock scientists. It makes sense that, living in a small town, they really devoured zines like *Maximum Rocknroll*, and internalized all the information. They had to dig to find all this music; in Atlanta it was all right there and easy to access.

Jim Wilbur I don't think they would've ever been together without the band. I think they got together because Mac was like, "I'm going to teach you how to play bass. And we're going to start a band. And from there, I'm going to start dating you."

Mac That was probably the motivating factor. But it was also like – "Well, I spend all my time making noise and playing in bands, so Laura should spend all her time doing the same thing!" In my narrow view of the world, it was like, "Why wouldn't someone want to be in a band?" That sounds fun, doesn't it? We called it Quit Shovin'. It just seemed like something fun to do.

Amy Saaed Laura and I lived in an apartment with six people, and we had a roommate named Sue Hunter. And Mac was actually supposed to be teaching Sue to play bass. And I came home one day, and he was teaching *Laura* how to play bass. Mac's a smart man. He knows what he wants, and he goes and gets it. He had his little plan all ready.

Jim Wilbur He basically stole her from Scott Williams. And I was always like, "Mac, you are in deep, deep trouble." And he was like, "I know, they're going to find me in an alley with a bullet in my head and Scott Williams's name on it."

Scott Williams I was going through a bad period in my life. My band was breaking up, I got kicked out of my house. It seemed like everything was falling apart at the same time.

Wayne Taylor Mac and Laura were a unit, and it was obvious. They were headstrong to be in love and the world was their oyster.

Amy Saaed In the beginning, Mac just had stars in his eyes. Laura could do no wrong. Not that Laura really did wrong.

Jonathan Neumann Quit Shovin' was me, Mac, and Laura. I was playing guitar, he was playing drums, and Laura was playing bass. It was to make Laura more comfortable playing bass – we were all new on our instruments, so we're all on the same skill level. Mac was

Quit Shovin', a.k.a. Rodeo Clam, at a house party.
Left to right: Jonathan Neumann, Mac, Laura.

Merge Records' first release:
Winterspring by Bricks.

very encouraging that way. It didn't go very far. We had ten or so songs. We played at one party. Redd Kross was in town, and they came. Which was a little nerve-wracking.

Lane Wurster   I literally remember Mac showing Laura where to put her fingers, onstage. I didn't really get it.

Laura   I was terrified the first time we played. And messing up a lot. I don't remember a whole lot about it — and not because I was drunk. My brain would seriously seize up in these situations. Yeah, I remember it being really bad.

Jonathan Neumann   Laura was kind of a reluctant partner. I know she enjoyed playing and everything, but I remember her being sort of conflicted about being in music. Mac was pretty persuasive. Cajoling. And I don't mean that in a negative way.

Laura   I think about myself back then, and I wasn't very in charge of my own life. I was kind of going through life not wanting to hurt

anyone else's feelings, and being kind of easily manipulated, you know? This is not really very flattering to myself, I know. Honestly, I did not want to get onstage. It was never a fantasy of mine.

Mac   After Quit Shovin' we also had Metal Pitcher, which was me and Laura and Jeb Bishop. We practiced in COC's practice space. And we just decided, "We're going to exist and we're going to make a record. Why not make a record?" So we recorded some songs on a four-track in a basement somewhere, and that ended up being the first Merge 7-inch — "A Careful Workman Is the Best Safety Device."

Wendy Moore (Former roommate of Laura's)   There was a house party in Carrboro where Metal Pitcher played. Laura was very tentative. She was just learning the bass at that point, and that was kind of clear. But still, it was a lot of fun. I think Mac just begged and pleaded for her to play. "C'mon, it'll be great!" And he's got so much charisma that you can't help but go along with it. He's really inclusive to people he cares about. And that was who he cared about.

Mac　I went back to Columbia after my year off. During my junior year, in 1988, I started Bricks with my roommate, Andrew Webster, and myself, recording on my four-track in my bedroom in our apartment on 108th Street. It was tiny and overcrowded – someone had to sleep in the living room all the time. We recorded what would become the *Winterspring* cassette, Merge's first release, in that apartment. One night, I was sitting in my room recording with headphones on, and I heard what sounded like a gunshot in the alley. I hit the floor. It was fucking loud. Turns out some kindly neighbor had tossed a brick through our window. That's how Bricks got its name.

Andrew Webster　We didn't really have space for a drum kit, so we played with Tupperware containers filled with rice, or cranberry juice bottles that we'd drained, and banged on with sticks and whatever we could find. We eventually added Laura Cantrell and Josh Phillips. We'd heard that Josh was taking drum lessons, and we didn't realize that he wasn't quite far enough along to be the whole rhythm section of the band. So we added Laura as an additional percussionist. She had the great benefit of being a good singer as well.

Josh Phillips　I'm pretty sure that I have the privilege of being the absolute worst musician that Mac has ever played with in his life. I literally couldn't keep the beat. And instead of just kicking me out of the band, they brought in Laura Cantrell to try and get me on beat, and have two drummers. I thought that was really nice.

Mac　I always had the impression that Laura was slumming it a bit being in Bricks. She could actually sing, compared to us, and she was just more of a serious person, so I felt lucky that she agreed to come over and mess around with us goofballs and our goofy songs.

Laura Cantrell　I joked with Mac at one point that I had secretly tried to turn Bricks into my country band. I suggested a Doug Sahm song or something for us to cover. And Mac said, "I don't think that's quite the direction we're going with this, Laura. Here's our new song, 'Smoking Hooch with the Flume Dude.'"

Brandon Holley (College roommate of Mac's; former editor of *Jane* magazine)　The songs were all written about our life in the apartment, and what was going on. The rehearsals were in our living room. It was kind of like an extension of making dinner.

Josh Phillips　One of us was studying the history of Albania. So we did an Albanian Christmas record, and all the songs on it had to be about Albania, and also about Christmas. The big hit from that tape was this thing called "Don't Hog the Nog, Zog." Apparently, in Albania there actually was a King Zog. We played with Fugazi once, and it was ridiculous. There's 350 rabid Fugazi fans, you know, and we're singing about the girl with the carrot skin.

Mac　In the summer of 1989, between my junior and senior year, Laura [Ballance] and I drove across country to take some friends who had graduated back to the West Coast. We were headed to Seattle, where our friend Aubrey Summers knew Bruce Pavitt and Jon Poneman, who had started Sub Pop the year before, and we were hoping to catch a Mudhoney show while we were out there.

Jason McLachlan (College friend of Mac's)　Mac had his dad's van, which had two twenty-gallon fuel tanks that were linked, so you could go forever without stopping for gas. And they had set it up with an eight-track tape deck and Laura had figured out how to record on to eight-track tapes, so we had this box of punk-rock music on eight-track.

Josh Phillips　We tried to go to the Grand Canyon, but we got there at two a.m. and everything was closed, so we left. And when you leave the Grand Canyon at night, there are hundreds of rabbits in the road. Aubrey was driving. At first she was swerving and

Bricks at CBGB's Record Canteen, 1990: Laura Cantrell, Josh Phillips, Andrew Webster.

Mac's parents' van after catching fire in New Mexico in 1989.

People ask the question a lot: Why did you decide to put out your own records? But it's not like there was anyone else asking to put them out.

— Mac McCaughan

going slow, but we had sixty miles to go to get to a hotel, and at a certain point she was just like, "Fuck it." It was just *badump, badump, badump.* We ran over literally hundreds of rabbits.

Laura   We were in the middle of New Mexico, and had spent the day driving to see the Anasazi ruins at Chaco Canyon, on these gravel roads for miles. We were on our way back, and were about to get back on the highway, when smoke started coming through the air-conditioning vent.

Mac   And then flames started shooting out from under the steering column.

Laura   I put the van in park, put on the emergency brake so it wouldn't roll into the brush and start a brushfire, turned it off, and jumped out. And then the van turned back on! By itself. It was like *Christine.* I jumped back in to try and turn it back off, but couldn't, since the key was already in the off position.

Jason McLachlan   We were trying to get our hands in there to pop the hood — Mac had a fire extinguisher — but it was too hot.

Laura   We managed to get all our stuff out except all my eight-track tapes. And my favorite pillow. We were on an Indian res-ervation, next to some sort of general store, which was closed. And I remember when we hopped out, I realized things were bad when I saw the side reflector just melting off.

Mac   We just sat there and watched it. The tires exploded.

Josh Phillips   Mac and Laura just kind of went off over by themselves, and then Mac came back crying, just to look at it again, and then ran away again to be comforted.

Laura   By the end, the windshield was draped over the steering column. Somebody called the fire department. We were so far from civilization that it took hours for them to show up.

Mac   I called my parents and they rented a car for us, and we shipped a bunch of stuff home. And we piled into the Taurus, or whatever it was. When we got to Seattle, Aubrey took us to meet Bruce and Jonathan, and we got to go see their office.

Aubrey Summers   It just seemed like one of the best tourist things I could take them to. It was definitely bustling. Lots of people running around in their band gear — their nighttime clothes, it looked like. Lots of makeup. I don't think Mac and Laura were blown away. It was more like, "Okay. I could see doing this."

Mac   It was the week that the Mudhoney single "You Got It (Keep It Outta My Face)" came out. So we got copies of that, and Bruce got us into the first Sub Pop Lame-fest, which had Mudhoney and Nirvana was opening. We already were fans of Sub Pop, so it was cool to be able to see that. We dropped everybody off and then it was just Laura and me on the way back to North Carolina.

Laura   And that's when Merge started.

Mac   We were talking about all these recordings we had — I'd done a bunch of Bricks recordings on four-track, and Wwax had some stuff, and we had done the Metal Pitcher stuff. And we had already done the box set, so we saw how it could be done.

Laura   The label was totally Mac's idea. To call it "Merge" was my idea. We were driving through Colorado, and I started reading road signs while I was thinking about a name for it. I actually thought it was a pretty dumb name for a long time. But it's certainly better than "Pronghorn Antelope," which is another thing I saw while I was driving on that trip.

Jonathan Neumann   Here's the thing — Mac lived and breathed music. This was his life. When I went to visit him in New York for spring break, I mean, sometimes it was insufferable. I had to go from fucking record store to record store while he looked for the reissue of this, or that. Looking for the early punk rock records, you know, the seventies stuff. These folks that scrapped it, and did it a lot on their own.

Mac   People ask the question a lot: Why did you decide to put out your own records? But it's not like there was anyone else asking to put them out.

Wendy Moore   When they started Merge, it didn't seem like they were starting much of anything. It just seemed like an art project. They would give singles to the record stores, and they would get bought up. At the beginning it was teeny, you know?

Jenny Toomey   There's a great line in a Destroyer song: "Formative years wasted / In love with our peers, we tasted / life with the stars." I couldn't have found language that was more clear about that whole idea of what we were doing. The twenty people who understand what you're talking about are the twenty most important people in the world. Maybe that's the difference between professional culture and outsider culture. Our antennae were tuned very specifically for like minds, as opposed to sending out a signal to convert people. There are some kinds of art that are trying to find their peers, and there are other kinds that are trying to make peers.

Laura   It was a lark. I had no idea it would last this long.

Mac   Everything we knew how to do, we just knew how to do from the box set. But also because we were consumers of music. I

read a lot of fanzines, so I knew where there was a place to take out an ad, or where to send a copy for a review. I eventually started working for Schoolkids, so then I was on the phone talking to Dutch East India, buying albums from them. Well, there's a distributor. Let's just use them. Revolver and all these other distributors — how hard could it be? I'm buying stuff from them at Schoolkids, why can't they sell our stuff at other stores? Merge was in Laura's bedroom at first, until she moved to an apartment where we had a separate room for it. Every six months or so — however often we were putting out the singles — we'd have a single-stuffing party. Get the singles, get the sleeves printed at Barefoot Press, order plastic bags to hold the sleeves, and go through repetitive motions.

Wendy Moore   Laura had a loft with a bed on top, and a desk underneath. There were boxes of singles in her room, boxes of T-shirts. A little money box.

Amy Ruth Buchanan (Former roommate of Laura's)   We had a little tiny room devoted to Merge. And it had this little red table, and like some stacks of singles. No windows. It was just this little, tiny, closet-y kind of room. And Laura would work away.

Mac   We would borrow money. Like a few hundred dollars from one person, and then do a release and then pay them back. Lydia Ely lent us money for the Chunk 7-inch. Glenn Boothe paid for the Angels of Epistemology 7-inch. My dad lent us the money for the Metal Pitcher single. So it was piecemeal — borrow money, pay it back, borrow money, pay it back. We did a Wwax double 7-inch that I helped fund with $2,000 that I got as a graduation gift from my grandparents. We were making enough to pay people back, and then we'd just sock away whatever else we made — $50, $100, so we wouldn't have to borrow as much next time.

Ralph McCaughan (Mac's father)   Mac's mother and I were "executive producers" on some records. But we were well-compensated: We got free records.

Amy Ruth Buchanan   I remember one single-stuffing party, and Mac brought over a VHS tape of *Seinfeld,* which none of us had seen. It must have been the first season. We sat and watched those episodes while we stuffed singles, and thought it was howlingly funny. But it was perfectly in tune with Mac's sense of humor, actually. Isn't that such a counter-culture thing to do? Watch *Seinfeld*?

Laura   Mac went back to school for another year in the fall of 1989, and I ran the label pretty much by myself, except when he'd come back for breaks. I was also still in school, and working at Pepper's and then Kinko's. At first, calling distributors to try and get them to buy singles made me really nervous. But after a while, I developed relationships with them, and it was fun. But I also had to harass people to collect payment. Not so fun. There are also hazards associated with having a record label in your bedroom. The tape gun nearly killed me a few times.

Mac   When a record would be done, Laura would send it up to me at school. I remember taking one to Pier Platters – taking the PATH train out to Hoboken, and saying, "Hey, I don't know, you might want to buy some of this 7-inch." And they were all these cool, beautiful girls who worked at Pier Platters who I was scared of. But it turns out they're like, Sure, we'll take sixty. Even if they'd never sold them it would've been cool because Pier Platters has our record on the shelves next to a Melvins single.

Kevin Collins   It was pretty easy to play shows, and Jerry Kee's place was cheap and right around the corner. People played in bands, and Mac would see them. And he'd say, "Can I put out your record?"

* * *

Typical Merge 7-inch-sleeve-stuffing affair, 1994.
Left to right: Colin Dodd, Laura, Joe Ventura.

Facing Page: Laura, Jason McLachlan, Josh Phillips, and Aubrey Summers at the Grand Canyon, 1989.   Next Page: Mac at Bryce Canyon, 1989.

Seaweed
Superchunk ☆
Geek
YOUNG ROCK REVOLUTION
1990

Chapter Two

Wet Behind the Ears

1989 to 1991

There was all this new music, and no one knew what to call it. You could trace its roots; you could hear Hüsker Dü and Black Flag and the Fall. But this stuff was more complicated, sincere, and self-aware than those bands. Or in some cases less complicated, affected, and deliberately clueless. But it was different, and there was a lot of it. Teenage Fanclub, Pavement, Sebadoh: They shared an approach, if not a particular sound — an abiding reverence for pop, a self-effacing disdain for artifice — and deserved a moniker of some sort.

Someone came up with "indie rock," a coinage that has frustrated music writers and fans for decades. Sonic Youth was an icon of indie rock, yet they were contract employees of David Geffen's DGC, which was a unit of MCA Records, which was in turn a unit of MCA, Inc., which was in turn a unit of Japan's Matsushita Electric Industrial Company. Ani DiFranco operated entirely independently of the corporate music business, but her crunchy diatribes were anathema to the indie-rock school.

In Chapel Hill there was an alternative coinage: "young rock." It's unclear who came up with it. Some say Norwood Cheek, who directed a documentary of that name about the Chapel Hill scene. Some say Stephen Akin, the lead singer of A Number of Things, who worked with Mac at Schoolkids and used it pejoratively to describe the flood of melodic, guitar-driven 7-inches making their way to the store. For a while in the early nineties, it was what you would say at the record store if someone asked you what the new Doughboys record sounded like. But "young rock" never quite caught on, and despite numerous competitors — "college rock," "alternative rock," "modern rock" — "indie rock" won the day.

Indie rock's emerging impresario was Gerard Cosloy, the acerbic former proprietor of *Conflict*, a zine out of Boston, who would go on to become a partner in Matador Records. Cosloy had managed Deep Wound, J. Mascis's pre-Dinosaur band, and by the late eighties was running Homestead Records, home of Dinosaur, Green River, and innumerable other indie progenitors. Mac had Boston friends at Columbia who knew Cosloy, and during his junior year played in Burn, a short-lived band featuring Jon Easley of Sorry, a Boston band that Cosloy was friendly with and that had released an album on Homestead.

Mac and Laura wanted to put a full-length record out. Merge was doing 7-inches, but neither of them had the know-how or money to manage a full-length release. Mac gave Cosloy virtually everything he recorded, and hassled him from pay phones on the Columbia campus in between classes to find out if he liked any of it. Cosloy's response to the Slushpuppies was "They're one singer short of being a great band." But he liked Bricks, and he liked Wwax, and during Mac's senior year he and Mac went around and around about the possibility of a series of records featuring Mac's various bands. It never really went anywhere.

It was Chunk that went somewhere. Chunk formed in the summer of 1989 out of the ashes of Quit Shovin' and Metal Pitcher. Mac recruited Jack McCook, a then-twenty-five-year-old UNC grad, to play guitar. McCook had never played in a band before, but he and Mac had bonded one afternoon over an impromptu thirty-minute rendition of Television's "Marquee Moon" in Laura's basement. The drummer was Chuck Garrison, a curly-haired, slovenly, lovable math whiz Mac lived with during his year off in Chapel Hill, who also played drums in Zen Frisbee, a spastic three-piece that recalled the Meat Puppets. Mac sang and played guitar, and Laura played bass. They got the name when a new Chapel Hill phone book came out with a listing for "Garrison, Chunk."

Chunk's first show was in Raleigh on Saturday, July 29, 1989, at a party celebrating the opening of a new space for Barefoot Press.

Scott Williams   When you start reaching your early twenties, you find out there's a whole world outside this little thing that you're living in. And that's what happened. People just grew out of hardcore. You could feel something happening around '88 and '89. The thing that really changed everything

All I remember is being petrified.

— Laura Ballance

was the Barefoot Press party, and that was when the first incarnation of Chunk played.

Sara Bell   There was a lot of excitement about that show — "Oh, Mac's new band, they're great!" And because of Chuck Garrison, who was a really great drummer from Zen Frisbee, who we all loved.

Bill Mooney (Cofounder of Tannis Root; Barbara Herring's husband)   From the beginning with Chunk, it was like, this sounds really good and this is catchy. People were bouncing around immediately.

Mac   Barefoot Press had moved into this giant warehouse. The bands were set up on the floor; there was no stage or anything. There was probably a keg. It went pretty well considering Laura didn't know how to play the bass, Jack was probably wasted, and we'd never played a show before. What we were doing was pretty basic. It was kind of hard to screw it up too much. And it seemed to have broader appeal than hardcore, or some of the noisier things that I'd been involved with. It just seemed like a natural progression and something we had a grasp on pretty quickly.

Jack McCook   We sounded pretty crappy at the Barefoot Press party. We hadn't practiced very much, and that was terrifying to me. It was, "OK, we've got this show coming up!" Like, "Oh fuck!" You know? I was not as much of an indie rocker as those guys. They were into some bands I'd never heard of. I was a college kid, a frat boy who got a job at this record store. I was aware of Wwax and the Slushpuppies, but it certainly wasn't like, "Gosh, I've got to see Metal Pitcher!"

Laura   All I remember is being petrified.

Mac   Chunk felt like an easy fit for everybody. But I don't think anyone was thinking of it beyond, Here's this band we have for six months, or who knows how long?

Jack McCook   I was surprised when people really liked it. We were kind of thrown together, you know? The songs kind of fell apart. But people really liked it.

In August of 1989, just weeks after their debut, Chunk recorded three songs at Duck Kee in Raleigh: "What Do I," "My Noise," and a cover of "Train from Kansas City," by the sixties girl group the Shangri-Las. The songs were brash, tuneful, and recorded very, very quickly. That month, Chunk played shows at the Brewery and the Cat's Cradle before Mac returned to school, leaving the rest of the band in Chapel Hill. He came back down on holidays and long weekends to play and record. In December, Merge released the first Chunk 7-inch.

Mac   I'd been talking to Gerard about Bricks, and Wwax, and Slushpuppies, and Chunk, and eventually he just said, "Look I'm leaving Homestead. But my friend Chris Lombardi from Boston is starting this new label." Gerard gave Chris the single, he liked it, and that's how we ended up on Matador. Then Gerard ended up partnering up with Chris a couple months later.

Matador signed Chunk to a three-record deal, with the understanding that Mac and Laura could continue to put out their own 7-inches on Merge, and paid a $2,500 advance for the first record. Mac, Jack, Laura, and Chuck spent two days recording and mixing it in January 1990, during Mac's winter break, at Duck Kee.

Laura   I'm always amazed, when I listen to those early recordings, at the takes that we accepted. I certainly didn't think my playing was very good. But in the interest of time — and money — we had to keep going.

Jack McCook   I was pretty nervous about recording. It all seemed very rushed, you know? It wasn't really what I was expecting. We're this little band, why are we — we're playing, now we're recording? It's ridiculous. Absurd.

Glenn Boothe   I remember once saying to Mac, "Hey, we should do something tomorrow." And he was like, "Oh no, we're going to the studio." And then the next day I saw him at like 1:30 in the afternoon. I said, "Oh, I thought you guys went to the studio." And he said, "Oh yeah, we were. We already recorded it." But that was their whole thing — go in, bang it out, and be done with it. And you know, those early recordings are all rough, but there's still something about them.

Mac   We were recording super-fast. We certainly weren't going for anything fancy. I basically wanted two things — lots of guitar tracks, and to bury the vocals.

Jack McCook   That single was the first time I ever heard Mac sing. When we practiced, he had a shitty little guitar amp that was our PA. He'd plug his mic into it. So there was no vocals for me at all when we'd practice. So during playback in the studio, that was the first time I heard his little voice. And I was like, "You've got to be shitting me!" It was a scratchy little boy's voice! As a total neophyte to the recording process, I thought, 'Gosh, well maybe everyone's voice sounds like this? And then there's something done to it in the process to make it sound, you know, real?' But I grew to like it. I like it now.

The first Chunk single.

I know my voice is like a broken saw /
I know my voice is like a tightening screw
— "Sweetness and Light," *Be Still Please*,
Portastatic, 2006.

Jon Wurster (Superchunk) In 1990, I was sitting in with this band the Accelerators, and Chunk opened for us. I wasn't terribly blown away by any means. But I remember really loving this one song. So afterwards, I said, "That last song you guys did was really great. What was it?" And it was the one cover — "Train from Kansas City."

Josh Phillips The first time I saw them, they were playing at a party in North Carolina. They were all just really drunk. Jack was really drunk and just knocking over the drum set and stuff, and falling to the ground. And pretty early on I remember talking to Jack and him having reservations about being in the band altogether. I think he just wasn't into that kind of music.

Laura Cantrell, visiting from New York, saw Chunk at the same party.

Laura Cantrell That was the first time I got to see the Laura/Mac dynamic. And it definitely felt like Mac wanted to have his girlfriend in the band. I knew that Laura had a taste for music, but it didn't seem like she was the most natural person to play that role. She just stood in one little place.

Jack McCook Sometimes Chuck and I didn't get along. We'd travel up to play New York when Mac was at school, and it sucked that I had to sleep with this guy. Mac and Laura would be in someone's bed, and we're doing the couch tour.

Jonathan Neumann Chuck was a very likable guy. He just had organizational issues. We got along quite well, but I didn't have to tour with him, and play with him, and live out of a van with him. I think I would have gone nutty. When Mac and Chuck were living together, I don't think Chuck ever put sheets on his mattress. And that was a hard thing for Mac to understand. Like, "Dude — get some sheets. C'mon." Chuck was a really bright guy, but he lived in his own little world.

In May, Mac graduated from Columbia, and Merge released its second Chunk 7-inch, "Slack Motherfucker," a propulsive and compressed blast of contempt for inertia. The epithet was aimed at a lazy coworker at a shitty job — "I'm working / But I'm not working for you / You slack motherfucker."

Glenn Boothe I tried to talk him out of releasing "Slack Motherfucker" as a single. I said, "You can't play it on the radio! You say, 'motherfucker'!" And he said, "I don't care." And he was right. That single put Chunk on the map.

Jeb Bishop (Angels of Epistemology, Egg, Stillborn Christians, the Ken Vandermark Five) I remember seeing them do "Slack Motherfucker" for the first time. That song stuck. It was a hit. The shows were really great. Like really cranked-up and flat-out, just really good.

Jack McCook It was a song that couldn't lose. When the "Slack Motherfucker" 7-inch came out, I did the painting on the sleeve, a bad painting of a face. And it says on top of it, "Slack Motherfucker," in yellow. So I gave it to my parents back in Greensboro, to show them what I'd been up to. And my mother, she was real proud of it. She displayed it on the bookshelf. And she cut off the fucking top of it! Ridiculous.

Sue McCaughan (Mac's mother) As a mother, I had to deal with that word becoming the emblem of Superchunk. And when we'd think of sending out clippings to family and friends when Superchunk was mentioned in the paper, we couldn't.

Ralph McCaughan We did, actually — we would make a copy so that we could smudge out the "motherfuckers."

"Slack Motherfucker" sold out of its initial pressing of 1,000 copies. At the time, Merge was spending about $1.35 to produce each single, and selling them for $1.95, making about $600 in profit.

Glenn Boothe   When I became the music director of WXYC in 1988, the 7-inch single was so unimportant that when we got in the first 7-inch by Nirvana, I just gave it away to one of the DJ's: "We're not going to play this, it's a 7-inch, here you take it." Two years later, the 7-inch single-handedly launched a lot of indie labels — it obviously had a lot to do with the initial releases of Merge, but you also had bands like Pavement, and Mudhoney, and other acts. It was an economical thing. I never really took 7-inches seriously until "Touch Me I'm Sick" by Mudhoney. That was the one where like, everyone was talking about it, and you realized, instead of spending all this money making an album, you could spend a couple hundred bucks on a couple songs, and still get the notoriety, you know? You could get your music out there on a national level, not just locally. It wasn't just something to sell at your shows, it was something you could service to radio and maybe the press. I financed the first Angels of Epistemology 7-inch that Merge put out in 1990. And I sent it to *Rockpool* magazine, which was a college-radio trade magazine, and they put it on the cover. So that was kind of like, "Wow, this is cool!" You spend a few hundred bucks, and people are taking note.

Andrew Webster   It was the dying age of vinyl, but also sort of the recovering age of 7-inch vinyl. Everybody had a 7-inch collection. We'd spend weekends going to the record store, and buying whatever new 7-inches had come out from some bands, near or far. We'd spend weekends just flipping through bins at In Your Ear or Pier Platters.

> From a practical and economic standpoint, the 7" vinyl single is still the only inexpensive way a person can document music in any sort of durable fashion. So it is the people's medium, the punk rock kid's and the garage band's and the home-taping hermit's medium . . . . [B]ut finally it is not about the colored wax and the limited edition, because it is about the adrenalin rush, the conceptual greatness of the 7" single: What can you do in three-and-a-half minutes that will make us get up and put the needle in the groove time and again? The single must be a distillation of one's powers, the most exciting slice of noise a person can cram between the lip of the disc and the edge of the label . . . . Thanks for listening.
> — from Mac's liner notes to *Tossing Seeds: Singles 89-91*, Superchunk's 1991 singles collection and Merge's first full-length release.

By February of 1989, an avant-garde percussion trio was gigging in New York under the name Chunk. When Cosloy invited Mac, Laura, McCook, and Garrison to play a show he had booked at CBGB's Record Canteen on New Year's Eve 1989, the listing in *The New York Times* read, "Sunday's performers include Chunk, a group of three percussionists led by Samm Bennett, who sings sustained melodies in a quizzical voice above the band's acoustic and electronic sounds. The bill also includes Unsane, Unrest, Johnny Cohen's Love Machine and H. P. Zinker. Admission is $12. Music starts at 10 P.M." Needless to say, it was not a percussion trio that ended up playing with Unsane at the CBGB Canteen that night. Since Bennett had been using the name slightly longer, Mac and Laura agreed to change theirs.

Chunk at CBGB's Record Canteen in New York City, New Year's Eve 1989. Left to right: Jack McCook, Laura, Mac.

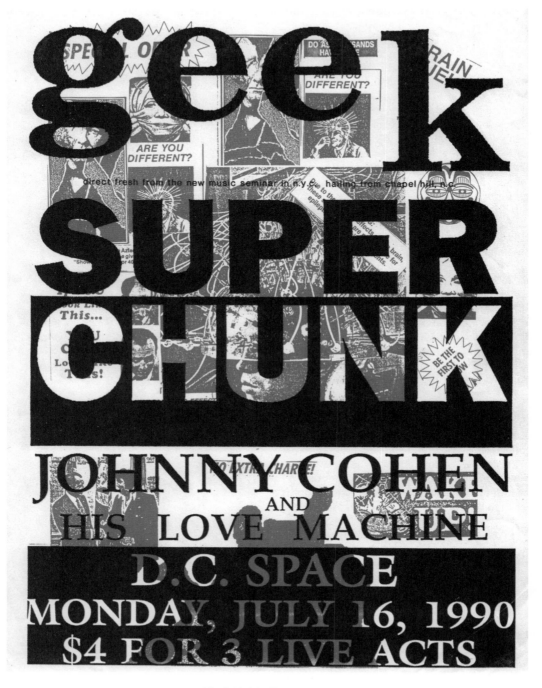

Wet Behind the Ears tour flyer.

Mac   My mom actually came up with the idea of just adding the "Super."

Sue McCaughan   He didn't jump on it, but he didn't dismiss it. And I guess he and Laura later decided they liked it.

Mac   In 1990, toward the end of my senior year, I had been talking with Aaron Stauffer from Seaweed, a Tacoma, Wash., band that was friends with people I went to school with, and Jenny Toomey of Geek. And we started planning this three-band tour for the summer after we all graduated. It was a big production. We made letterpress posters, and pressed a 7-inch called "Three's Company," with songs from all the bands. We called it the Wet Behind the Ears Tour. You know, what are your plans after graduation? Go on tour!

Ralph McCaughan   We thought it was great. Better than grad school, you know? If he's going to be a musician, what better way to learn the business than to go on tour, and start a band, and start a record company? You can't get in too much trouble, and you can learn an awful lot. More than you would getting an MBA, that's for sure.

Jack McCook   I remember that being proposed, and me thinking, I don't really want to do this shit. And at that point I realized they were taking it a little more seriously than I was. So I thought, "I should step out of this, before I get in too deep." I regretted it maybe the first year or so after it happened, because my girlfriend split on me, and I was kind of bummed out. I was like, "Shit man, I wish I was with Superchunk. Maybe I could get some chicks on the road or something."

Jim Wilbur   I was a schoolteacher. I could barely play guitar, and just got in with the right group of people. I met Mac through Andrew Webster, who was my best friend growing up in the tiny village of Noank, Conn. Andrew and I had a hardcore band in high school called Woodsmen Crusade, and then I went to Fairfield University and he went to Columbia and was roommates with Mac. I joined Superchunk for three months. That was the agreement. I said, "I'll come

down for three months and do this tour." But I was planning on going back to Connecticut and being a teacher. The tour was sort of a goof. You know, it was highly ambitious — it would be cynical to call it a marketing ploy — but it was sort of an armada. We were in like seven or eight cars. It was like a camping trip. We played to you know, ten people here, two people there. We got as far as Minneapolis. But then there would be like, really good shows. When we got to Boston, we were blown away that we got $300. We were like, "Holy shit! We made $300! Between eighteen people!" We were just cold-calling people saying, "You know we've got a three-band bill. We have a 7-inch."

Frank Heath   A lot of bands around here just never toured very much. Superchunk was probably the first one that actually did the national, touring, support-act kind of stuff. And I think that they helped bring a lot of other bands into that. Especially bands that were on Merge, into that mindset of being able to go out on tour, and understanding, well, you're going to do this, you're not going to make any money, but it's good. It's good for record sales, it's good as a way to get your name out.

Aaron Stauffer (Seaweed)   We just went on tour blindly, with no idea of what was going to happen. It was just like, "We're a rock band, we've been waiting to go on tour, now we're out of high school. Let's do it." We drove straight from Tacoma to North Carolina, six of us in a full-size pickup truck with all of our equipment, without stopping. We calculated that we could do it in two and a half days. We didn't even stop and sleep — just for two or three meals. That was miserable.

Jenny Toomey   This was like the most fun anybody could have in the world. I worked all summer just to make sure I had enough money so that I could ping around and go on tour. My friend Kristin and I made tour jackets for everyone, and on everyone's jacket — we used golf jackets — we put their band logos on the back and then we put their names on the front and the name of their label. We just stenciled it out and painted them.

Jenny Toomey (Geek), Wade Neal (Seaweed), and Mac on the Wet Behind the Ears tour in 1990.

Aaron Stauffer We didn't really have any expectations. But people came to the shows. Even if it would be like five or ten people, or maybe twenty, there'd be five people who had our singles, or had Superchunk singles, or heard us on the radio, or knew about us.

Andrew Webster Superchunk asked me to come along as a roadie. It was a bunch of college kids going on a road trip. It was all chaos – funny, and messy, and full of jokes and boy comedy all the time. We slept on floors. There was maybe fifteen of us traveling. I mean, who's going to put up fifteen people they don't know? Somebody always did. No one knew about riders, and you just hoped you would get some beer at the show, and maybe they would pay you enough to get gas money to go on to the next thing. It was a little bit skin of the teeth all the time. The shows were sparsely attended and kind of random. I was just wandering around, carrying amps and hoping we could figure out how to get dinner before everyone had to go onstage.

* * *

Peter Margasak, publisher of the ever-irreverent, ever-insightful 3-year-old local rock fanzine *B--- Rag* (that's a family-newspaper abbreviation, folks), is now booking bands at Czar Bar, 1814 W. Division St. Margasak jokingly (I think) says he "hates most music," which means he'll go where few bookers have gone before to find the great, grating unknown bands of America. In that spirit, Sunday's lineup features at least one clear winner, Superchunk, whose two independently released singles sound like the most explosive thing to come out of the festering Northwest noise rock scene [sic] since Nirvana.
— Greg Kot, the *Chicago Tribune*, August 16, 1990.

Peter Margasak (Staff writer for the *Chicago Reader*) It was in the summer, it was hot as hell, and this was the second show I booked at the Czar Bar. The guarantee for all three bands was $150. I lost $15. And Mac gave me a deal because I was indie, you know? We were just two people – me and John Henderson, who ran a label called Feel Good All Over – and it was coming out of our own pockets. At the time I was, as many people were, completely

Wet Behind the Ears tour flyer for Chicago.

Laura at O'Cayz Corral, Madison, Wisc., 1990.

smitten with Laura right off the bat. I thought Mac was great, but I was kind of pissed that he had such a great girlfriend.

Aaron Stauffer   In Chicago, Nash Kato from Urge Overkill — I assume he was coked up — grabbed the mic before Superchunk played, and said, "Superchunk-*chunk-chunk-chunk*!" He did this long intro and kept doing that, and then he'd grab the mic after a couple of songs and be like, "Superchunk-*chunk-chunk-chunk*!" Definitely that show at the Czar Bar was one of the best-attended shows of the tour. People were very excited to see Superchunk. It definitely had the feeling of like, "Wow, something's going on."

Laura   In Madison, Aaron started to threaten me. He started saying, "You've got to rock out! I want to see a foot up on that monitor tonight, or I'm going to come up there on stage and knock you over!" And it seriously took that kind of thing. He was obviously joking, but it made me realize that I needed to try. That this is not acceptable. So the pogoing began there.

Aaron Stauffer   I was just trying to give her a pep talk. She's a shy person, for sure. And she definitely was shy with us at first, but we didn't take shyness. That wasn't part of our deal. We were just like, "We're fucking out here rocking and rolling! This isn't shy! This is rock!"

Frank Heath   "Slack Motherfucker" was a big deal. What I see happen with bands a lot of times is that a song will sort of define them, and show them what they can actually accomplish. I don't think that Superchunk was planning on being a serious band so much. They didn't seem like they were as focused on it until they started actually getting asked to do shows with other bands, and stuff like that, and they were like, "Wow, people like us. This may be something we should actually, like, try and do." And the bands that Mac had been in before then, were always this very DIY, we're playing for our friends, this is fun, we're playing at parties. It wasn't as driven as Superchunk became within a couple of years. I felt like it sort of

got more — a lot more professional, and a lot better. But the key is always having the songs. And Superchunk was one of those bands that had that thing that people needed to hear.

Wendy Moore   There wasn't any talk or concept of doing anything but Superchunk. No real jobs were talked about. Nobody was thinking about doing anything else, or being any other kind of person. I think they had such a good response, and they didn't maybe set out with a mission to become this super-successful indie-rock band or anything. But as they became more successful, they definitely were ready to step up.

Steve Albini (Big Black, Shellac; engineer for the Pixies and Nirvana)   I first met both of them at a Sonic Youth gig at the Cat's Cradle, 1990. I was doing sound for the Jesus Lizard when they were opening for Sonic Youth on an East Coast tour. And they both showed up at the merchandise table and introduced themselves. I think their first album had just come out, and I had heard of Wwax. But I didn't know Superchunk. They were physically quite tiny people. I think Laura was either beginning or maintaining a dreadlock phase at that point, and I had a generally low opinion of dreadlocks. But I don't think I let it affect my opinion of her.

> The fledgling Matador label has already yielded one of the year's most highly praised releases, Teenage Fanclub's *A Catholic Education*, but it's this offering by Chapel Hill, N.C., quartet Superchunk that really gets my blood boiling. Sure, the distorted guitars, bludgeoning bass and snarled vocals are de rigueur at the moment, but these 10 songs offer something more than postmodern nihilism: unwashed melodies and gobs of genuine feeling. In the aptly titled "My Noise," Mac McCaughn [sic] wails, 'It's my life and it's my voice,' and his passion is infectious. The production is a big, sloppy mess, but time and again these guys mold the mud into a great pop song.
> — Greg Kot, the *Chicago Tribune*, October 1990.

Bob Lawton (Founder of Twin Towers Touring; booking agent for Superchunk, Sonic Youth,

Chuck Garrison in the Superchunk van's rear loft, February 1991.

Erectus Monotone in front of CBGB's, February 1990.

and Yo La Tengo)   They had this incredible energy. And for a punk band — if you want to call them a punk band — they had songs. So many bands don't have songs. They may have an attitude, they may have a shtick, they may have figured out something that appeals to people. But Superchunk could actually write songs and play them. They weren't going to be on the radio, and weren't verse-chorus-verse-chorus, and they didn't use the word "love" in the title. But they could still really write good songs. And the abandon! The way Mac played, running and jumping, and so physical — god they were a fucking good band.

Superchunk came out in September 1990, but the band couldn't book a tour until Laura graduated from UNC in December. In the spring of 1991, they embarked on a nation-wide tour to the West Coast for the first time, where they opened for Sonic Youth — then at the height of their powers, having released *Goo* on DGC the year before — at the Whisky a Go Go.

Aaron Stauffer   When they opened for Sonic Youth at the Whisky, they just rose to the occasion and were amazing. It was the first time I saw them on a big stage, and they were playing all those *No Pocky for Kitty* songs. And they were just fucking great. I remember thinking, "They're going to be popular." They played "Cast Iron," and Mac had the total star power at that moment. He was glowing.

On the way back, they scheduled a three-day stop in Chicago to record their second record, *No Pocky for Kitty,* with Steve Albini. They stayed at Margasak's apartment.

Peter Margasak   The next time they came through, in April 1991, they insisted on playing Czar Bar. They could have played at a much bigger club. And Bob Lawton was already booking them, and wanted them to play at the venues he had relationships with. But they said we have to play the Czar Bar in Chicago. Which made me respect them more, because it was like payback for the $15 we lost on them the first time.

Mac   Steve suggested we do the record at Chicago Recording Company, a fancy place downtown where Styx had made albums. We had to record at night from six p.m. to six a.m. to get the good rate, but even with the good rate we could only afford three nights. Steve kept saying my leads were like the guy from REO Speedwagon, which was intended as an insult. But I secretly took a small amount of pride in that, because I was a big REO Speedwagon fan when I was twelve.

Steve Albini   They were pretty lighthearted. There wasn't a lot of farting around. Coming from an independent background, Mac understood the economics of making a record independently. You have to try to save as much money as possible. And it's much more efficient and it costs less money to have your shit together and be well rehearsed. Less money than it does to sort of hope that things come together in the studio.

* * *

Laura   Oh, god. Chuck. The whole thing with Chuck.

Bob Lawton   How indie is that, blowing out the drummer? It was kind of weird, you know what I mean? Those days, you're all friends, you're all in it together, and all of a sudden: "New drummer! Total rock!" And he was fucking pissed!

Wendy Moore   Chuck was really bitter about it. I mean, they named the band after him, kind of. So that was kind of harsh. But there wasn't a lot of agonizing. They just did it. And I think probably Laura felt bad about it. I don't know if Mac felt too bad about it.

Mac   I felt bad about it. I don't remember Laura agonizing too much. Jim and I walked over to the house on Pritchard St. where Chuck was living. This was October 1991. Right after we played the release party for *No Pocky* at the Cat's Cradle. I'm fundamentally uncomfortable with any kind of conflict, but Jim is not, and he did all the talking. Laura didn't come. There were a lot of reasons why we needed to do it, and I'm sure we could

The Superchunk van.

have handled it much better than we did. Some of the reasons now sound kind of petty. But those reasons were symptoms of bigger reasons. We were all new at being crammed together in a van for days at a time, and being on tour was hard because there were no boundaries between your space and anyone else's. I like Chuck, and when we see each other now it's friendly. And he's actually been on Merge since then as a member of the great Pipe band. It didn't have anything to do with his drumming. Chuck made punk rock swing.

Jim Wilbur   Mac and I went to talk to him, but I was the one who had to say, "You're out." And then he called me later, and it was ugly. It was just ugly. I don't want to say anything bad about Chuck.

Laura Cantrell   I think there was a period where Mac really did things that he enjoyed with his friends, and then, all of a sudden, it was also business. And that could be a totally different animal. That was a moment where everybody grew up a little bit.

Garrison declined to be interviewed for this book.

Mac   I actually didn't think he would take it as hard as he did, because he was going around telling people he didn't want to be in the band anymore. It's not like Chuck was so happy being in Superchunk.

Ron Liberti (Pipe)   Chuck claims that "Slack Motherfucker" was written about him. Because, god bless Chuck Garrison, but he's just not the most reliable dude. He claims that he fell asleep during practice at some point. And then, the next practice, Mac's like, I've got a new song — "Slack Motherfucker." And Chuck's like, "Hey! Hey!" Chuck's a badass, but I think they just traded for somebody that might have been ready in their life to go tour Japan and to take this maybe more seriously. I don't know. Chuck's a sweetheart, but he is a slack motherfucker, you know? I do love the guy, though.

Mac   "Slack Motherfucker" is not about Chuck. It's about a guy I used to work with at Kinko's. That's the most bizarre thing. And it's such a weird idea. I mean, he was in the band at the time, and he recorded the song! Not that you couldn't write a song about someone that you're in a band with, even if they're still in the band. But it's just not what it's about.

Jon Wurster was raised in Philadelphia. He grew up thoroughly ensconced in the world of late-eighties hardcore — his high school band, Psychotic Norman, opened for the Minutemen in 1985, just months before Minutemen frontman D. Boon was killed in a car accident. But he had an equal affection for the southern dreampop of bands like R.E.M. and Let's Active that was then emanating from Mitch Easter's Drive-In Studio in Winston-Salem, N.C. In 1983, when he was fifteen, Wurster read a zine review of a record by a Winston-Salem roots-rock band called the Right Profile, sent away for a record, and struck up a correspondence with the band. Three years later, the Right Profile was looking for a new drummer; Wurster flew to North Carolina to audition, and joined the band. Two months after that, Clive Davis signed the Right Profile to Arista Records.

The Right Profile's experience on Arista was a farcical tour through the major-label machinery, which included a commemora-tive Polaroid, taken in Davis's office at the contract signing, of Davis handing the band members a gold record (it was a Whitney Houston record that Davis took off the wall); recording sessions at Sam Phillips's Memphis studio; and requests from the label that the band record a song called "I'm Not Your Lover But I Was Last Night," an outtake from Bon Jovi's *Slippery When Wet*. By 1991, the band had been dropped and changed its name to the Carneys. Wurster was living in Chapel Hill, working as a window washer. His brother Lane lived there, too, and was friendly with Mac. After a particularly disastrous Carneys tour in 1991 — "We were supposed to do an outdoor show in Lubbock, but it was rained out, so the promoter says, 'I have good news: You're all getting in free to the Dread Zeppelin show I'm putting on down the street!'" — Wurster returned home to a message that Mac was interested in talking to him.

Jon Wurster   I was at the record release party for *No Pocky*, and I watched them play, and it was a whole different band, I thought, than when they opened for the Accelerators. Because they'd been out on the road, and the band was totally tight. The songs totally came across for the first time, for me anyway. Like, "Wow. They're great." So I talked to Mac after that and said, "Yeah, I want to do it." My first show was just a couple days later, at the Madonnathon, which was a benefit for WXYC at the Cradle.

Frank Heath   The Madonnathon. It was ridiculous. But that was so typical of our scene. Sort of this cerebral, like, how are we going to put on a show without seeming to be pretentious? We're going to have a stupid enough theme that it's obvious that we're making fun of ourselves.

Jon Wurster   We were billed that night as Super-duper-chunk, because Jack was playing with us also. It was the only time that ever happened. And we opened with a cover, but not a Madonna cover. The first song that I ever played with Superchunk live was Metallica's "Enter Sandman."

Tom Scharpling (Founder of zine and record label called *18 Wheeler*; television writer; comedy partner of Jon Wurster)   I thought Chuck was great. But Jon, to me, he was like a force back there. All of a sudden there's this drummer who was pushing the whole thing to go as hard and as loud and as fast as it can go. And it just matched Mac perfectly when Jon joined the group. And then they became my favorite band.

* * *

Next Two Pages: Superchunk circa 1992.

Mac McCaighan guitar

Jim Wilbur guitar

Laura Ballance bass

Chuck Garrison drums

Superchunk trading cards from the Wet Behind the Ears tour.
Note the misspelling of Mac's last name, above, and Laura's
last name on the next page.

JIM WILBUR

a.k.a "shloopey shloppy"
Instrument: guitar
Personal Description: six feet and all man
Secret geeky thing: hasn't got a guitar yet
Three favorites:
1. tofu pups
2. scotch
3. skunk

All time best makeout tune: "Mom I gave the cat some acid" by the Happy Flowers
Fantasy gig: Dinosaur, Sockeye, Patsy Cline all appearing at a high school auditorium with crepe paper
Quote: "Lookin' good, feelin' good, soundin' good!"

MAC McCAIGHAN

a.k.a "Ralph"
Personal Description: 5'8 1/2", dusky green build and thin as a stick, missing three fingers on the left hand.
Instrument: mid 20's Gibson Melody Maker, cherry red, through a Mesa Loud amp, and sometimes I spit on the mike.
Secret geeky thing: original instigator of young rock
Three Favorites:
1. peanut butter and banana sandwich with a glass of chocolate milk
2. the now-extinct giant sloth

All time best makeout tune: "Moonlight Mile" by Maggot Brain
Fantasy Gig: opening for Blondie and Cheap Trick at a bowling alley in Champlain, IL in 1977
Quote: "Less talk, more rock."

CHUCK GARRISON

a.k.a "Chunk"
Personal Description: 6'6" 312 lbs., black hair, black eyes
Instrument played: circa 1933 termite ridden piece of shit
Secret Geeky thing: Huh?
Three Favorites:
1. raw version
2. raw version
3. raw version

All time best makeout tune: any recent power-ballad
Fantasy gig: to be the Scorpion road manager/drug and girl gopher
Quote: "...Hey! Has anybody seen my keys?............HEY! HAS ANYBO-.........Damn, what's this shit on the floor?..................."

LAURA BALANCE

a.k.a "scar patty" or "twingette"
Personal Description: kinda short with big hips, but others say "dark and lovely"
Instrument: bass
Secret geeky thing: puts her boogers on the bottoms of her shoes
Three Favorites:
1. ravioli
2. meer cats at the zoo
3. knitting

All time best makeout tune:
Fantasy gig: "One where I don't have to play"
Quote: "Life is too deliberate to be random."

Mac, wearing a Star Crunch
cookie box, at O'Cayz Corral,
1990.

Sign posted in Seaweed's pickup truck on the Wet Behind the Ears tour.

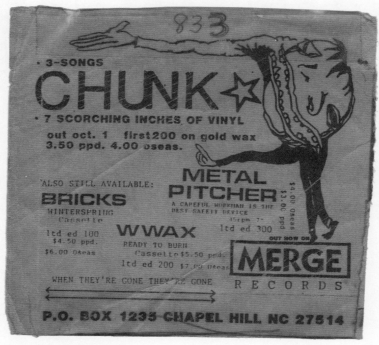

Merge insert circa 1989.

wet behind the ears tour 1990

from washington, d.c.

geek

...from Tacoma, WA...

Seaweed

SUPERCHUNK
SUPERCHUNK
SUPERCHUNK
SUPERCHUNK

simple machines

Leopard Gecko Records
P.O. Box 45486 Tacoma, WA 98445

MERGE
RECORDS

appearing at :   on this date :

Wet Behind the Ears tour flyer.

Laura in the van on the Wet Behind the Ears tour, summer 1990.

MY NOISE (mod)
1-2-3-4
RIFF (4X)
HALF TIME
VERSE
FILL (2X)
HALF TIME
VERSE
FILL 2X
STOP
RIFF - FAST (1X)
FILL 2X?
AFTR OCT - (4)
4X - RIFF
RETARD or 7X
END (4)

Jon Wurster's chart for "My Noise."

Wet Behind the Ears tour group photo, summer 1990.

"The Cow"—purchased at the Mousehouse Cheesehaus in Windsor, Wisc.—carried all Superchunk's tour cash and receipts.

FALL 1990

Here we are at edition #2 of the Merge newsletter/ catalogue fun factsheet etc. hope your summers were all sexy and filled with melting things and hot pavement. Hot off the presses is the WWAX double 7" containing seven fine tunes you can dance to and packed into a thick and texturally delicious brown sleeve that opens out into a semi-gatefold sorta deal, plus fun inserts. Features the songs "Seven" and "The Price of Gas". The songs span two recording sessions and the massive one year career of the band. Grab it. Available by October 1 is the "Vertigogo" ep by Raleigh band Erectus Monotone and it kicks up a dense, catchy swirl of guitars. Following on the heels of that monster are singles from Breadwinner, two heavy jerky songs featuring the impossible guitar heroics of ex-Honor Role Pen and the acrobatics of Breadwinner's incredible rhythm section , and one from Finger, a Raleigh band that plays catchy rock with a capital "R" and a cigarette hanging out of your mouth. The Finger will have three songs most likely and the band contains ex-members of No Labels (you wouldn't know), the Accelerators, and Sink. Breadwinner and Finger will be out by November 1 at the latest. A Zen Frisbee 7" is still pending but a date at this point would be premature. It'll be worth the torturous wait, believe us. Superchunk recently returned from their two week jaunt with Geek and Seaweed and the tour was highly successful, enlightening the masses from Boston to Minneapolis and stops in between . A grand thanks to anyone (Pete Margasak, Brian Welker, Pete Davis, Joel in Flint, John Cook) and everyone too numerous to name who put us up or helped out in any way. We are now selling the hot tour single here at Merge. The "Slack Motherfucker" 7" is sold out, but after 3 test pressings and a pack of lies Rainbow has decided to allow us a Superchunk LP, still coming out on Matador Records and it should be in stores soon...Ha - you say you've heard that before, well so have we . Get it when you can and it will rock you. enough enough...bye fer now

Merge's second newsletter.

Superchunk and Erectus Monotone tour flyer.

Laura and Mac on tour with Erectus Monotone, February 1991.

Superchunk at O'Cayz Corral, 1990.

SUPERCHUNK

Superchunk's first publicity photo.

Laura in the hotel on Superchunk's first European tour, 1992.

Jim Wilbur at O'Cayz Corral, 1990.

NUMBER FOUR $2.00

EIGHTEEN WHEELER
F A N Z I N E
SUPERCHUNK
cooler than you!

· a year with sebadoh
· volcano suns break up (almost)
· happy flowers say goodbye
· first annual dave rick celebrity roast
· and less

Cover of Tom Scharpling's zine *Eighteen Wheeler*, 1990.

Chrysalis

Chrysalis Records, Inc.

645 Madison Avenue
New York, New York 10022-1010
Telephone: 212-758-3555

Telex: 971860 CABLES CHRYSALA
Fax: 212-319-0685 or 212-754-4076

April 25, 1990

The Angels Of Epistemology
Merge Records
Box 1235
Chapel Hill, NC 27514

Dear Label Manager:

I read a very favorable review on The Angels Of Epistemology
material. I would appreciate receiving a copy of some of their
songs for review by the A & R department. Please feel free to
call me if you have any questions or comments at (212) 326-2343.
Thanks.

Sincerely,

Evon Handras
A & R

Letter to Merge from Chrysalis Records' A&R department requesting
a copy of the Angels of Epistemology 7-inch, 1990.

Chunk in 1989.

Chapter Three

Where's Your Patience, Dear?

Matt Suggs, Butterglory, and White Whale

Facing Page: Matt Suggs on the set for the video of "She's Got the Akshun!" shot by Roman Coppola in Tulare, Calif., December 1995.
Previous Page: Butterglory in Milwaukee, Wisc., 1995.

My gripe of the month: People calling about their demo tapes. Please. What are you thinking? If we were floored by your demo tape obviously we would call you. I'm afraid to answer my phone anymore. I hate to tell people that I don't like their music (or admit that I've had their tape for the last six months and still haven't listened to it). So maybe I have a problem of being overprotective of people's feelings, but I'd like to work on it at my own speed. So. On that positive, uplifting note, I end. Thanks for being there. LAURA.
— from Merge's August 1992 newsletter.

In 1992, Mac and Laura popped in a cassette they had received from a band called Butterglory.

It would become the first unsolicited submission that Merge ever released, and it would launch a fifteen-year, seven-record relationship with Matt Suggs. Not very many people know who Matt Suggs is. He never sold a substantial amount of records. While Butterglory enjoyed a brief period of low-grade indie-rock cachet, they broke up before they could find a wide audience. Unlike many bands on the label, Suggs never attracted next-big-thing buzz. He never affected the look of the indie-rock antihero. But Suggs writes aching, clever, and timeless songs, and Merge has always put them out.

Laura **Matt's records are prime examples of how you can put out the best record in the world, and it doesn't mean shit. If the timing is wrong, or the right people don't notice it — I cannot explain what makes a record happen big. Not that it matters. I love putting out good records. And I don't care if it sells 500 copies or 250,000.**

Suggs was raised in Visalia, Calif., a small agricultural community between Fresno and Bakersfield in California's central valley — a red county in a blue state. He has a self-deprecating wit, a laid-back, California attitude, and a nervous suspicion of mainstream culture, honed during years making music in his bedroom that few, if any, of his neighbors would care for or understand. There wasn't much of a Visalia scene.

Matt Suggs   It was pretty isolated. I was pretty much just discovering all these bands — Hüsker Dü, the Replacements, Dinosaur, Sonic Youth — through the fanzine networks. None of my friends really listened to what I listened to. I would save up money whenever I was going to San Francisco or L.A., to go to record stores. And when I'd finally get a chance to see these records I'd read about, it was like seeing celebrities — "Oh, this is the record I've read about for the last year, and now I'm seeing it in person."

When Suggs was fifteen, he started recording songs in his room on a four-track cassette recorder.

Matt Suggs   That was really critical, especially when you're a loner who doesn't have a band to work with. It was so hard to find people to play with, and the four-track became that person.

In 1990, Suggs met Debby Vander Wall at a community college in Visalia. They started dating, and Suggs recruited her into playing a rickety drum kit he had. Initially, it was just the two of them, making four-track tapes. They called themselves Butterglory, and played the occasional house party when they could find someone to fill in on bass, but it was mainly a recording project.

Matt Suggs   It was just these little home-made tapes. We made little potato-print covers with handmade-looking stuff and just ran off maybe fifty of each to hand out to friends. It wasn't like we were trying to even be a real band.

Four-tracks had been around since the late 1970s, and Bruce Springsteen famously recorded *Nebraska* on one in 1982. But the early nineties saw a flourishing cassette culture, based on bedroom noodlers who dubbed copies of their output with mocked-up covers to mimic "real" releases. Small-scale labels and distributors — like Chicago's Ajax Records, which published a catalog of cassette releases with capsule reviews that readers could order from, and Dennis Callaci's Shrimper, which sold

An early self-released Butterglory cassette.

cassette-only releases from Nothing Painted Blue and the Mountain Goats — sprung up to meet the demand.

Matt and Debby were happy just making cool-looking tapes — the designs were simple, with block lettering and stark line drawings — for their friends, but they occasionally sent out copies just to see what would happen.

Matt Suggs   We sent a few out to labels and stuff, more or less just to get some acknowledgement, because we felt so isolated. If I just got the letter back on label letterhead saying, "Thanks for sending the tape," that would be enough.

Matt had read about, and bought, Superchunk's "Cool" 7-inch, but he had never seen the band, and knew next to nothing about Merge aside from the occasional reference to their early releases he'd seen in zines.

Matt Suggs   I had bought these padded envelopes that came in a package of three. And I was sending a tape to Ajax, and a tape to K Records. And so I had this third envelope. And it was like, "Oh, let's just send it to Merge." I didn't even put down a phone number or anything.

Mac   I'd never heard of them, and it kind of reminded me of Pavement a little bit. But the more I listened to it, I thought the songs were really there, and catchy.

Mac wrote Suggs and Vander Wall a letter saying Merge would like to put out a 7-inch with a couple of the tape's dozen or so songs. In the interim, Matt and Debby had decided to leave Visalia for Lawrence, Kansas, a college town that was capable of supporting a music scene.

Matt Suggs   I got it literally the day before Debby and I were leaving to move to Kansas. I thought my friends were playing a prank on me, like it was a plot to keep us from moving. I had to check the postmark on the envelope. It actually came from North Carolina.

Matt and Debby drove from Lawrence to Columbia, Mo., to discuss the details with Mac and Laura a few weeks later, when Superchunk came through town. One day in the fall of 1992, a UPS deliveryman knocked on Suggs's door in Lawrence with a box of 100 copies of the "Alexander Bends" 7-inch.

Matt Suggs   I'll never know how that feels again. You open the box and pull a record out, and you just can't believe it. And you turn it over, and the Merge logo is on the back. I was beside myself. And I played it. Even though I knew all the songs. I put the needle on and listened to it. Well, it's on there. Wow.

"Alexander Bends" is a defining document of the lo-fi recording movement. The songs were built around simple, repetitive, almost childlike guitar lines, undergirded by Vander Wall's hesitant drumming. The pair traded vocals on the record's five songs, and their laconic, unpolished voices lent the record a sense that the whole thing was on the verge of falling apart. Rendered through the depredations of a four-track, Butterglory sounded like a wind-up toy — a plinking, wheezing, pop contraption.
   "Alexander Bends" was well received by several zines, and sold out of its 1,500-copy pressing within a year. In April 1993, Superchunk was playing in Lawrence with Rocket From the Crypt, and Mac and Laura asked Butterglory to open.

We made little potato-print covers with handmade-looking stuff and just ran off maybe fifty of each to hand out to friends. It wasn't like we were trying to even be a real band.

— Matt Suggs

Matt Suggs   I thought, "Oh shit, we don't even have a band." We've come out of the bedroom, and we have to get our shit together. A friend of ours who was living on the West Coast came out to play bass. We practiced a few times. It was a well-attended show, because of Superchunk. And it was the first time we played what I'd call a real show — a real stage with a real sound system. I had to get drunk the whole day, pretty much.

It was a strategy Mac and Laura would use repeatedly to help build the label — asking their lesser-known bands to open for Superchunk.
   Butterglory followed "Alexander Bends" with another four-tracked 7-inch, "Our Heads," one year later. In 1993, Suggs dropped out of school — "always a good idea," he says — to take Butterglory on tour.

Matt Suggs   It was intimidating. I had never been to New York before. And I remember thinking, "Oh, God, we have to drive into Manhattan! That's going to be fucking freaky! Where are we going to park?" We played a show in Chapel Hill in 1993 that was one of our first out-of-town shows. Mac actually played second guitar with us. I was real nervous, because I still hadn't played on stage that much. And it was awkward, because no one was standing for us. They were all sitting Indian-style. All of a sudden, this dude starts heckling me like crazy. I look over, and it's Jim Wilbur. I wanted to shrivel up.

Jim Wilbur   All I said was something like "Hey, why don't you play the slow one from the good record!" That was a standard heckle from the Wet Behind the Ears tour.

Matt Suggs   We camped out a lot on that first tour. We'd just play a show and then put up a tent somewhere. It was only like $10 a night. You could not convince me to do that again.

In 1994, Butterglory decided to leave the four-track behind and make its first studio record. The cost of recording the 7-inches had been zero dollars, but if Butterglory were to go into a studio, they would need an advance. Mac and Laura refused to use contracts with its artists, insisting that all deals be based on a handshake.

Matt Suggs   It was just an agreement kind of thing. They're friends of mine — people I would invite over to my house. So it was, "Hey, let's do another one! Let's do this, let's do that." We had done two 7-inches, and weren't going to just continue doing 7-inches. We wanted to do an album. I don't know what else we were supposed to do. It was all really casual.

Laura   We weren't thinking of it as a business, we were thinking about it as this fun, cool thing. Contracts seemed like a gesture of mistrust. We were putting out records by people we knew and were friends with, and that could trust us and that we could trust. We'd talk about the basic premise, and that was that. In hindsight, I think that was really naïve. But at first, there really wasn't that much money involved, so it didn't really seem to matter.

Brian McPherson (Attorney for Merge and Superchunk)   I always thought it was a bad idea. I wrote a book called *Get It In Writing*. But that's obviously their way.

Merge gave Suggs and Vander Wall a small advance, and Butterglory went into the studio to record *Crumble*.

Matt Suggs   I was really scared of having big sounds on anything. We were really going for this rickety drum sound, and buzzing little guitar. I was worried that it would sound too produced.

Crumble, and even more so its unforgettable follow-up, 1996's *Are You Building a Temple in Heaven?*, did sound produced. And the production — crisp drums, gorgeously fuzzed-out guitar drones, anachronistic keyboards, and the addition of bass player Stephen Naron as a permanent band member — liberated the songs. No more was Butterglory a quaint shambles — they were a tight and taut, slightly Anglicized pop band, with Suggs's sedated vocals overlaid against Velvet Underground vamps. *Temple* opened with "She Clicks the Sticks," a duet that narrated the band's dissatisfaction with itself, with Suggs and Vander Wall alternating lines: "She clicks the sticks and hits the drums / This song is such a bore / As the guitar player's amplifier hums / It's all been done before."

Matt Suggs   I guess we kind of abandoned the lo-fi roots and accepted the speedy allure, to the alienation of some of our fans. A lot of them were into the lo-fi arty thing. But we were just working within the technology we had at our disposal at the time. It was because we couldn't afford the thirty dollars per fucking hour! And you can only get so much fidelity out of a little fucking tape machine.

Crumble and *Temple* each sold about 5,000 copies. They were well received, with write-ups in *Spin* and *Magnet*. At the time, Suggs was working a food-service job at the local college cafeteria.

Matt Suggs   The records would help out. And we'd go on tour for a month, come back with maybe $700 apiece. But it wasn't enough to live on. I remember a big goal at the time was like, man, if we could just get that to 10,000 in sales, that would really open things up for us. But we just never got there.

Still, Butterglory's name was sometimes mentioned in the same breath in the mid-nineties

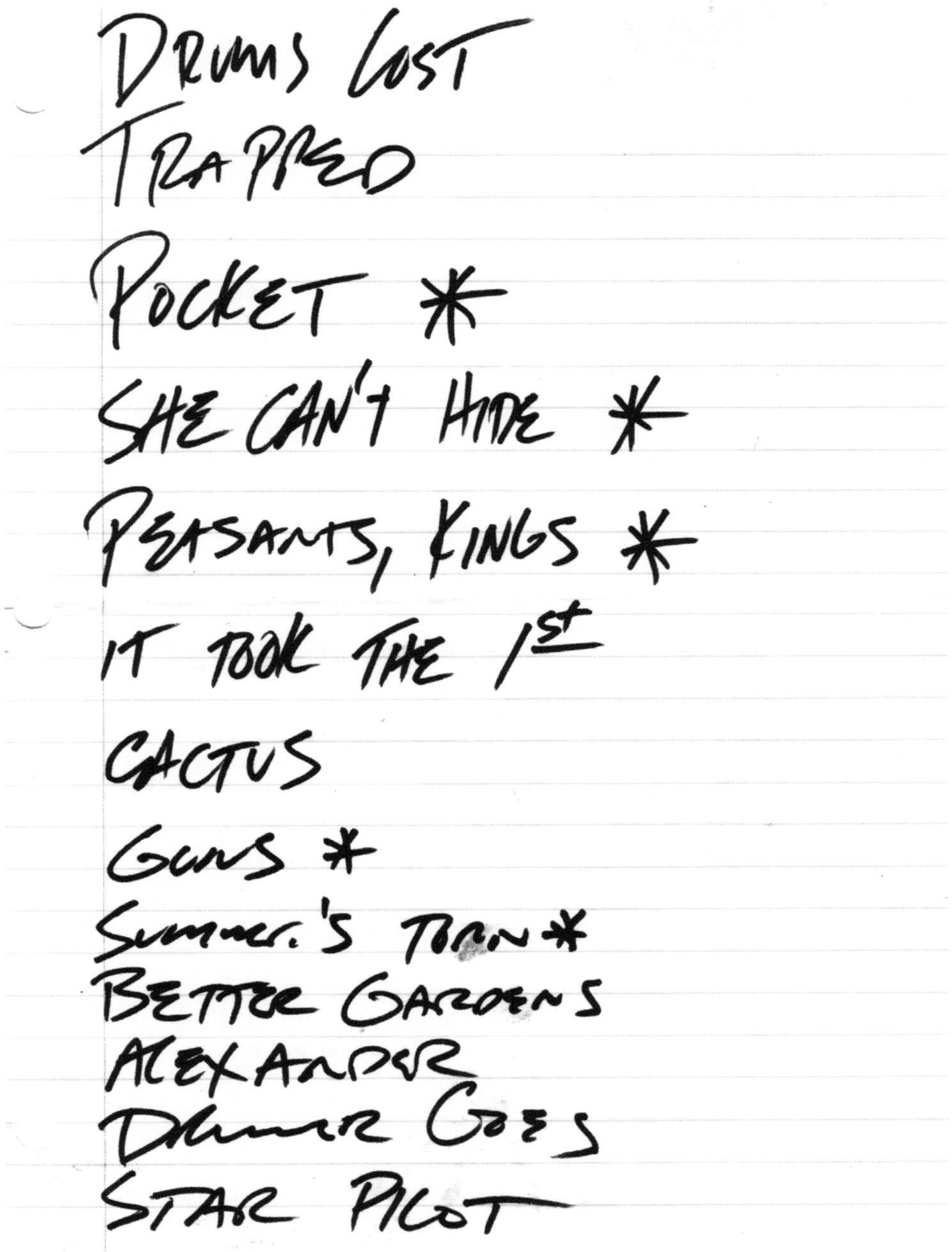

DRUMS LOST
TRAPPED
POCKET *
SHE CAN'T HIDE *
PEASANTS, KINGS *
IT TOOK THE 1st
CACTUS
GUNS *
SUMMER'S TORN *
BETTER GARDENS
ALEXANDER
DINNER GOES
STAR PILOT

Mac's setlist from a 1993 Butterglory show at Margaret's Rock'n'Roll Cantina in Chapel Hill;
Mac sat in with Butterglory (who were listed as "Butlerglory" on the sign outside the club) on guitar.

I wanted to say, "Have you listened to the record? This is not going to get played on the radio."

— Matt Suggs

as Pavement, or Archers of Loaf, and they attracted major-label interest.

Matt Suggs I got talked to by a lot of completely cheesy-ass industry people, which always freaked me out. I wanted to say, "Have you listened to the record? This is not going to get played on the radio."

In 1996, Butterglory was offered a $50,000 publishing-contract advance — wherein a publishing company buys a songwriter's catalog copyrights, in hopes that the songs blow up one day.

Matt Suggs They were offering a ridiculous amount of money. It started out at 30 grand, and then it was 40 grand. And we kept saying no. It was ridiculous, because I'm like a twenty-three-year-old working a deep-fryer, making $6 an hour, and I'm saying, "No, thirty grand is too low." So when it got to $50,000, I said to Debby, "Look man, we should take this fucking money, because there's no way we're ever going to sell enough records for them to recoup even half that. So let's just take their fucking money."

The publishing company sent a $10,000 check as first payment, and Debby and Matt went to Santa Monica to sign the papers.

Matt Suggs We're in the office with the big cheese. He comes in with a fucking camera and starts taking pictures of us. I felt like we were the band on *Beverly Hills 90210* or something. He said, "Buddy, let me see you smile," and we had to pretend like we were signing something for the camera. So this guy

could sort of sense from me that I felt wrong. I wasn't very animated. And he starts grilling me. He asks, "How bad do you want it? From a scale of one to ten, where are you?" He's kind of needling me. And I said, "Man, it depends on what you mean by *it*. We have a different idea of what *it* is." And he says, "Well, you don't want it bad enough." That's how these people operate. So we basically sent the check back and said, "Fuck it." I had a friend who was a lawyer helping us. He called the company and said, "So how do we do this?" They said this had never happened in the history of the company, where a band sent back the money.

In fall of 1996, Butterglory toured Europe with Guv'ner and Cat Power, headlining shows in Holland and Belgium. Jim Romeo, who worked for Bob Lawton, tagged along as a working vacation.

Jim Romeo (Ground Control Touring) That was kind of an odd tour, because I think that was the Butterglory-breaking-up tour. I could tell that something was going on.

Laura Superchunk toured with Butterglory a lot, and we spent a lot of time together. And it was really fun and great. Until it got to that point where it was clear that Matt and Debby were having problems. I remember we were on tour once with the Wedding Present and Butterglory, and Debby was hanging out with one of the Wedding Present guys too much.

Matt Suggs We had recorded our next record, *Rat Tat Tat*, in 1997. It was coming out in the fall of 1997, and we had a tour planned. And things between me and Debby just weren't working out. At the time I never really thought about being in a band and being on tour with a girlfriend. But I think now it would be extremely difficult to do something like that. It was just strange. We weren't very affectionate towards each other on tour. We pretty much broke up, and I found it hard to continue with Butterglory. Mac and Laura said, "Okay, I understand. But let's not tell anyone." Because they were worried about sales — that some distributors might not pick up *Rat Tat Tat* if they knew we weren't touring. So I would do interviews where people would ask about the future, and I'd say, "Oh, yeah, we're going to do this and that." When I knew the whole time that the band was breaking up. We were scheduled to play a Merge showcase at CMJ that year, which we cancelled. And Stephin Merritt said from the stage that Butterglory had broken up. And it was kind of just done.

Suggs left Lawrence and moved back to Visalia, taking a job in the kitchen of a local restaurant. It was two years before he decided to make a solo record.

Matt Suggs   In my relationship with Mac and Laura, I never assumed anything. So I went to them and said, "Look — it's not Butterglory, so I can't say if you guys will want to put it out."

Suggs recorded *Golden Days Before They End* — the name comes from Roy Orbison's "It's Over" — in Lawrence in 1999, with Naron playing bass and Ranjit Arab, who had toured with Butterglory and played on *Rat Tat Tat*, on guitar. In other words, it was Butterglory with a different drummer. But it sounded nothing like Butterglory. *Golden Days* is epic; *The New York Observer* described it as "visceral music that incorporates honky-tonk piano with elements of spaghetti-Western scores: taut, twangy electric guitars, mandolins, snare drums, castanets and the mournful howl of Mr. Suggs' lap steel guitar." The four-on-the-floor propulsion of Butterglory was replaced by shuffles and waltzes; the Velvet Underground debt had been repaid, and new accounts opened with the Kinks and Neil Young. Populated by circus performers, skeletons, vultures, palm readers, and ghosts, *Golden Days* is as visceral and punishing a document of a failed relationship as *Blood on the Tracks*.

Matt Suggs   It was a real cathartic time for me making that record. Part of me wanted to prove to myself that I could still do it. So I gave the tape to Mac and Laura at a Superchunk show in L.A., and they called and said, "We love it."

Merge released *Golden Days* in June 2000. Suggs only did one brief tour, out to New York to play Merge's 2000 CMJ showcase. At the CMJ show, Suggs shed the shoegazing indie-rock pose that he had struck with Butterglory, stalking the stage in leaps and bounds like he was playing a monster in a children's play and conducting the band like a maestro. But not many people got to see Suggs on stage that year.

Matt Suggs   The economics of touring got tough, because we were all spread out. Ever since I went solo, tours were pretty much a money drain. Guarantees for shows weren't the best. And touring can start to get old. Especially if you're sleeping on the boards. I didn't really care about it in my twenties. But you get into your thirties, and I'd rather just be at home watching some bullshit on TV.

Golden Days sold 1,500 copies, far less than the Butterglory records. A follow-up, *Amigo Row*, recorded with Lawrence's Thee Higher Burning Fire, expanded in several directions from the territory staked out with *Golden Days*. Suggs wrote the songs on piano, which he had recently learned to play. They flirted with seventies rock and piano balladry, and sixties soul, all while keeping one foot in the Western milieu of *Red-Headed Stranger*. It didn't sell any better than *Golden Days*.

Matt Suggs   Every time I finish a project post-Butterglory, I've always thought that might be it for me. *Golden Days* pretty much bombed, and *Amigo Row* didn't do any better. A lot of people were surprised that it didn't do better. But that's almost been the story of my life with this shit. "Oh, I would have thought that record would have done better." What can you do? It sold 1,500 copies. I never got into this for the fame and fortune, but sometimes the frustration of never really achieving any kind of success does wear on me. Like, if no one's listening, maybe I should do my own thing and not worry about putting it out.

Laura   I know he wants more to come out of — or I feel like he wants more to come out of — putting out a record than it just selling a few copies. And he *so* deserves it.

After touring for *Amigo Row*, Suggs returned to Visalia and stopped playing — but not writing songs — for two years before his friends in Thee Higher Burning Fire and Robbie Pope, the former bass player for the Get Up Kids, coaxed him into forming a new band and moving back to Lawrence.

White Whale was a different animal entirely, so to speak, than anything Suggs had done before. It was a collaborative effort, with all five members pushing and pulling the songs, which Suggs wrote with keyboard player and guitarist Dustin Kinsey, into more explosive and strange directions. The band's only record, *WWI*, released by Merge in 2006, is a sprawling, circuitous progrock concept album worthy of David Bowie, with driving anthems devolving into overprocessed diversions of burbling electronic keys, guitar feedback, and treated vocals. Lyrically, *WWI* hews to a nautical theme — the spooky Western plains imagery of Suggs's solo records had given way to admirals, yeomen, fetching damsels, and talk of going down with the ship.

Most dramatic, however, was Suggs's transformation from self-effacing singer-songwriter to enthusiastic frontman. *WWI* features, for the first time, Suggs delivering his songs with full-throated bellows and urgent couplets. "As capably as the band . . . rocks," *Pitchfork* wrote, "it's Suggs' theatrical charisma that steals the show."

Matt Suggs   **The guys kind of pushed me in that area. And I went with it. It was kind of fun to try something new.**

WWI received more and better press than either of Suggs's solo records and, owing to the enterprising lobbying of Merge publicist Christina Rentz, the record's release was accompanied by a proclamation from the Kansas state legislature that July 25, 2006, was "White Whale Day" throughout the state. It sold 4,200 — better than *Golden Days* and *Amigo Row*, but not as much as Suggs had hoped. The band tried to persuade Mac and Laura to put more money behind the record, but Merge wouldn't budge from its frugal philosophy — Suggs's previous sales just didn't justify an outsized investment.

Robbie Pope   **Merge did really good with the record. But there was a while where I was on the phone arguing with Laura over money every day. Which sucked, because I love Laura. I think Merge had higher expectations, and was expecting us to tour more. But I wouldn't rather have had it come out on any other label, that's for sure.**

Matt Suggs   **My favorite part of my relationship with Merge is that I feel like we're a part of a community. Which makes it awkward sometimes to deal with the business part of it. A lot of times, doing business, you have to kind of be a jerk. It's easier to be businesslike with people you don't care about.**

White Whale toured in the fall of 2006.

Matt Suggs   **It was okay. Some shows were better than others.**

Robbie Pope   **I was going from playing to over a thousand people a night with the Get Up Kids to playing in front of fifteen drunk people in Louisville. But when we got back, we had actually made money. I was shocked. We were a brand-new band, and we went on tour for the first time, and we all came home with money. But those guys had higher expectations, and they were just kind of ready to not do that again for a while. I don't blame Matt for not wanting to do it full-force. He's done it in the past, and it hasn't really paid off for him. He has written these amazing songs, and it just doesn't seem like he ever caught a break.**

Not long after *WWI* came out, fellow Merge artists Spoon asked Pope to come aboard as bass player. He accepted, and White Whale went on a hiatus. Suggs is working at a record store in Lawrence, and going to school. He hasn't performed or written songs since White Whale stopped playing.

Matt Suggs   **I'm just kind of taking a break. Part of me still wants to write, and create. But so much of it isn't about that. It's like touring, and talking to people. It's not just about writing and creating. The thing about me is I feel like I'm always starting over.**

* * *

The Popular Music

1991 to 1993

Matador released *No Pocky For Kitty* in October 1991, one month after David Geffen's DGC had released *Nevermind* by Nirvana. In November, *Rockpool* featured both bands on the cover, giving Superchunk almost as prominent billing as Nirvana. Within three months, *Nevermind* had replaced Michael Jackson's *Dangerous* as *Billboard*'s top-selling album; Geffen was moving 300,000 copies of the record each week. By May, it had sold 4 million. The newly discovered affinity on the part of a generation of fourteen-year-old suburban kids for loud, overdriven guitars and earnest melodies played (mostly) by young men wearing thrift-store clothes and T-shirts bearing the names of obscure bands was an epochal shift in the music business.

The Seattle scene that Mac and Laura had toured through in the summer of 1989 had gone from a cool and inspirational DIY uprising to a potential goldmine. Aaron Stauffer was working in the mail-order room of Sub Pop when *Nevermind* came out — when Seaweed signed to the label, he had negotiated a job for himself — and remembers the day it hit number one. "Bruce came in with a copy of

Billboard, and he started punching the air and going, 'Yes!' Then he got down on the ground and did some crazy Elvis pose. It was the moment." Sub Pop, which had been on the verge of bankruptcy, had sold Nirvana's contract to Geffen, and was earning three percentage points of *Nevermind*'s sales.

Nirvana's success sent well-heeled A&R reps from New York and L.A. scrambling to excavate, catalog, and monetize every mane of hair and distortion pedal extant in the Emerald City. In a matter of months, Seattle had been conquered, and previously unknown bands such as Pearl Jam, Alice in Chains, and Soundgarden were suddenly bringing in enormous amounts of money for major labels. Even Mudhoney signed to Reprise. Sub Pop and Matador — the latter of which at the time had released just ten full-length records, two by Superchunk — were suddenly seen as gateways to a fortune in previously unexplored musical territory. Pavitt & Poneman and Cosloy & Lombardi were ornery, visionary prospectors who had left the suits behind, lit out for the territories, and hit pay dirt. And now the suits were catching up

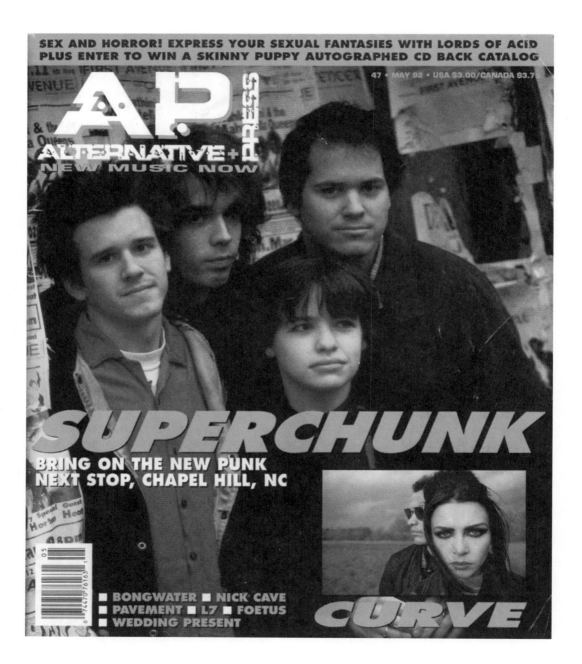

May 1992 cover of *Alternative Press*.

to them, checkbooks in hand. If there was no one clamoring to put out Superchunk records in 1989, there was now.

The same month that Nirvana hit the top of the charts, Danny Goldberg was named a senior vice president at Atlantic Records. Goldberg, a former music journalist and executive for Led Zeppelin's Swan Song label, was at the time Nirvana's manager, not to mention Hole's and Sonic Youth's. In other words, he was plugged into the underground that was going to make everybody rich.

Danny Goldberg I don't think people were so silly as to think there was going to be another Nirvana. But there was an awareness that there was an audience that Nirvana had, that there was kind of a new constellation. There's no question that there was a shift in the taste of a mass audience that was dramatic, and it was dramatized by the success of *Nevermind*.

Jon Wurster We played in Bloomington, Ind., on my first tour with the band, in 1991. And we get there to load in, and there's these frat guys playing "Smells Like Teen Spirit." On the floor, not even on the stage. Like that's where they rehearsed. They were wearing flip-flops, back-hatting. I thought, "Wow. It's happening, man."

Glenn Boothe When I started at major labels in 1990, the watchword was always "artist development." During the eighties, bands like the Cure, and R.E.M., and U2 started slow, but by ten years later, they're the biggest acts on the label. So the emphasis at the time was, we need to get in with these bands early. But all that really changed with Nirvana. All of a sudden, these bands who could have been the future R.E.M.'s and U2's and Cure's were expected to do it in two years, not ten years. Because the labels saw that money could be made.

Aaron Stauffer Everybody was trying to sign everybody. I think the line from Danny Goldberg was, "Sign anything that moves." That was the party line. And that's how they put out a Surgery album.

Ian MacKaye Nirvana was a band that would have opened for us. When they signed, Nirvana was selling 40,000 records. Fugazi was selling 200,000 records on Dischord. Keep in mind that the general rule of thumb in the early nineties was that anything you could sell on an independent, the major would be able to sell double right out of the box. So suddenly they're like, Hello? We want you! Once Nirvana hit, the labels were like, "Oh my god, this is such fertile soil, let's go and grab some more farms."

Peter Margasak I thought, "Oh, well, Superchunk will probably be on a major label within six months."

In April 1992, Superchunk toured Europe, opening for Mudhoney in Holland, Italy, and Germany. They played a few headlining shows in England, where the response was overwhelming. The British music press fawned. *New Musical Express* and *Melody Maker*, England's most influential music magazines, sought out the band for interviews. *NME* devoted its cover to Superchunk, photographed through a shredded American flag, with the tagline, "The Yanks Are Coming! Superchunk Lead the American

May 1992 cover of *New Musical Express*.

Invasion." By the time the band returned to the states, they were selling out the Knitting Factory in New York.

Jon Wurster   We played at the Underworld, in London. Which is kind of like the show-case place for a lot of new bands who are just coming out. We start playing the first song, and it was almost like being at the Oscars. A wall of flashbulbs. It was professional photographers who had just been assigned this show, because we were part of this new thing that's coming over. It was my first time overseas. I remember playing in the Netherlands on that tour, and going in to the van after soundcheck, and just crying. I don't know why. It was all too much.

Despite the newfound popularity, there was little debauchery on the road with Superchunk.

Jon Wurster   I wasn't sure what it was going to be like on my first tour, so I brought a box of twelve condoms along. Having no idea what was going to happen. But I might want to have twelve of them, you know? I didn't use any of them. Never opened it. Still have them.

DeWitt Burton (Superchunk roadie; equip-ment manager for R.E.M.)   Maybe somebody might have too much to drink one night and have a bad stomachache the next day, but that's the extent of the excess on a Superc-hunk tour.

Jason Ward (Superchunk sound engi-neer)   They definitely came down on the nerdier side. Like, "We're real tired, where can we go be quiet and go to bed?" The usual thing would be to get back to the hotel and just go to someone's room and drink about a six-pack and watch some TV. Hang out by the pool and talk or whatever. That was about it really.

Laura Cantrell   You'd try to always hang out with them after shows. I was starting to get a little annoyed by the hanger-on factor. Superchunk was enjoying some attention. And for some of their older friends, it was, you know, it could be a little awkward to like watch your friends kind of go off with their new friends. They used to play this goofy game called Celebrity, which is like a version of charades only you put a bunch of celebri-ties' names onto slips of paper in a pile.

Laura   They would be playing Celebrity. Not me. I would be like, "Shut up! I'm going to sleep." I can't play Celebrity, because I don't retain celebrity information.

Laura Cantrell   Watching Laura in those settings, she would always be counting the money. You could see that it was like, "Okay guys. You're all drinking beer and having fun, but I'm actually finishing the work of the night. You know, we're not done yet."

Laura   In addition to doing all the account-ing for Merge, I did all the business stuff for Superchunk. I did the taxes. I advanced the shows. I booked the hotels. I ordered the T-shirts and CDs to sell on tour. I got paid at the end of the night. I was a den mother deluxe. I put myself in that situation to keep myself sane, and I also didn't really see anybody else doing it.

Mac   We didn't have a manager or anything. Which meant that there was no one for labels who wanted to talk to us to channel all the stuff through. Labels are obviously more comfortable dealing with managers because they're like, "Oh, you're a business guy, you understand." I think that we kind of warded off a large group of people just from the start because there was no one for them to call except for us. We exuded a sense that we weren't that interested in whatever you're selling, but we're happy to talk to you. You're nice people, but we're not that interested in the company you work for.

Laura   It was just noise. I had grown up with that whole concept of, "Dude, so and so sold out! That's not cool!" And the fact that Nirvana had done it didn't make me want to do it. When the industry folks would come around, I would leave the room.

Not every Superchunk show, of course, was beset by industry types.

Mac   We made an effort to branch out into areas, like the South, not known for supporting indie rock. We played a show once in Virginia Beach with Erectus Monotone in the early nineties at the Peppermint Beach Club. We knew Virginia Beach was a total redneck town, but we figured it's a trip to the beach — how bad could it be? We showed up and the sign literally said ALL YOU CAN EAT SEAFOOD BUFFET SUPERCHUNK. After Erectus played, all of a sudden there were these bleached-blonde girls on stage wearing half-shirts that say 'Kool' on them, and they're throwing out tube socks with the Kool cigarettes logo on them. Then they announced a contest where the girl who can take off her bra under her shirt the fastest gets a free carton of cigarettes! To top it all off, Jim ate sand trying to body surf and skinned the side of his face. You can see the scab in our promotional photos from that time. When it was time to get paid, I went into the office, and the club owner took his gun out and put it on the desk before telling me how little they made that night. He then gave me the reason for why the show went so poorly: It's "the niggers" who came into town on weekend nights. *Holy shit what world am I living in?* So that's Virginia Beach for you.

In early 1992, Superchunk opened for Hole at the Whisky a Go Go in Los Angeles.

Jon Wurster   Courtney Love was nuts. Hole only played for a little while and then just stopped. Backstage, she went up to Laura and said, "I hear you're the hot new rock chick" or something.

Laura   I just ran away and went to the merch table. "I'm not going back there anymore! It's scary!" And Perry Farrell was backstage hanging out with Courtney. Yeah, that was a scene.

Mac   While we were in L.A., Danny Goldberg called us and asked for a meeting.

Andrew Webster was traveling with Superchunk as a roadie at the time.

Andrew Webster   It was impressive. It was everything you thought a record label was

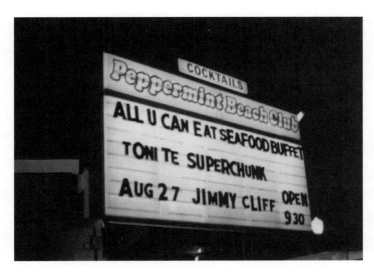

Peppermint Beach Club, Virginia Beach, Va., 1992.

going to be. It was shiny, in a big building with a nice view over L.A. It was a very cultured environment. You felt like you were at a five-star Hilton somewhere.

Mac   At one point, the secretary buzzed in and goes, "Danny, Bonnie Raitt is on the phone." And Danny says, "Tell her I'm in a meeting with Superchunk." I was like, really? She really called? It would be normal if she called, I guess. But did the secretary really tell her he was in a meeting with Superchunk? Would Bonnie Raitt have any idea who Superchunk was?

Jim Wilbur   It was comical. He said, "I'm gonna make you the center of my world! We don't even have to put the Atlantic logo on the records! I want to use you to look cool. All I want is to be associated with you, and not be a dick." He actually said that.

Jon Wurster   At one point, Mac had to go to the bathroom or something, and Danny left the room, too. Like, I'm not going to talk to you. It was kind of insulting.

Mac   No money was ever even mentioned. It was just implied that there was a lot of it. Part of the thing that people would always offer was, you can still have all that stuff on your own label too. Or maybe we could buy your label. Like it wasn't just the band that's interesting, but the label also. But none of these things ever got to the point of a deal

They weren't desperate for cash; they weren't desperate for fame. The only thing they were desperate for was the thing that they were doing.

— Jonathan Marx

memo even. It was more like, "Hey, anything's possible."

Andrew Webster   That same day, we also met with Danny's wife, Rosemary Carroll, who was a lawyer for a lot of bands. Which was funny, because her take on the whole industry play was totally different from his. Danny was quite anxious to get them all signed and tucked away. She was a little bit more reticent and a little more encouraging to forget about the money, because the money would go away.

Mac   The old Good Cop Bad Cop routine!

Jim Wilbur   She said, "You know, I love my husband. But I don't necessarily think that you should sign with him."

Andrew Webster   She told a story about fIREHOSE. They knew that Sony was trying to get rid of cassettes, and so they wrote into their contract specifically that Sony had to produce cassettes of their albums. None of this all-CD bullshit. And when the album came out, Sony pressed however many cassettes they needed to fulfill that contractual obligation. But they neglected to press vinyl, which no one thought would go the way of the dodo. It was sort of an object lesson — you can't control this process as much as you think you can. You can't outguess these jokers. You do the best you can, and take the things you can get. But don't expect you're going to outwit an industry designed to get their own best out of this.

Jim Wilbur   We left the meeting with Danny, and went and sat in the van. There was horrible flooding in California at the time, and there was this deluge of rain pouring down on us. And Mac said, "Well, there's pros and cons to be considered here."

Mac   Those guys are all real good talkers, so sometimes you start thinking, "Oh, maybe he's right. It could be really cool." We listened to what he was saying. We didn't just say, "Fuck you!" But if you think about it long enough, where are the examples of a band like us being happy, or successful, on a major label? Hüsker Dü signed to Warner Bros., and I thought the records got worse. And then they broke up. Maybe they would have made the same records on SST, but it's easy to look at it and say, That's what happens when you work with a major label. Same with the Replacements. I like *Tim*, but those Sire records got progressively worse. Is that because they were on a major label? I don't know. You can never really pin it on something, but it always seems to happen. If our records are going to sell less and less, I'd rather have them sell less and less in a creative situation – a cool situation – than a depressing one where it's just a job to do. There's all this money, but that's only appealing to people who don't know how it works.

Laura   Or for people who don't see a future.

Jon Wurster   I think it was obvious we weren't going to. I'm the only person in the band who's ever been on a major label. And I know how awful it can be. It can be really good if the stars are in your favor and everything kind of falls into place, and somehow you connect with one song that everyone else connects with. But that's two percent of the people who sign to major labels. I had already experienced the worst of it, and I didn't really want to do that again.

Jim Wilbur   We talked about it for twenty minutes, and said, "You know, I don't think it's worth it." And the meeting was done. It was like, Okay we're not signing to a major.

Danny Goldberg   You don't win them all. They just were interested in doing their own thing. And now that they've built this spectacular record company, so obviously it was the right thing for them to do.

Phil Morrison (Director, *Junebug, Upright Citizens Brigade,* and countless music videos)   The real reason Superchunk never signed is that they knew that labels were mistaken to want to sign them. And why should Superchunk participate in that mistake, just because there might be something glamorous or exciting about it? It shouldn't

be surprising that a really excited music fan who's an A&R person at a big label would want to sign them. There were really enthusiastic music fans who then got these jobs, and so of course they wanted to sign these bands that they loved. It was a faulty system.

Jonathan Marx (Lambchop)   They weren't desperate for cash; they weren't desperate for fame. The only thing they were desperate for was the thing that they were doing.

Tom Scharpling   That thing was over before it was started, that whole revolution. You see guys like Tad signed to major labels. Guys who had no place on a major label. Surgery, all these bands getting signed and it's like it was a morbid correction in a way. Like the stock market will take a hit and occasionally correct itself, and all of a sudden the floor will fall out and everything recalibrates. That's all that was. That was not meant to happen.

Aaron Stauffer   So Superchunk was totally against it. And we were initially against it, and then once '93 rolled around, and we'd done this big long tour on an indie record, and we were on MTV pretty regularly and yet we weren't selling — we were bottoming out at 20,000. And we were fucking poor, and we were like, "Let's just sign. Fuck it. We can't stand each other, and we need hotel rooms."

Phil Morrison   Seaweed had come through Chapel Hill, and we were all at this diner called Breadmen's the next morning, after a show at the Cradle, having breakfast. And Aaron says, "Dude, we're signing to a label. Guess who we're going to sign with?" And Mac says, "Geffen?" "Worse." "Um, A&M?" "Worse." And Mac named every label, and every time he said something, Aaron said, "Worse."

In 1995, Seaweed signed with Disney's Hollywood Records.

Aaron Stauffer   Mac and Laura said, "You should just put your album out with us." Mac was definitely like, "It's a bad idea. Don't sign." He was right. But we decided to go for the money.

In 1993, Steve Albini wrote an article for Chicago journal *The Baffler* called "The Problem With Music." It was an astringent and clear-eyed case study of the process by which a band is signed to a major, beginning with the seemingly hip A&R rep who first makes contact: "After meeting 'their' A&R guy, the band will say to themselves and everyone else, 'He's not like a record company guy at all! He's like one of us.' And they will be right. That's one of the reasons he was hired." It ends with a detailed accounting of how, after lawyers, managers, producers, promotional budgets, and all the other fees necessitated by the major-label system are taken into account, a band can sign a $1-million contract, sell 250,000 copies of their first record, and end up $14,000 in debt to the record company. Its final line is, "Some of your friends are probably already this fucked."

Brian McPherson   They were traditional record deals. They were worldwide, up to seven records. Usually the seven records were all at the label's option, with perpetual copyright ownership vested in the label. And everything was recoupable. So they'll give you anywhere from $150,000 to $500,000 per record. You'd pay for the recording out of that fund. And they'd own it and you'd have to pay all that back even though they own the master.

Danny Goldberg   People like Steve Albini have always said the majors are evil and you're going to compromise by being there. I think some artists were better off with majors, and some were better off with indies. I think it was good for Nirvana. Nirvana had a lot of problems, but they didn't derive from their record company. I think it was fine for Pearl Jam, I think it was fine for Rage Against the Machine. I think it was fine for Sonic Youth, who continued to spend another fifteen years in the major system doing great work. There were acts that may have done it for the wrong reasons, or have been lied to. But there are people on indie labels that have bad experiences, too. Not every indie label is like Merge. There are indie labels that stole from people. These generalities are good if you want to get quoted and act like some self-righteous person. I have a lot of respect for Steve Albini, but my experience with him when he produced Nirvana was that he got $100,000 for a few weeks' work. That seemed to be good pay from a corporate company. And he earned it. As far as I know he kept the money. I thought *In Utero* sounded kind of like the other Nirvana record.

Lou Barlow (Sebadoh, Folk Implosion)   I had this radio hit with the Folk Implosion called "Natural One," and we signed to Interscope. The Interscope thing was just so bizarre. We'd go to meet the head of the label. And he's sitting in his office with the Mellotron that John Lennon used on "Strawberry Fields." And you're wondering, what the hell is it doing in his office! Why isn't it in a studio?

Danny Goldberg   It depends on the kind of music that they wanted to make, and it depends on what their ambitions were. Not every artist was happy selling 50,000 records, which in the nineties was what you often would get at indie labels.

Lou Barlow   When we were meeting with labels before we signed, we met with Sylvia Rhone, who ran Elektra Records. And she was just totally full of shit. She was this older woman, with her hair pulled back and this little designer sweatsuit on. We had this totally bizarre conversation about music. And I left the room, and immediately she tells the person who accompanied us in there, "He doesn't have what it takes." And I kind of got mad about that when I heard about it. But you know what? She's right. I don't have what it takes. At all. I'm not even going to argue that point. It's just a bummer. Dealing with the amounts of money that those people deal with — it's just a bummer.

Aaron Stauffer   We fucking met with the head of Disney. That's how we ended up signing to Hollywood Records. Michael Eisner came and had a meeting with us for a half an hour. If we got Eisner in the room for a half an hour, that's kind of big, right? It meant they were serious. They wouldn't have had him in there, you know? But it was awful.

The whole thing was awful from the moment that we signed the contract. We got to spend an ungodly amount of money and make the rock record that we'd always dreamed of. That was great. And being on a bus, and that kind of shit. But the price to pay was that we basically fucked ourselves.

Ian MacKaye The truth is that if Fugazi had signed to a major label, the pressure of the label, the structures of the label, the kinds of compromise that would have been necessary to engage in that machinery — I think that would have broken us up.

Aaron Stauffer They were like, "I don't hear the hit." Which pisses you off. So you go back and write the hit. But it was annoying. I just remember one of the A&R guys playing us the Alanis Morrisette album, in his car. And saying, "This is going to be the next big thing." And we were like, "This guy is on crack. This is fucking awful." And he's in this purple suit and what the fuck? Why do we even have to listen to this Canadian shit? And lo and behold, he was right. But who would have fucking thought?

Ian MacKaye I've heard early demos of the songs that I think are just insanely great, and so beautiful. And then by the time they come out on a major label, they're packaged in a way, and they've been treated in a way, that has just made them — there's just nothing there. There's no substance anymore. I'm in a band called the Evens with my partner Amy Farina, and we have a song with a little melodic hook on it that happens once in the song. And this friend of mine who's in an extremely popular band listened to the record. And he said, "I can't believe you just did that hook one time. We would have to do it like twelve times." Because there would be a producer going, "That's it, that's the hook!" I said, "But it sounds so right just once." He goes, "It *is* right. But we would have done it twelve times."

Danny Goldberg I never was involved in creative problems like that. There have been people in major labels who've tried to interfere with artists, and intimidate them

into doing things that they didn't want to do. After the nineties, most artists that had decent lawyers or managers were able to negotiate legal creative control. Then it was just a question of, psychologically, if they get intimidated when somebody says, "We want you to change this." But in those situations, artists had the right to say no.

Ian MacKaye You have full creative artistic control. Sure you do. There's no doubt about it. That's what the language says. But if the label says, "You know, we'd be a lot more excited by this if you'd just do this" — you're essentially the object of a huge investment. And you want to please the investor. And I just can't help but think that — though you have full artistic control — those decisions are going to be heavily influenced by wanting to please those people who have given you this opportunity. And also, you want to sell a lot of records. That's why you get into that world.

The next Seattle? For months, music fans and record-company execs have been searching for another town to crown as the alternative-rock capital of the U.S., now that so many feel the Puget Sound city has grown passé. Plenty of places . . . have been very eager to oblige, but it's the sleepy college burg of Chapel Hill, N.C., that has caught the fancy of the music world, including rockers themselves . . . . Superchunk is a noisy band that plays superpower-pop by blowing melodies out of the water into a stinging spray. When it toured England last spring, Superchunk gained added cachet by being featured on the cover of the British weekly *New Musical Express*, but the group and its lead singer, Mac McCaughan, seem genuinely indifferent to mainstream success, despite interest from major labels.
— Peter Kobel, "Rock This Town," *Entertainment Weekly*, January 8, 1993.

Throw me a cord and plug it in / Get the Cradle rockin' . . . / Too bad the scene is dead.
— "Chapel Hill," Sonic Youth, *Dirty*, 1992.

Glenn Boothe **People were noticing North Carolina. And people at the labels**

I worked for knew that I was from North Carolina, and they would ask me, "Can you introduce me to Superchunk?" Basically it was kind of this feeding frenzy, and that led to the whole "next Seattle" thing. Which was funny because we never had the Pearl Jam, or the Nirvana. But for some reason everyone thought this area was going to have that. All these bands got signed based on speculation.

Jeb Bishop   It had a flavor-of-the-month vibe about it. People were bemused that this was happening, but also trying to keep some kind of perspective on it, and realize that this didn't mean we were all going to get rich overnight or anything. It just meant that somebody was trying to make a buck.

Ron Liberti   The people that were down scouting the bands, I think that they were looking for the Chapel Hill sound. And there wasn't a Chapel Hill sound. So it was tough for them to scoop us up as easily as they did in Seattle. And we were going to do it whether they helped us or not. We were already doing it. We didn't need them. We had Merge.

Jack McCook   I thought it was absurd. That's when there was an influx of shitheads coming to this cool little town. Every band was "great" for a while. And everyone had a band. Yeah, that was a nightmare. I couldn't stand it. Everyone had a label. That's when I moved to New York. It's much more interesting up there than some guy from Kernersville, N.C., trying to be a music mogul. Or living the rock'n'roll life. When I lived in New York, these fuckers were calling me from Chapel Hill, people I hardly knew, to ask me if I knew any managers. I guess they thought I'd moved up there and jumped into the music industry.

The early nineties indie boom didn't just take in bands. Hundreds of labels popped up, hoping to find a diamond in the rough and ride them to glory and riches. Or at least to a sustainable business model. Moist/Baited Breath, a Chapel Hill label, found early success with *Beyond the Java Sea*, by a short-lived band called Metal Flake Mother whose frontman,

Jimbo Mathus, went on to found the Squirrel Nut Zippers. They moved into nice offices and cosponsored 1992's "Big Record Stardom Convention" in Chapel Hill, and promptly went out of business. And the bigger indies had the same stars in their eyes.

Lou Barlow   Sub Pop totally, really went for it. They really tried to go whole hog, fucking big time.

Karen Glauber (Editor of *HITS*, independent radio promoter)   They expanded, and they started hiring all these people. They put all their eggs into a Sebadoh record. It wasn't that successful, to say the least.

Lou Barlow   We had started writing all these electric songs, which became the *Bubble and Scrape* record. And I was kind of looking for a label. So I sent four songs to Mac, and Merge offered to put it out. And I was actually going to do that. But that's when Sub Pop kind of stepped in and said, "We'll give you $20,000." And that was it. There just wasn't any question at that point. Do we work day jobs? Or do we sign this record contract and get $3,000 apiece to live on for the next three months? It seemed like an astronomical amount of money.

Aaron Stauffer   Sub Pop was always spending money. And they were also putting out the illusion that they were spending even more money than they actually did spend. They weren't ever trying to be a little label. They had these stoner, heroin-addict fucking rockers doing their accounting. It was just unbelievably mismanaged.

Lou Barlow   I kind of wish modesty had stepped in at that point, and that we had gone about it a bit slower and not answered record sales by spending tons more money — more money than we had — to sell even more records. They sat down at meetings and said, "One hundred thousand is good. But if we turn this over we could be looking at a million!" That's how Bruce Pavitt was talking back then.

Steve Albini   The sort of opportunist labels, like Sub Pop and Matador — labels that sort of sold off their bands at the first opportunity, those people were looking at it as, not as a cultural enterprise, but as another in a series of business enterprises. They were thinking of it in monetary terms before they were thinking of it in cultural terms.

Laura Cantrell   I think Mac and Laura kind of got some schooling in the Matador experience. I'm not saying that it was distasteful to them, but I think they were just, 'We're going to North Carolina and doing it our own way.' I don't think they were impressed.

Mac   Our first statement from Matador was a lesson in record business accounting. We could see that *Superchunk* had sold some copies and made a bit of money — more than our advance, which was only $2,500. But we had recorded *No Pocky*, which hadn't come out yet, so the cost of that recording was cross-collateralized against the earnings from our first album. In other words, we wouldn't see any of the money our first record earned until we started making money from the second record. It's totally standard, not something Matador was doing in an underhanded way, but it just made me think, "This isn't so simple."

Jon Wurster   Honestly, no slag to Matador or anything, but it was sort of hard to find our records in stores sometimes. If you wanted to buy our record, you'd almost have to come to the show and buy it from Mac and Laura.

Mac   We were introduced to Corey Rusk and Touch and Go through Albini. Sometime during the process of making *No Pocky for Kitty*, we were talking about Merge and Steve said, "You should talk to Corey." All I knew about Touch and Go was that it was a pretty heavy punk-rock aggro label that had put out Steve's bands — Big Black and Rapeman — and Scratch Acid records.

Touch and Go is a legendary label founded in Michigan in 1979 by Tesco Vee and Dave Stimson, who published a hardcore zine of the same name. Rusk took over managing the label in 1981 and moved it to Chicago, and put out records by the Butthole Surfers and the Jesus Lizard. Rusk did not use contracts,

It was sort of hard to find our records in stores sometimes. If you wanted to buy our record, you'd almost have to come to the show and buy it from Mac and Laura.

— Jon Wurster

and worked on a fifty-fifty profit-split basis with bands, as opposed to the industry-standard 12 percent royalty paid to bands.

Corey Rusk   When I first heard Superchunk, they instantly became one of my favorite bands, and I couldn't stop listening to them. Merge had just been putting out 7-inches, and wanted to put out this compilation of Superchunk singles. The proper new Superchunk album had been on Matador, but they wanted to put out this compilation on Merge. And they knew that the demand for it would be quite high, and that they hadn't really done anything on that scale with their label before.

Mac   It's one thing to get together a few hundred bucks for a 7-inch and fold your own sleeves, but making a bunch of CDs was a bit beyond us. By the time *Tossing Seeds* came out, we weren't just talking about a thousand or two — I think we initially made ten thousand copies of that collection. At two bucks per CD, $20,000 wasn't an amount of money we had lying around to manufacture, much less promote, that record. But we wanted it to be on Merge, and not Matador. We had put most of the singles out on Merge and wanted Merge to benefit from that. Plus, we were already thinking that Merge would be the home of Superchunk in the future.

John Reis (second from right) getting too much advice from the band during the recording of *On the Mouth* in Los Angeles, September 1992.

Corey Rusk   The typical person who starts an indie label is someone who loves music and really enjoys working with artists and promoting their music. But that same personality type, more often than not, is not that organized, and just can't wrap their head around all the logistical things that need to be in place for their company to function smoothly on the whole sort of nonmusic side of things. It was a really brutal environment for indie labels to try to exist in back then. Basically, the labels only got paid when the distributors needed something from us. They'd tell you the check was in the mail, and they had not mailed it. How can you run a business when you just couldn't even predict your cash flow? I recognized that some of my peers just didn't have their shit together in this sort of back-end, just boring stuff — getting the records pressed, taking care of cash-flow management so that you don't run out of money to press the new records, dealing with distributors, getting paid from distributors, keeping track of all the accounting. Touch and Go was just really good and efficient at that stuff. So I thought, maybe I should offer this as a service to some other labels that I like. And if we formed a small group of labels, we would be more likely to have a new record each month that the distributors would want, so they'd pay us on time.

Steve Albini   The people that survived are the people that became competent businessmen sort of by necessity, like Corey Rusk and Ian MacKaye. Corey actually went to a community college and took business classes. This is a guy who *hated* school with a passion. When he realized that he was going to be handling hundreds of thousands of dollars and, you know, the lives and careers of a bunch of his friends, he decided he had to take it seriously.

Mac   So we put out *Tossing Seeds* on Merge, but with Touch and Go handling the production and distribution — basically, they put up the money to produce all the CDs, dealt with getting all the CDs and artwork printed, sold it to distributors, and took a 30 percent cut. It did really well, and the whole process was exceedingly smooth. We were *actually*

getting paid by Touch and Go. I remember the first check from them blew me away. It was like $18,000 or something, at a time when we'd put out two records on Matador and hadn't seen a cent yet beyond the small advances.

In the fall of 1993, Superchunk delivered its third record, *On the Mouth,* fulfilling the band's deal with Matador. Recorded and mixed over six days — the longest time the band had spent recording to date — at West Beach Studios in Hollywood with Rocket From the Crypt's John Reis.

Once they got to L.A., recording *On the Mouth* was a sometimes frustrating experience.

Mac   They were having trouble getting a kick drum sound. It was taking a really long time, which meant we had to hang out in the tiny little lounge with the engineer's vast and "eclectic" porn collection, which we really did *not* want to be watching.

Laura   I wonder who was making those guys watch the porn collection? Those damn tapes must have been putting themselves in. Recording studios are *so* sophisticated.

Mac   At some point the engineer, Donnell Cameron, suggested that we just throw a fat-sounding kick-drum sample on there that would be triggered by Jon's kick.

Jon Wurster   That was like spitting on the Bible. The band whose sample we were talking about using was a hardcore band called Jughead's Revenge. And I remember Mac saying plain as day: "I am not going to have a sample from a band called Jughead's Revenge on my record."

Mac   Just someone please capture how it sounds in the room! Did Fleetwood Mac need a sampled kick when they recorded at West Beach?

* * *

Three years into the Nineties and nostalgia for the Eighties has already begun. Bands like

Seaweed, Rocket From the Crypt and Drive Like Jehu are bringing back the DIY attitude and heartland punk-rock sound of Hüsker Dü and the early Replacements, recalling a time when SST was *the* cool indie label and corporate America had never heard of Sub Pop. Superchunk, the unofficial flagship group of this quasi movement, has been predictably labeled the next Nirvana — and not entirely without reason. Both bands share a penchant for hummable melodies mixed with blaring guitars, unintelligible lyrics, good drumming and a wariness of major-label sellout. *On the Mouth*, Superchunk's first offering since grunge took over the charts and fashion magazines, is no *Nevermind*, though, and doesn't try to be. Instead, the album refines and tightens the sound Superchunk established on its previous releases long before anyone considered punk rock commercially viable.

— *Rolling Stone*, review of *On the Mouth*, April 15, 1993.

Tom Scharpling   I liked the first album a lot. I liked *No Pocky* a lot. But *On The Mouth* — that's an album with a capital A.

In January 1993, the month before *On the Mouth* came out, Atlantic announced that it had purchased 49 percent of Matador. By that point, Superchunk had already decided to put out its future releases on Merge, with the help of Touch and Go.

Danny Goldberg   I was close friends with Kim Gordon and Thurston Moore and Sonic Youth. They said to me that Matador was a very special place and the people that ran it had exquisite taste and credibility. So Atlantic bought half of Matador. The two most interesting bands that Matador had at that time were Pavement and Superchunk. The only act that didn't stay with Matador was Superchunk. Pavement did, Liz Phair did, Yo La Tengo did. And none of them had long-term contracts so any of them could have left. But you're not going to get everything you want, and there are artists that just wanted to stay in the indie world.

Brian McPherson   These guys in the suits, they look down and say, "Oh let's buy these

Artwork from *On the Mouth* cover

little things." Which is why Merge has always been so unique, because it's never sold out. Even Gerard and Chris, you know, have sold Matador several times. And done really well.

Mac   Matador was the far "cooler" place to be. They had Pavement and Teenage Fanclub, working with Chris and Gerard was great, plus walking into their office in the Cable Building on Broadway just *felt* cool to us kids from North Carolina. But for Merge, Touch and Go seemed a lot easier to understand, and a lot more profitable to boot. Corey knew we had another record we owed Matador, and he said, "Why don't you see if Gerard would be interested in having Matador put the next record through Touch and Go, like Merge did with *Tossing Seeds*?" I called Gerard. I remember standing in Laura's kitchen on the phone with him. He just kind of laughed and said, "I don't think we're interested." And why would he be? Matador was a real label, and I was basically saying, "Do you guys need a little help from Corey?" So that was probably a little insulting. But what did

[Continued on page 77]

On Paper It Makes Perfect Sense

— Dan Kennedy

I was maybe twenty-seven years old, living in Seattle. I lived on a street with a liquor store on the corner, and every holiday season there were some reindeer, holly leaves, and whatnot painted on the windows of the place. There were some elves on there, too, and there was a big Santa. Nobody ever seemed to think it was dubious, funny, or sad that the list Santa was reviewing said CIGARETTES, MAGAZINES, BEER, WINE. People just walked in and out, bought their cigarettes, magazines, beer, or wine, and maybe a lottery ticket. Those holiday window decorations went up ambitiously early, around the end of October each year, and they summed up how I saw the world: a place that was equal parts funny, sad, dubious, and seemingly not noted by the people wandering through it.

Further down the hill on Queen Anne Avenue was, and certainly still is, a bar called The Mecca, the kind of dive where big, angry Northwest lugs made for violent and eventually sad and emotional drunks. My friend Dave and I would kill time sitting across the street in front of Uptown Espresso and laughing at the big, violent, and eventually oddly intimate and loving near-fisticuffs that these roughnecks would choreograph on the sidewalk after spilling out of The Mecca. We would sort of give it this play-by-play. "Wallet Chain is pissed off and he's not gonna take it anymore!" and then within fifteen minutes, "Ah, Wallet Chain is sorry, Car Club Guy. He loves you man. Give him a tough-guy hug like he wants. There you go, yeah, pound each other on the back so everyone knows its not actual love, since you guys are so tough." We had the sense to keep our comments low, but more than once we were laughing too hard and staring too obviously and one of the knuckle-draggers would cross the street and give charge — like a Bison letting a family sedan in Yellowstone Park know who's running the show.

One night I got up the courage to go into The Mecca and hit on the waitress — she was tall and pretty and maybe five notches out of my league. I had a crush bigger than the sky on this girl and always saw her around the neighborhood. I sat at a booth and ordered coffee from her. Made her laugh with some riff or joke about the place she was working in, and then asked her what she was doing when she got off from her shift. She said she might be meeting some guy — hinted at a sort-of boyfriend. At any rate, some guy was maybe picking her up at closing time. Most likely one of the ham-fisted cavemen that coated their brains in this smoke hole. So I pulled some huge heart and guts out of nowhere and said that I had some writing to get done, but I'd swing back by around closing time and if the guy didn't come around I would take her out to a late dinner at this Twenty-four-hour place called Minnie's. Anyway, she smiled and said that sounded good, the guy never showed, we went to Minnie's and six months later she's moving to New York City with me. Where does a twenty-seven-year-old shut-in / wannabe writer get the guts to taunt (from across the street) tattooed bruiser thugs with shaved heads and goatees, then sneak into their dive to steal their waitresses or girlfriends? That's where this record comes in.

I bought *On the Mouth* completely by accident, three years after it had come out. Bought it at this little record store by the espresso place. Superchunk wasn't a band I knew anything about. Merge wasn't a label I had ever heard of. I wasn't an alternative-rock snob searching out new releases from hip bands to get into — I was a bartender/dreamer/ loser geek with a pocket full of tips taking a chance in a record store; something that more often than not left me feeling just as alone or as uncool as I felt before I walked in. I can't tell you why I picked this CD up. Once I got it home I listened to it, and then again, then once more, once after that — pretty much constantly. I would honestly be surprised if there were seven days in 1996 that I didn't play it at least once all the way through. *On the Mouth* might be the one prefect top-to-bottom American pop punk album. I'm no record producer, but I think I've figured out a few things about how they made *On the Mouth* so perfect. I think their guitar tone in the studio was achieved by patching the first guitar track through a long history of D-minus grades and day jobs that somehow didn't break your spirit, then it sounds like maybe they did the guitar overdubs a decade later alone in a studio apartment, where self-doubt makes you wonder if you didn't make a big, big mistake by being such a smart-ass in class way back then. The drum sound, I think, is achieved by recording the drum kit with four separate mics set up in the four separate basements of each best friend you've made since the sixth grade. The bass sound is crafted with a more complex recording technique. In order to understand it, you must first sleep alone for at least a few years contemplating how it seems nature has designed the heart to beat strong and steadily in the chest, always a solid low boom with solid meter, no matter how half-hearted or half-assed life might seem when you're lying there alone staring at the ceiling. And Mac's vocal, loud and shy at the same time, is something you can't hear half of the time, yet you somehow understand every word. I'm not sure how the vocal is recorded, but I'm pretty certain it has to do with setting up a mic in a separate room, then asking Mac to recite every string of words that everyone with any heart has ever had floating around jumbled in their head and not even known it. And I think there's a program you can run the vocal take through that will automatically put it in the tone and manner of every single feeling you've had on the tip of your tongue and haven't been able to articulate since age twenty-one up until the day you play track one of this set of songs. But like I said, I'm no engineer or producer, so don't quote me on the recording techniques used in making *On the Mouth* as I could be off base here.

One night in the autumn of 1996 I was bartending at this place where I worked a few nights a week to supplement my eating and writing habits. It was maybe my fourth year bartending, and at this point I was starting to wonder if maybe bartending at this place was all I was ever going to get around to doing with my life. Not that bartending is a bad gig and not that the place was a bad place to spend your nights: a quiet little upscale bistro with five barstools where patrons were keen to buy expensive drinks, keep conversation clever, and tip accordingly. But it was starting to seem like maybe whatever guts I thought I had were gone or temporary and this job was going to be the long haul for me. And if you know anything about bar stories, you know that this is the point that goes, And guess who walks into the bar and orders a drink? That would be Mac from Superchunk. A regular of mine was with him, a guy who did publicity and lined up interviews and things for bands and clubs in town as far as I could figure. Superchunk was playing somewhere that night while I was slinging drinks, and he and Mac stopped in for something before the show. I don't think I said a word past hello and what can I get for you. I remember overhearing Mac asking the publicist something skeptical like, "Why does some big music magazine want to follow around some loser band from North Carolina for a week?"

I was just some guy who felt like a loser most of the time, too, and I couldn't believe the guy who was in that band that made that record could feel like a loser as well. How could that be? And that might have been the moment I realized this whole "loser" thing was an odd con job of sorts from the brain. I don't really know what snapped or changed, but I found my guts again. I quit my job after the holidays and was moving to New York that spring no matter what. Tonight as I type this, the huge guitars are fading out on the last bash and feedback at the end of "Swallow That," that part of the album where the meter slows and staggers to an end just before "I Guess I Remembered It Wrong" takes a deep breath and kicks in to bring everything full speed again. It's thirteen years later, and I'm up too late with these songs like I've always been. The sky's already getting a little bit light outside, and in a few hours an October sun will rise and start making downtown New York orange in transition. Then I'll grab some coffee from the café down the street from my place on Eleventh Street and get back to writing — maybe read this over and make sure I wrote about Mac enough to conceal the crush I had on Laura.

I know? I guess they did end up getting help from Atlantic, though. After we left, they took out an ad in *Spin* that joked: "Superchunk Blew Us Off! But we still have suckers like Jon Spencer," or something like that.

Ron Liberti   Matador was king shit back then. I thought, God, Superchunk really does care about this place. And they can do it.

Jon Wurster   I don't even remember there being like a real discussion about it. I'm sure at some point, Mac just said, "You know we're thinking about putting the next record out on Merge. Is that cool?"

Laura Cantrell   I was friendly with They Might Be Giants, who were on Warner Bros. at the time. I was talking about Superchunk with John Flansburgh, and I said, "Oh yeah, they're not going stay with Matador. They're going to do their own thing." He was like shaking his head, like, "They'll be back. They'll find out they need the money to do what they want to do. They'll need to be back on the corporate bandwagon." I said, "I don't know."

Andrew Webster   They said, "We're going to put out records that we like. We're going to do it in an honest, transparent way." *That's* how you get successful.

Jim Wilbur   The whole "indie rock" thing irritated everyone in the band. This isn't an ideology or a religion. It's just business. It just makes sense to do it this way. I mean, we're all highly educated people. And we weren't trying to be rock stars. We're trying to make a sustainable way of living. And you know, pay rent.

Mac   Touch and Go basically taught us how to be a record label. You can put out 7-inch singles and cassettes and stuff all day, and you're just kind of paying bands with copies of their single and then it goes out of print. But once we started doing albums, it was real. And we essentially patterned ourselves in almost every way after Touch and Go. We adopted their profit-split deal and just kind of learned everything we could.

Corey Rusk   We gave them advice all the time, whether they were asking for it or not. We'd be analyzing every release that went through us on spreadsheets: What are all the costs involved here, and how many do we think we're going to be able to sell? Are the two wildly out of line? That is where so many indie labels get in trouble. They're really well-intentioned people, who are so enthusiastic about the music they're putting out that they just feel sure; their gut instinct says, "Spend this money. It'll work out, we're going to sell so many, because this band is so great." But at the end of the day, that's the downfall of so many labels, because it's easy to get carried away beyond the point of reality. I think with a lot of labels that we work with, for better or worse, we're kind of the voice of reason. Quite often, labels don't want to hear it. They're like, "No you don't understand." And our job is to try to show them — "Look at this spreadsheet. Even if you sell this many, we're still in the red. We really have to make some changes to how this is being set up so that it doesn't work out that way. And you stay in business and we stay in business." I'm sure I had plenty of those discussions with Mac and Laura along the way.

Mac   The Touch and Go folks definitely thought it was kind of novel to be working with a label from a small town in North Carolina. So that became kind of a running joke — "Where do you guys get a fax machine in Mayberry?"

Ed Roche (Label manager, Touch and Go)   I was born and raised in Chicago. I had absolutely no idea whatsoever what North Carolina was like. One time when I called down there to talk to Laura, John Williams — Merge's first employee — gave me her home phone number. I asked, "Are you sure it's okay that I'm calling her at home?" And he told me, "Yeah, you just have to wait a little while because she's going to have to climb up the pole to answer the phone." And I'd seen *Green Acres* as a kid, and I fully believed him. I did not question that in the slightest.

Laura   Touch and Go took 30 percent off the top. And then we were left with the rest, the other 70 percent. To try and compensate for Touch and Go taking 30 percent, we gave the band 70 percent of what Touch and Go gave to us. Leaving Merge with 30 percent of 70 percent. It was the only way we could think of to make it viable for the bands to be on Merge while we had this distribution deal. And it definitely made things hard for Merge. And as time went by and we started to sell more records, it became apparent.

* * *

Merge's early catalog reads like the manifest from an indie-rock ghost ship that haunts the shoals off the Outer Banks. Aside from the Superchunk, Wwax, and Bricks singles, it's a list of now-defunct — and often then-defunct — bands that once populated the bars of North Carolina. There were the already-gone Angels of Epistemology; Erectus Monotone, a four-piece featuring Subculture's Kevin Collins that fused eighties dreampop, spastic rhythms, and vestiges of hardcore aggression; Pure, an Asheville, N.C., band, equal parts Joy Division and Dinosaur; Finger, Raleigh's trash-rock heroes; and Seam, a Chapel Hill band fronted by Bitch Magnet's Sooyoung Park that Mac briefly played drums for. There were occasional forays out of North Carolina, mostly involving the projects and friends of Pen Rollings, who had been in an influential Richmond band called Honor Role. Rollings's dark, complicated new band, Breadwinner, was Merge's tenth release, and Coral, another Richmond band featuring Honor Role's frontman Bob Schick, was its fourteenth. Many of the early Merge bands were so short-lived that Mac complained of the "Merge curse" in a 1991 newsletter.

Superchunk's relentless touring also brought folks such as John Reis into the fold, and began to relieve Merge of the burden of being perceived as a regional label. Mac and Laura met Reis on tour in 1992, when Superchunk played with Rocket From the Crypt, which sounded like a Jerry Lee Lewis–Misfits hybrid. In addition to asking him to produce *On the Mouth,* they put out 7-inches by Rocket and by his other project, Drive Like Jehu (both bands ended up signing to Interscope).

But Merge was still, by and large, the Superchunk label. That changed in July 1992, when, following the success of *Tossing Seeds,* Mac and Laura released another record through Touch and Go, this time from Polvo, a Chapel Hill four-piece featuring the perverse guitar heroics of Dave Brylawski and Ash Bowie. Polvo was a disheveled and detuned glorious mess that reveled in unusual time signatures, unconventional song structures, and Eastern tonal scales. They were hailed as leaders in the math rock movement, but played with an orchestrated imprecision that implied access to some sort of alien logic system.

Bill Mooney   The first time I saw Polvo was at a house party. They were playing in the basement. I was upstairs and it sounded like this kind of a growl in the house.

Mac   I was at that same party. They were completely out of tune and completely great.

Cor-Crane Secret came out in July 1992, three months after *Tossing Seeds.*

Matt Gentling (Archers of Loaf)   One of the coolest things I remember was the whole town getting excited when that album came out. We went to a party, and the Polvo record was on, and it was brand new, and everybody just got kind of swept up in it.

The record, a guitar-rock classic, garnered international attention. A *Melody Maker* critic described Polvo as "the first new American guitar band I've heard for months who owe no debt to the fuck-art-let's-rawk Sub Pop aesthetic" and praised *Cor-Crane*'s "effortless command of the more vibrant hues of the Nineties guitar spectrum." Sonic Youth invited the band on tour.

Mac   That was a big deal for us. Because it made it clear that Merge was not just about Superchunk and a couple cool 7-inches here and there. It was a full-length record, that we put out, by a really good band in its own right.

* * *

Facing Page: Mac in Europe, 1996.   Next Page: David Doernberg manning the merch table in Europe, 1992.

MERGE RECORDS

P.O. Box 1235

Chapel Hill, North Carolina
27514

MERGE insidious tract July 26 1991

New stuff: mid aug. should bring the appearance of a new BREADWINNER 7" with 3 awesome "pieces" recorded in some guy's basemet in Chicago. Also a 4-song ep from MTV stars SUPERCHUNK with "Seed Toss" (a preview of upcoming Matador LP #2) and three Sebadoh covers you'll love. The New Music Seminar was some kinda slippery fun, huh? Merge Nite was a rousing success, CORAL, ERECTUS, and BREADWINNER knocking everyone outta their collective socks, not to mention the sensitive acoustic set by certain fearless members of Superchunk. If you haven't already, you must check out the Coral (ex-Honor Role vocalist Bob Schick and some hot tunes) and Erectus Monotone (5 new serrated pop hits) 7" 's before you melt, OK? Superchunk's new Matador single is finally out as well...ok so I wimped out on the mock Cristina action, but I figured why bother trying with that kinda competition? in my ear quite a bit: Pavement, Mark Eitzel, Chris Knox, the 3D's, Seaweed, live Bastro. Lament: the premature disintigration of locals Willard and Merge stars Pure, both no more. Soon we'll reveal our plans for the Fall, but for now thanks to our NYC hosts Josh n Jess, and numerous others I can't remember...drink lots of liquids

xxxoox   Mac & LAURA

Anti-Superchunk flyer from 1991 for Garbageman, led by Scott Williams, Laura's ex-boyfriend.

Wurster and Matt Lukin of Mudhoney on tour in Europe, 1992.

Merge newsletter, summer 1991.

Wurster examining Mudhoney's van in Europe, 1992.
The band traced "porno crew" into the road dirt.

Superchunk tour manager Dino Galasso, Mac, Wilbur, and Wurster in Europe, 1992. Wilbur is wearing the free pair of British Knights sneakers he earned when Superchunk recorded a song for a BK ad.

Laura after a good cry, 1990.

A 1991 letter from Steve Albini to Mac and Laura.

Steve Albini
Post Office Box 442
Evanston, Illinois
USA 60204
Telephone (312) 539-2555
Fax (312) 539-4495

M&L:

After I spoke with you, the check from Matador bounced. I hope you will understand if I don't send the masters until the check clears. Since there is no immediate hurry to manufacture the record, I don't think it would be wise while they still owe me money.

The invoice from CRC was a little higher than I expected ($1,700), but all in all, this was pretty cheap for them. They always needle me for more money, and if I had another place in town that was as reasonable and nice, I'd go there, but I don't.

To ameliorate the increased studio cost, I have knocked off a few of the more paltry charges from the invoice, reducing the total by $24.00. It's not much, but hey, that's as nice as I feel like being today.

I have also enclosed a collector scum item which you may be able to trade for a yellow vinyl Greek Misfits picture sleeve 45 or something.

The Mouse tape is a rough mix of their ablum, and I like three or four of the songs quite a bit. the song titles are: "Emmet," "The Mayor," "Johnny Cash (swims through my tears)," "Ceasar Salad," "The Bike Song," "Titanium Man,""The Claw," "Systems and Processes" and "Bohemian Rhapsody (just the good part where everybody dies)".

The Mouse (Jenny) is also becoming a fan of the "Supperchucks," and whenever she borrows my car or I drive her anywhere, she has to play the Supperchucks tape or she gets quite mad. I think she imagines a species of little squirrel-like groundhogs or something.

Oh, and two members of Rifle Sport got busted for having a few pot granules on them in Pennsylvania. I had to wire them $10,000 for bail. Thus endeth the trip to Madagascar. I cry salty lemur tears daily.

Goodnight, I'm
Steve Albini

-S

Laminate from Superchunk's 1992 tour of Japan.

Superchunk in Europe, 1992.

Superchunk getting ready to sleep on the floor of Die Insel,
a club in the former East Berlin, 1992.

New Zealand's the 3Ds, the first non-U.S. band
to release an album through Merge.

Phil Morrison and Mac in the early 1990s.

Wurster in Europe, 1992.

Glitterhouse
RECORDS
Grüner Weg 25 3472 Beverungen
West Germany
Ph.: 05273–4137
Fax: 05273–21329

Sept. 25

Hi Mac,

first of all please forgive me for writing this by computer. Someone told me this is considered impersonal in the US, but since I do most of my stuff on this thing, my handwriting has become hard to decipher and I get cramps after half a page. Thanks for sending those 45's, I actually had them all apart from the WWax double. I like them a lot, especially Chunk and Superchunk. I have to admit that Superchunk is my main interest, coz I had the 1st 7" and when in NY I went to the Matador show early to catch your band, If I would have known that you are running Merge and that you licensed the album to Matador I would've talked to you right on the spot. Anyway, Gerard sent me the Superchunk album tape and I love it!! Would love to put it out over here. Unfortunately Gerard hasn't replied to my faxes yet.

Concerning the other Merge stuff let me explain the european market a little. I think it would be impossible for me to license the 7"-es for Europe, as I could probably sell only about 1.000 each. It is also the fact that the harder the music on independent 45's is, the more they sell. As much as I like your 7"-es, I see problems selling them over here if manuafctured here. You would also loose some of your sales, coz I'm sure some get over here thru importers/exporters. On the other hand I am no distributor or wholesaler. I have a small mailorder, were I sell about 20 copies of your stuff each (which is ok by my standards) which I get from Semaphore. If you want to get your stuff distributed more or less all over Europe you should contact Semaphore in Holland. They're quite good and sell a lot of 45's (and care about them). Biggest problem might be the payment, they pay me quite ok, but I've also heard other things. Best way to get your money is probably putting out new product which they want.

The upcoming stuff sounds interesting and I wish I could do more for you. On the CD front things look a bit different here. Independent-wise it is still more vinyl than CD's, so I'm pretty sure European-wise a CD-only thing would fail. I do mostly vinyl and sometimes a simutaneous CD-release (which I would do in case of the Superchunk LP, if I would do it).

What I'd be probably interested in is doing that Merge- Singles-Compilation together with you, in one way or another. If you don't have the money for it, maybe I manufacture both LP and CD over here and I send over manufactured copies as payment/advance. This is just an idea and can be brainstormed.

Back to Superchunk: As I said, I don't actually know with whom I have to deal (you or Matador), but I'd very much like to do it. I'd also be interested in licensing the upcoming Superchunk 7". Could only help your band.

Anyway, find enclosed 5 bucks which hopefully cover the cost for that Three's Company 7" (I like Seaweed a lot), which I simply have to own.

If you have a fax-number you can use, please let me know, coz it makes correspondence so much easier.

Bye for now. Sorry I couldn't help you more with distribution/licensing.

A 1992 letter to Mac from Reinhard Holsten, the co-founder of the German label Glitterhouse Records, declining to distribute Merge's releases in Europe.

MERGE RECORDS

P.O. Box 1235

Chapel Hill, North Carolina

27514

September

breezes are getting cooler and
so are you everytime you pick up
a hefty slab of Merge Vinyl ... with
this letter you may have just
purchased a new 3-Song Breadwinner
ep that'll slap you silly or a snazzy
Superchunk "Freed Seed" record ...
whichever, we hope you enjoy
it immensely. Victims of the
Merge curse: Pure broke up,
Coral are on hold until Mr. Right
shows up to play bass, and Breadwinner are sans drummer at
the moment ... what's the deal?
Who knows but the last few
Breadwinner shows have levelled
just about everyone. Superchunk
have a couple of tours planned
for the Fall, so Merge's Fall
Schedule is sketchy right
now since we won't be in town
much to deal with the shit.
Rocking us baby: new Metallica,
Cake Kitchen, Seaweed, plus
the FUCKERS demo! bye! Mac

Merge newsletter, circa 1991.

Pen Rollings and Bobby Donne of Breadwinner.

Backstage deli tray, Munich, 1992.

Phil Morrison directing the video for Superchunk's "Fishing" in a field
behind Jon Wurster's house in North Carolina, 1991. At right are
Wurster and Pier Platters co-owner Bill Ryan at the same shoot.

Butterglory: Debby Vander Wall, Stephen Naron, and Matt Suggs
in Lawrence, Kansas, 1995.

Raleigh's Finger, 1990.

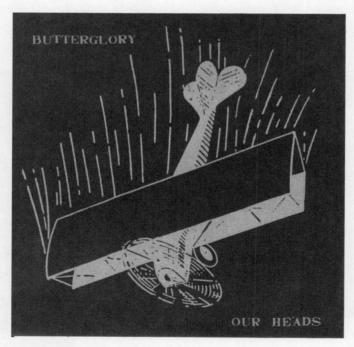

Our Heads, Butterglory's second Merge release.

Chapter Five

Signals That Sound in the Dark

Neutral Milk Hotel

Ruston, La., an old railroad town of 20,000 about 35 miles south of the Arkansas border, is something of a puzzle. It is "very redneck," as the Apples in Stereo's Robert Schneider, who endured the rather drastic shock of moving to Ruston from South Africa in the second grade, puts it. It is the seat of a parish that voted three-to-two for George W. Bush in 2004. But it is also the home of Louisiana Tech University, which has one of the stronger art departments in the region and attracts enough creative types to sustain a tiny counterculture amid the surrounding Bible Belt. And it has KLPI, the school's student-run radio station, which in the mid-eighties saturated the muggy Piney Woods air with signals bearing Black Flag, Daniel Johnston, and the Sex Pistols. And somehow — whether by the vicissitudes of the local water system or the munificent effects of KLPI's frequency radiating through the expecting mothers of Ruston — it produced Jeff Mangum, Bill Doss, and Will Cullen Hart, all of whom would go on to form the Elephant 6 Collective and make some of the most outlandish, obsessive, gorgeous, and influential pop music of the late twentieth century.

Mangum, the son of a Louisiana Tech economics professor, was a tall, shy, absent-minded teenager with a childlike fascination with music. He'd been friends with Schneider — also a university brat — and Hart since grade school.

Robert Schneider   I met Jeff on the first day of second grade. He came up to me in recess with a Wiffle Ball bat, and invited me to play. I had just come from South Africa, and I didn't know what Wiffle Ball was, so I assumed he was going to hit me with the bat. So I turned around and ran, and he chased me all the way around the playground going, "Do you want to play Wiffle Ball?"

In high school the trio, along with Doss, who lived in a small town just north of Ruston and met the rest of the gang at Haymaker's Guitar Store, became consumed with making and documenting their own music. It was, to hear Schneider tell it, a cocooned life of adolescent whimsy, with innumerable "bands," all featuring the same players, each with a sillier name than the last, forming and dissolving on a weekly basis. Some were commemorated to tape, at first by a laborious process of jury-rigging a dual-cassette boom box into a primitive multitrack recorder, and later via the proper four-tracks that all four of them purchased and obsessively twiddled with. They traded the tapes amongst themselves; each pop song or noise exploration from one was a challenge to be met and overcome by the others. Mangum played drums in a junior-high noise-punk band called Maggot; he and Cullen recorded psychedelic songs in Cranberry Lifecycle, which begat Synthetic Flying Machine, which begat, after they left Ruston, Olivia Tremor Control. Schneider and Mangum recorded a project under the name Mr. Burton Says Hello; Mangum and Louisiana Tech students Scott Spillane, Ross Beach, and Will Westbrook were in a noise band called Clay Bears. And Mangum had another name for his own four-track songs: Milk. When he learned that another band had already taken the name, he changed it to Neutral Milk Hotel.

It was a self-generated Willy Wonka world of music in the middle of nowhere. "In school I was surrounded by racist, sexist jocks," Mangum told *Puncture* magazine in 1998. "From an early age, my friends and I all felt we didn't belong there. We all kind of saved ourselves from that place. The little world we had there was beautiful."

Robert Schneider   **We were making these four-track recordings. What we were trying to make was symphonies, but we did it in such a sloppy and haphazard manner, because we were young, and we didn't know how to make symphonies. But we felt like we were.**

At the same time, Mangum and Hart both played high school football — no mean feat in a town where Louisiana Tech alum Terry Bradshaw played college ball — and Schneider successfully ran, as a goof, for class president. They were sociable enough, Schneider says, to avoid too much trouble. Mangum also attended what he described approvingly to *Puncture* as a "crazy church camp" in central Louisiana each summer.

Absolutely no thought was given to whether anyone else might be interested in hearing their symphonies, or how to engage the mysterious and confusing levers of the record business.

Robert Schneider   **We took our recordings seriously. But it was for each other. I don't think we even considered ourselves musicians. That involved some sort of long hair, or leather pants or something.**

If anything, Mangum was slightly more aware than his peers of the realities involved with getting records made, by virtue of his two-year tenure, ending in 1990, as program director of KLPI.

Robert Schneider   **He seemed more experienced in understanding that stuff. He just knew people from labels and stuff like that, and where you could possibly send your DAT tape or cassette or whatever to get the record mastered. But just a little bit. More than anybody else. But the extent of it was that he had a list. He had a handwritten list.**

After high school, the Ruston boys scattered to the winds. Schneider went to school in Denver; Mangum briefly attended community college in Ruston before lighting out on a peripatetic cross-country journey, guitar and four-track in tow, that essentially never ended.

Robert Schneider   **He has a nomadic streak. Maybe he's seeking different experiences, or some sort of perfect place that isn't quite there or something. But he's always moved around.**

They all continued to trade tapes through the mail, or swap them whenever Mangum would swing through on his travels.

Robert Schneider   **I remember there was one moment when I was listening to a Cranberry Lifecycle tape that Will and Jeff had done. I was on a Greyhound bus on the way to summer vacation. I remember looking out the window, and it occurred to me that this was different. This is a style of music that I'm making with my friends.**

In 1992, not long after the Ruston diaspora, Mangum, Hart, Schneider, and the rest of the gang began affixing a logo, designed by Hart, to the cassettes they traded among themselves and gave to friends: ELEPHANT

6 RECORDING CO. There was, of course, no company. There was little more than the distinctiveness of the style that Schneider heard — an obsessive fascination with the border between pure pop and pure noise — and a desire to somehow mark it as their own. It was also a self-mocking appropriation of the slightly pompous language of the business world that was so alien to them. Atlantic got to put their logo on records, and the Beatles got their very own Apple label; why shouldn't Mangum et al. get one too?

Sometime around 1990 or 1991 (it's best not to try to pin anyone down to dates when dealing with Mangum and his friends), Mangum and Hart both found themselves living in Athens, Ga., which had returned to sleepy Southern tranquility after a brief heyday in the early 1980s as the hippest town in America and home of R.E.M. It was there that they met Julian Koster, who would become a member of Neutral Milk Hotel and release his own records, under the name the Music Tapes, through Merge.

Julian Koster   Athens was a place where you could be poor. It wasn't like the real world. It was like a sleepaway camp.

Koster was born and raised in New York. In high school, he had formed a band called Chocolate USA that signed to Bar/None Records, an independent label that had put out records by They Might Be Giants, Alex Chilton, and Yo La Tengo. Koster's experience with Bar/None ended badly; he doesn't like to recall the details.

Julian Koster   They had put out some of my favorite records, and I thought they were a part of that magic world of records, and that it was like, if you went into the office, it would be a room full of the world of those songs. I'm completely oblivious to reality.

Mangum was in many ways oblivious, too.

Julian Koster   Will and Jeff were much like me, in the sense that none of us could keep jobs. Our attempts at working were always hilarious and absurd and ended in immediate dismissal.

We were extremely suspicious ... because a lot of people who had made really wonderful things stopped making wonderful things, and it seemed to have something to do with their interacting with the real world.

— Julian Koster

Robert Schneider   We were all working at a telemarketing job once in Denver, doing phone surveys. And Jeff wasn't comfortable with calling people and having to schmooze them, so he would go hours getting zero people to do surveys. So the boss called him in and goes, "You're going to have to pick this up if we're going to be able to keep you." And he goes, "I'm just learning how to do this. Please don't be like that. I'm a person." And she says, "Go back to your desk now and get to work." And Jeff says, "Come on. Please don't talk to me like that. Can't you just talk to me like I'm a person?" And she says, "You're fired and I'm calling security."

Mangum didn't stay long in Athens. He headed off to Denver, where he lived in a walk-in closet that he believed to be haunted and in the utility room next door to Schneider's apartment. He was four-tracking all the while. Around 1993, he moved to the West Coast "for a girl," Schneider says, living in Los Angeles and then Seattle for a time. Seattle was at the height of its frenzy.

Robert Schneider   He hated it. He recorded a whole record on four-track, called *Hype City Soundtrack*, that was critical of everything going on there. That sort of mainstream business-y culture has always been repulsive

to all of us, but to Jeff especially. He's really sensitive about what's pure in his music.

There was a brief time, for some in the Elephant 6 world, when the notion of taking the steps necessary to put out an actual record beyond their small circle of tape-traders was fraught with peril.

Julian Koster   We were extremely suspicious, because we were conscious of the fact that a lot of people who had made really wonderful things stopped making wonderful things, and that it seemed to have something to do with their interacting with the real world. But I also remember being in a convenience store with Jeff, and he was looking at a magazine with some band on the cover. And Jeff pointed at it and said, "We could do that." And we all kind of laughed when he said it. But it was clear that he meant it.

Mangum was the first of the Elephant 6 folks to overcome his suspicions. In Seattle, he got in touch with Nancy Ostrander, who had a tiny label called Cher Doll. In 1994, she put out the first Neutral Milk Hotel 7-inch: "Everything Is" b/w "Snow Song Pt. 1." The songs were raw and nearly swallowed by tape hiss, but "Everything Is" was a two-chord slow burner with a cool, detached vocal style that recalled Beck and self-consciously psychedelic lyrics ("Everything is beautiful here / It's spinning circles 'round my ears").
   Somehow a copy of "Everything Is" made its way to Mac. He liked it, but not enough to pursue Mangum on his own.

Tom Scharpling   Mac and I were talking about that Neutral Milk Hotel single. And Mac's like, "Yeah you should put something out by that guy." And I said, "Maybe. I don't know." I kind of wish I did now because I'd have money. From any scrap of having put that out, I could buy a boat from that.

Schneider was also becoming less apprehensive about trying to make a living off his music, and released an Apples in Stereo 7-inch under the Elephant 6 Recording Co. name shortly after the Cher Doll release (1994 saw a short-lived attempt by Schneider

Koster with Neutral Milk Hotel, Portland, Oregon, April 1998.

to turn Elephant 6 into a real label, selling 7-inches and cassettes via catalog; it didn't take). Jeff was playing bass in the Apples at the time, so Neutral Milk Hotel and Apples in Stereo embarked on a West Coast tour that summer. They played a music festival in Olympia, Wash., and shows in Seattle and San Francisco before heading down to L.A. to hang out for two weeks. The Apples 7-inch had gotten some attention from Warner Bros.

Robert Schneider   I think they heard hit potential. At that time there was this alternative pop thing happening, so a band like us could've had a song like a Fountains of Wayne thing.

Schneider eventually decided on indie label spinART, but the Warner Bros. A&R rep had recommended that he talk to a lawyer — Brian McPherson. McPherson had been working with Merge off and on — the no-contracts policy cut down on their need for legal advice — for two years at that point. McPherson, who was friends with Shrimper Records founder Dennis Callaci, had approached Superchunk as a fan after a 1992 show in Pomona, Calif., and it was McPherson who had set up the dinner with Rosemary Carroll — his boss at the time — where she advised Superchunk not to sign with her husband.

Robert Schneider   He's a punk-rock lawyer. He was living out of his car at the same time he had Beck as a client. He had his files in the passenger seat.

Brian McPherson   I had this compilation that had "Everything Is" on it, and I'd been playing it to death. And I'd been trying to find out who Jeff Mangum was. So the Apples come into the office because they're going to sign with spinART, and they had this guy with them who had a Shrimper T-shirt on. So I said, "Who are you and where did you get that shirt?" And he says, "My name's Jeff Mangum." I said, "I'll take one of those please. I'm your lawyer now, too. Because I think you're great."

The following February, Mangum decamped to Denver, where Schneider had been building a studio, to make his first full-length. He was in love with the sound of his four-track, and highly suspicious of professional studio technology. But he wanted *On Avery Island* to sound more somber and substantial than his tapes did; Schneider decided to ease him into the studio by using a four-track reel-to-reel machine, rather than a more sophisticated eight-track he'd recently purchased, so that Mangum could still say that the record was "produced by Robert Schnieder [sic] on 4-track" in the liner notes. The two of them recorded *Avery Island* every day, all day, for four months.

They worked obsessively, with Mangum playing almost all the instruments and Schneider producing and playing some bass and keyboards. Mangum would record and erase guitar parts over and over again until they sounded right, constantly searching for melodies and parts that sounded special to him. One of the most fussed-over tracks, which took days to finish, was an eleven-minute drone created by slowing down a sample of a banjo riff over and over again until it was an unrecognizable, contorted shriek.

Robert Schneider   Jeff wanted to make something really meaningful. A classic that would blow people's minds. That even if nobody hears it, it's going to be a classic.

On Avery Island is a propulsive grab bag of eras and styles; there are trombones, but there is weird radio squall, too, and oversaturated acoustic guitars. It's a pop record that hearkens back to American music before the electronic age — to ragtime and circus-tent revivals — even as it revels in the chaotic noise of overtaxed circuitry. The juxtapositions are jarring and moving. There is carnival music over electronic noise over melodies that could have been written by Neil Diamond over distressing and dark lyrics about body organs and drug overdoses — "Your teeth believe / that teeth are for tearing / tear into me / the scent of your sweating / smells good to me" — sung with the tragic pop sensibility and vocal power of Roy Orbison.

Julian Koster   Everything before that had been completely chaotic and homemade, like this little thing that you do. But *Avery Island* felt like a real record.

Mac   Brian sent us a copy. It had a hand-made paper cover. And who knows how many generations from the original this tape was. I was just, like, "Whoa!" There were trombones, all kinds of crazy stuff. It was crazy-sounding, but so cool. It was one of those things where I was like, "Is it really good? Or is it just so weird that it's striking?"

Matt Suggs   Butterglory played a house party in Ruston in probably '93 or '94. And Jeff had opened for us as Neutral Milk Hotel. And I remember Mac calling me maybe a year afterward like, "You know this Neutral Milk Hotel?" Mac would do that from time to time. Kind of like put feelers out. I was like, "Yeah, we played with that guy. He was good." Mac said, "Well, you know, Laura and I are thinking about doing something with him."

Robert Schneider   I remember the day that Jeff told me Merge was putting it out. He was really excited about it. He worshiped Superchunk. Mac and Laura were to him like Lennon and McCartney are to me.

Merge released *On Avery Island* in March of 1996. The grand irony that one of the most strange, unambitious, and uncommercial pop musicians of the current era found his way to Merge through a Hollywood music lawyer is not lost on McPherson.

Brian McPherson   **How hilarious is that? That's such a traditional music-business way of music finding its way to the label. Through a lawyer.**

Just like Suggs and Vander Wall, Mangum found himself in a position of trying to put together a band after the fact in order to tour. He invited Koster to play bass, the singing saw, accordion, and any number of other odd instruments. Koster knew of a ferocious and unhinged drummer at DePaul University he'd seen while touring with Chocolate USA, so he and Mangum took separate trains to Chicago — Mangum from Denver; Koster from New York — to meet Jeremy Barnes, an eighteen-year-old whose parents were none too pleased to learn that he was going to drop out to play in a band. Lastly, Mangum swung through Austin, Texas, to visit his old Clay Bears bandmate from the Ruston days, Scott Spillane. Mangum found him at two a.m. at the Gumby's Pizza where Spillane worked. He was living in his van at the time. It was the post-bartime rush, so Mangum went behind the counter to help make some pizzas before telling Spillane, "This job sucks. You should come with me to New York."

Mangum, Koster, Spillane, and Barnes were the foursome that came to define Neutral Milk Hotel. They holed up in the basement of Koster's grandmother's house in Queens to put together a set. Even though Koster had toured with Chocolate USA, and Mangum had done some touring with the Apples, they were largely clueless as to the logistics of mounting a tour on their own as a virtually unknown band with no resources. Mac and Laura put them in touch with Jim Romeo, who set up a show at Brownies, in New York's East Village, to see what they were like.

The Neutral Milk Hotel that debuted that night was a beautiful shambles: Fast, loud, and giddy, with instruments being swapped constantly and impromptu wrestling matches and tickle fights erupting between, and during, songs.

Jim Romeo   **I felt like the roof was going to cave in. The building was structurally sound, but I just had this feeling it was going to happen. They just had this weird, out-of-control energy. I had to leave after their set. I was so blown away by them that I just had to go outside.**

Robert Schneider   **That band was never, in any way, what you would call tight or polished. They were like, if you took a carnival, and you played it on an AM radio, and then you stuck it in a bucket with a microphone and recorded it, and then took that recording and played it on a Victrola, and then rolled it down the stairs, and there's someone there to catch it — that's a Neutral Milk Hotel show.**

They toured during the summer of 1996 with Butterglory.

Matt Suggs   **Neutral Milk Hotel opening for Butterglory. It just kills me. Today, people are like Butter who? But I watched them on the first night of the tour, and they were fucking unbelievably amazing. And I remember turning to Debby and saying, "Fuck. You've got to be kidding me. We've got to follow this shit every night of this tour?"**

Mangum & co. were as confused and disorganized and lovable offstage as they were when they were performing, and every tour was a cascade of just-in-time arrivals, mislaid bags full of cash, and vain attempts to find places to crash.

Matt Suggs   **They had this Bad News Bears quality. They never had any information or anything. "Uh, where are we playing tomorrow night?" It's a wonder that they even made it to the gigs. Most bands who tour have a method of loading the van where everything just kind of fits. And with them, it always looked like a three-year-old had packed the fucking thing. They'd open the door and here would come a cymbal rolling out, and they'd go chasing it.**

Mangum's love of Wiffle Ball didn't end in the second grade. They would play games at truck stops and club parking lots on the road. In Cleveland, Suggs says, they got so wrapped up in one game that they showed up late to the club.

Julian Koster   **The thing that we were going to the club to do was being warmed up, or kept alive, more by what was happening during that Wiffle Ball game than it would by a soundcheck.**

On Avery Island sold roughly 5,000 copies. It caught the attention of some reviewers, ranking 35 in the *Village Voice's* 1996 critics' poll. In 1996, with a little money coming in from touring and from Merge, Mangum settled down for a while in Athens, where the Elephant 6 Collective had landed and taken hold. The fact that profit-sharing statements were coming in from Merge was "mind-boggling" to Koster; by that point many of the Elephant 6 folks had worked with all manner of labels, major and indie, and almost universally found the experiences to be excessively complicated and financially underwhelming.

Julian Koster   **Merge was the only one that did it in a way that was honest and real. I don't think we saw a penny from anyone else. That's a slight exaggeration, but it's an exaggeration that expresses a truth. When checks started coming from Merge, it was a miracle.**

In Ruston in 1995, a few days before taking a bus to Denver to record *Avery Island,* Mangum had come across a copy of *The Diary of Anne Frank* in a used bookstore. He read it in two days, and cried for three days afterward. He later told *Puncture* that the experience was like coming to know Frank better than he could know someone in the

flesh, only to see her "thrown away like a piece of trash." He began having insistent dreams every night in which he used a time machine to go back and save her life. The dreams found their way into Mangum's songs, and in July 1997 he headed back to Schneider's place in Denver to record them.

Making *In the Aeroplane Over the Sea* was, like *Avery Island,* a venture into uncharted territory for Mangum and Schneider. Where the challenge of *Avery Island* was to maneuver Mangum's four-track sensibility in to something approaching a "real" studio, the challenge of *Aeroplane* was to capture both the performances of an actual, existing band and the artificial, spooky noises that washed over the music when Mangum heard it in his head. The sessions lasted three months and were characteristically chaotic. Mangum brought out Koster, Spillane, and Barnes, paying their expenses while they stayed, and a steady stream of visiting musicians were dropping by at Mangum's invitation to add parts. Schneider clashed at first with the rest of the band, who already had a deep attachment to Mangum's songs and regarded with suspicion some of the seemingly traditional recording techniques he was bringing to bear.

San Francisco, April 1998. From left: Robbie Cucchario, Will Westbrook (at bottom), D'Azzo, Scott Spillane, Koster.

Robert Schneider We were very, very intense about making a great record. We were on this mission to defeat popular music. It was really our enemy. And we felt strongly about it.

During the recording, Mac called Schneider to ask how things were going. "Did you like *On Avery Island*?" Schneider asked.

"Yes," Mac said.

"THEN YOU'RE GONNA FUCKING LOVE THIS ONE!!!" Schneider screamed into the phone.

Aeroplane is bathed in fuzz. Not rock fuzz, or punk fuzz, but a sort of gentle disintegration of tones and notes around their edges that attempts to capture the surging and shambolic spirit of the band's performances. Lyrically, it is an astonishing and continuous fever-dream; songs blend into one another and cascade from an inchoate sonic soup to folk to pre-electric punk. It is shot through with images and moments from the life and death of Frank mingled with bits from Mangum's own life, reimagined as a Hieronymus Bosch tableau. There are two-headed boys trapped in glass jars who can be saved by stereo speakers and fed tomatoes and radio wires, there are brothers who erupt into flames, there are semen-stained mountaintops, there are ecstatic testaments to Mangum's love for Jesus Christ. There is a visceral and graphic sense of loss coupled with a child-like wonderment: "You left with your head filled with flames / you watched as your brains / fell out through your teeth / push the pieces in place / make your smile sweet to see / don't you take this away / I'm still wanting my face on your cheek." And somehow it all leads back to a tender and sad imagining of Frank's death and, as Mangum sees it, rebirth. Nothing like it had ever been made before.

"A lot of the songs on *Aeroplane* freaked me out," Mangum told *Puncture*. "It took other people to make me comfortable with them, and to see it was OK to sing about this stuff. . . . I would ask a friend, 'What the fuck am I doing?'"

Mac and Laura first got ahold of *Aeroplane* while on the road with Superchunk, and played it in the van. Mac and Laura did

FUCKING LOVE IT, as Schneider had promised. Wurster and Wilbur were puzzled.

Jim Wilbur I was like, "Are you out of your mind? This is the worst piece of shit I've ever heard in my life!" But I had a blind spot. I don't think that way anymore. It just took a while.

Jon Wurster Yeah, Jim and I just rolled our eyes. It's not my thing. And that song is like, "Jesus Christ I love you!" Whatever. Greatest album ever recorded. According to *Magnet*.

The initial critical response to *Aeroplane* saw a similar divide. *Rolling Stone* gave it three out of five stars and called it "scant and drab, with flat-footed rhythms and chord changes strictly out of the beginner's folk songbook." *Pitchfork*, which was at the time a relatively fledgling Chicago-based Web site devoted to chronicling the comings and goings of indie-rock stars, gave it 8.7 out of ten stars in a rather cursory 144-word review that commended its "credible job of blending *Sgt. Pepper* with early '90s lo-fi."

Elsewhere, the response was more ecstatic. In *Salon*, Caterina Fake wrote, simply: "Listening to this album is like watching someone fly."

Merge pressed 5,500 copies of *Aeroplane*, expecting sales to be in line with *Avery Island*. (A 1997 fax from Merge to Touch and Go authorizing reproduction of the master lists Jeff Mangum's phone number as "disconnected at the moment.") Initially, they were right. But slowly, over a period of months, the record gathered momentum. Had *Aeroplane* come out five years later, Neutral Milk Hotel would surely have been a "blog band": the beneficiary of an instant, white-hot outpouring of online enthusiasm from a core of fans who loved the record immediately. But 1998 was still the Web 1.0 era, and fans of the album had to actually talk to people to convey what was special about it. People had to hear it at parties and ask, "What the hell *is* that?"

Ed Roche It took a long time. I think it was about two months after it happened that all the great reviews were starting to pile

[Continued on page 103]

All You Need

—Joshua Ferris

In the Aeroplane Over the Sea begins with an acoustic guitar strumming a few simple chord changes and ends not quite forty minutes later, in the hushed silence of the recording studio, when the guitar strings squeak as Jeff Mangum stands up, bops the soundbox while setting the guitar down, and walks away. Four heavy, muted steps through the studio, then silence. If you listen to the album on vinyl, the next thing you'll hear is the rhythmic static of the needle stuck in the run-out groove, calling you back to the world.

The world without the King of Carrot Flowers. Without the Two-Headed Boy. Without the Aeroplane Over the Sea.

And without Anne Frank.

This isn't just an album. It's a mythology and a dream, full of anachronisms and transmigrations and violations of the laws of nature. "Your dark brother wrapped in white," the narrator of "Holland, 1945" sings, "says it was good to be alive / but now he rides a comet's flame / and won't be coming back again." The given world of historical record brushes up obliquely against the imagined world of whimsy, set to a street-corner carnival score that is baroque, fuzzy, layered, looping. It is a world unto itself, as beautiful and strange as the cover art featuring the tambourine-headed woman, the flying Victrola, and the ascending stilt-legged horn players.

A lyric from "Oh Comely" declares the album's prevailing spirit: "silly music is magical meaningful." The familiar mundane sneaks in — a dysfunctional family, a trailer park, a simple horn solo — but the major key is a fantasia of invention, restitution, and multilayered sound. The Two-Headed Boy comes to life, puts on his Sunday shoes, and dances around the room to accordion keys. Fathers make fetuses with flesh-licking ladies while holy water pours from the sky. The instruments involved include the flugelhorn, the euphonium, the zanzithophone and something called the wandering genie.

All of it is held together elliptically by "Anna's ghost" — Anne Frank. The narrator of "Holland, 1945" again: "The only girl I've ever loved / was born with roses in her eyes / but then they buried her alive one evening 1945 / with just her sister at her side / and only weeks before the guns / all came and rained on everyone." The real world elbows its way inside the fantasia. But what history makes inevitable, Mangum transmutes into a gem: "Now she's a little boy in Spain / playing pianos filled with flames / on empty rings around the sun."

Still, it can't be so, not even here. On "Oh Comely," when the warbling saws and whirling white noise that define the album soberly yield to a fuguelike hum, an acoustic guitar, and Mangum's uninflected voice, whimsy gives way to reality. It's the quietest moment, the most chilling, the most heart-rending: "I know they buried her body with others / her sister and mother and 500 families . . . I wished I could save her in some sort of time machine." For all the radical transmutation — the artistry — of the world of *In the Aeroplane Over the Sea*, there is, at its heart, a plaint, a naked submission to an unjust world, to sympathy's sad limitations.

In the album's final line, Mangum sings — about Anne? — "She is all you could need . . . but don't hate her when she gets up to leave." Then he himself does precisely that: he gets up and leaves. If Anne Frank haunts the world of *In the Aeroplane Over the Sea*, Magnum's four heavy steps out of the studio haunt the album. He is gone, and may never return. But no one should hate him for it, or so much as ask for more. *In the Aeroplane Over the Sea* is all you need.

CATT

(ED)

MASTER RELEASE INFO *MUST ACCOMPANY MASTER TAPES   7/11/97

DATE 10/16/97   REQUESTED RELEASE DATE 2/20

CATALOG # MRG136   BAND **NEUTRAL MILK HOTEL**
RELEASE TITLE   s/t

TIME LENGTH 39:56   **IMPORTANT! MUST ATTACH TIMESHEET!!**
SIDEBREAK AT ~~7/8~~ 21:54 BETWEEN TRACKS/SONGS   7/8
FORMATS   CD/LP   IF LP, SPEED   33 RPM
format length recommendations: 12" 33 18:00, 12" 45 12:00 and
                                 CD 78 min. or less

LIMITED EDITION?   NOPE

✱   PACKAGING (if anything other than the basics) __see attached__

MATRIX MESSAGE
A-SIDE: NONE
B-SIDE:

LP INSERT:FORMAT____SIZE____COLOR 4 over 1 PAPERSTOCK____ see attached)
(YES)─ STICKER:FORMAT ? SIZE/DIE# ? STOCK ?

POSTERS: SIZE 17 × 24   COLOR TBD   STOCK TBD
           TOTAL QUANTITY/BUDGET ~~~~ TBD
           QUANTITY TO YOU/LABEL   1500

IS THIS RELEASE LICENSED? (to who, where) NOT YET

IF IT IS NOT YET LICENSED, MIGHT IT BE? YES - UK/EUROPE

*WHAT ARE YOUR/LABEL'S SALES EXPECTATIONS?   CD 5500
                                             LP 1600
*LIST PRICES? CD $14.98   LP $10.98 (if 2x must be 13.98 or higher)

*TOURING? WHEN? WHERE? HOW MANY DATES? ~ 30 dates, FULL US tour

WHEN CAN WE EXPECT ONE SHEET INFO

DECISION-MAKING BAND MEMBER   JEFF MANGUM
           PHONE is connected at the moment
           ADDRESS

OTHER INFORMATION

The master release form for *In the Aeroplane Over the Sea.*

up, and the record was selling better than we thought. And then towards the end of the year, we started getting notices that like every writer in the country was going to put it in their Top Ten list.

Corey Rusk   I don't think anyone would have guessed that it was going to turn into the touchstone that it is. There was a period of time in that record's life where every year it was doing more than the previous year. It just spread and just became this cult record of massive proportions.

To date, *Aeroplane* has sold 254,000 copies. *Magnet* did, as Wurster pointed out, name it the best album recorded between 1993 and 2003. In 2003, *Pitchfork* ranked it the fourth best record of the 1990s, calling it "indelible and heartbreaking." Two years later, when *Aeroplane* was reissued in the U.K., *Pitchfork* took the opportunity to review it a second time, giving it a perfect 10. *Spin* would eventually name it one of the top 100 records since 1985. When *Rolling Stone* published a new edition of its album guide in 2004, *Aeroplane* had been upgraded to four stars.

Neutral Milk Hotel embarked on a grueling tour schedule for *Aeroplane*, opening for Superchunk in the spring of 1998 before summer and fall headlining tours of the states and Europe.

Laura   They were riveting. At that point, it was rare that I'd watch an opening band's whole set every night. But with them, I wanted to see it every night. It was so raw, emotionally.

By the summer of 1998, Neutral Milk Hotel was selling out the Bowery Ballroom in New York. Fans reacted to the record intensely and personally — one young woman drove from Arkansas to see Mangum in Tennessee so she could give him her grandmother's rosary before heading home without even seeing the show — which put Mangum in an awkward position.

Robert Schneider   He would never turn his back on somebody. But it's kind of like a private thing. Even though you made it for people to listen to, you didn't make it for *that*

many people. And so I guess people accosting him — he's very modest, and very shy.

He grew weary of explaining his songs in interviews, and came to regard the creeping advances of the music industry with an almost visceral fear. Capitol, Epic, and other labels went after the band. McPherson would get the offers, but he wouldn't even bring them to Mangum. He already knew the answer.

Julian Koster   Everything was snowballing. We were aware of that.

Magazines were calling, asking for photo shoots. Promoters were asking them to tour Japan. Labels were buying them dinner. The idyllic life of hanging out and playing songs and laughing while cymbals rolled down the sidewalk was suddenly taking on an adult, professional patina. Since Ruston, the only thing Magnum cared about was making music; now there were parts of making music — the adulation, the press, the money — that he felt he needed to protect himself from.

Julian Koster   There is a big world out there, that's very powerful and can be very crushing if you're on the wrong side of it. You can't tread under the foot of a thousand-ton animal, you know? You have to be aware of it.

To Mangum, there was something sinister about the attention. At an early Neutral Milk Hotel show in an art space on the West Coast, local kids had made flyers using a kitschy, '60s photograph of girls wearing bikinis on the beach.

Robert Schneider   It was like a Beach Boys thing. But Jeff got furious, and ripped them down. He thought they were marketing us like Warrant, or something. But it was just a retro, fun poster. He would rather have just had something scrawled with a Sharpie. He's just really sensitive to anything that's cheesy or glossy or commercial in any way.

In the winter of 1998, Neutral Milk Hotel did a grueling tour of Europe. Mangum suffered a nasty string of colds. Their last show was in London in October, and the band flew back to Athens. He played a solo set at a friend's birthday party in Athens in December. And that was, essentially, it. There was no press release. No dramatic meeting with the band. At first, it was just the normal break to exhale that you take after a year of touring. Everyone expected that another record was forthcoming. But it wasn't.

Mac and Laura never inquired about another record, even though it surely would have sold an enormous amount. There was no contract that said Mangum owed them one, so they kept in contact with him and waited. Jim Romeo, Neutral Milk Hotel's booking agent, would periodically forward Mangum e-mails with offers of shows, most of which were ignored. Occasionally Mangum would write back: "I'm sorry. I don't know what to tell you." The clearest indication that Mangum wasn't interested in continuing came in 1999, when R.E.M. asked Neutral Milk Hotel, Olivia Tremor Control, and Elf Power, an Elephant 6 band led by Mangum's ex-girlfriend Laura Carter, to open for them in Atlanta. Olivia Tremor Control and Elf Power both said yes immediately. Romeo called Mangum repeatedly, leaving messages, but couldn't reach him for days. When Mangum finally picked up the phone, he turned down the offer. Neutral Milk Hotel hadn't played in a year, Mangum told Romeo, and if they were going to reconvene after a long break, he wanted to do it in front of their fans, not in a giant amphitheater.

As recently as 2000, Schneider says, Mangum had talked about making another Neutral Milk Hotel record. But nothing came of it. In 2001, Mangum did release a record, through Carter's Orange Twin label, of field recordings he'd made during a trip the year before to a folk music festival in Bulgaria. Needless to say, it perplexed some of his fans. Mangum eventually left Athens for New York, where he briefly DJ'd an overnight radio show on independent freeform radio station WFMU, under the name Jefferson. His overnight disappearance, especially given the fact that he could, if he wanted, play a tour of sold-out shows, has lent Mangum a reputation as the J. D. Salinger of indie rock.

Brian McPherson   **When the guy sneezes it's on the front page of _Pitchfork_. It's freaky to me. Would you leave the guy alone? Maybe he would make a record if you didn't stalk him for years.**

Mac   **I think that he'll do something. I don't know if it will be Neutral Milk Hotel, or if it'll just be noise collages. He's an interesting person who clearly loves music, and is obsessed with it, in a way, but at the same time doesn't feel the need to participate in the music business. There are lots of people waiting to buy his record and see him play. Most people would be like, "Awesome!" But I think some people would react the other way — too much pressure.**

In 2003, a writer for the Atlanta weekly alternative newspaper _Creative Loafing_, for a story on the band's dissolution, called Mangum's father and asked him what he thought of his son's songs, some of which would seem to indicate a violent and unpleasant upbringing ("And mom would stick a fork right into daddy's shoulder / And dad would throw the garbage all across the floor"). The younger Mangum hadn't responded to the reporter's e-mails, but after his father was contacted, he wrote: "I wish you the best in everything you do. But please do not contact my family. I think [my dad] was caught off guard by you, and maybe a little intrigued at first, but now he is left wondering how a perfect stranger could know about his painful past. I don't wish to revisit the past either.

"I'm not an idea," Mangum continued. "I'm a person, who obviously wants to be left alone. If my music has meant anything to you, you'll respect that."

Mangum likewise declined to participate in an interview for this book, but he sent Mac the following e-mail by way of explanation: "I don't really have any desire to try and recapture the past, so any history of Neutral Milk Hotel is very strange for me to try and write about. But I would like to give you this: Merge is by far the perfect home for our music, a label that couldn't be more honest and true to its vision. It gladdens me to see that it's the human labels like Merge who are fully alive in this moment, while the giants of the music industry are all eating shit. May it forever be so."

* * *

Facing Page: Mangum in the Neutral Milk Hotel van, San Francisco, April 1998.   Next Page: Portland, Oregon, 1998.

The First Part

1994

This is our last show. We're breaking up the band. Jon the drummer and I just can't face each other anymore since the breakup. This is a song I wrote about our problems. It's called "Like a Fool," because, well — I was a fool.
— Jim Wilbur, at a 1995 Superchunk show in Detroit.

Wilbur and Wurster on the road in Van Horn, Texas, in the mid-1990's.

On a Saturday night in late July 1994, Laura took the stage before a capacity crowd at the Cat's Cradle. Though she'd done battle with an unruly Moog synthesizer earlier that evening as part of Double Dynamite, an infrequently convened cover band featuring Phil Morrison, Bob Lawton, and Yo La Tengo's Ira Kaplan, she wasn't there to perform. She wanted to thank the crowd, and the bands, for coming to Merge's fifth anniversary "hoo-hah."

"It was so great everybody came," she said. "I'm so happy you were here." It was, says Laura Cantrell, the most effusive she'd ever seen Laura.

Back in 1988, Mac and Wayne Taylor had kick-started the Chapel Hill scene by booking sold-out five-band bills at both the Cradle and the Brewery to celebrate the release of the ludicrously ambitious box set. And now here was a five-year-old Merge riding the crest of that wave and upping the ante a bit, with three nights of sold-out five-band bills at the Cradle. Polvo played a dissonant cover of the Steve Miller Band's "Fly Like an Eagle" on the final night; the Archers of Loaf, who had done one 7-inch with Merge earlier that year but had already signed a disastrous and onerous contract with Alias Records, headlined the first night. Chuck Garrison even showed up to play with Pipe, the fast and furious adolescent punk band he started with Ron Liberti after his ouster from Superchunk. In true insular Chapel Hill fashion, Pipe ended up releasing two 7-inches and a full-length on Merge, Garrison's hard feelings notwithstanding. "They're such a great live band," says Mac. "Ron is the ideal punk-rock frontman. He's aggro but really funny about it. And he has an arsenal of hilarious dances." (As for any lingering bitterness on Garrison's part, Liberti says, "We have a saying here: 'Chapel Hill it.'" In other words, learn to quash whatever inconvenient emotional hang-ups you may have with your fellow Chapel Hillians, because you're going to run into them on the street every day.)

Also playing was Squirrel Nut Zippers, a hot-jazz revivalist combo featuring former members of Subculture and Metal Flake Mother. The Zippers released a 7-inch of three creakily recorded, anachronistic torch songs on Merge in 1994 before jumping over to Mammoth a year later; by 1997 they had become the most commercially successful band to emerge from the Chapel Hill scene, with the genuine MTV hit "Hell" and a platinum record. They performed at the 1996 Olympic Games in Atlanta and at President Bill Clinton's second inaugural. At the Merge show, they played before Butterglory.

Merge also marked the occasion with *Rows of Teeth*, a compilation CD of songs that were either previously unreleased or released only on vinyl. *Rows of Teeth* was Merge's 10th full-length release and its fourth in the previous year. The Touch and Go deal meant more money, more records, more boxes, more promo materials, more phone calls, and more hassle for Laura operating a label out of her home. She got sick of getting out of bed in the middle of the night to answer calls from Europe on the Merge phone in a little room reserved for the label in the house she shared with Amy Ruth Buchanan, only to find herself still in there three hours later, in her pajamas, working. She also started to get strange visitors — fans who wanted to see Merge HQ up close, including a couple with two children in tow who knocked on her front door one day and just wanted to hang

out. Laura politely entertained them on the hammock in her yard before sending them on their way.

In mid-1993, Merge moved from Laura's house to a shabby two-room office space above a burrito joint in downtown Carrboro. When the Armadillo Grill fired up its neon sign each morning, Merge's phones would stop working.

The same year, Mac and Laura hired their first employee, John Williams, who worked with Mac at Schoolkids, to handle mail-order and run the show when Superchunk was on tour. A few months later they brought on Stacy Philpott, known as Spott, who was at the time serving as music director of WXYC, to handle publicity. It was Spott's first and only real job interview; he showed up hungover and pale. He got the job and has never left.

Of course Superchunk played the Merge anniversary, too, still blushing from an appearance three weeks prior on *Late Night with Conan O'Brien*. Their fourth record, *Foolish*, released earlier that spring on Merge, had sold 40,000 copies and was widely considered a landmark step beyond indie rock's postcollegiate affectations and into denser, more complex, and more grown-up territory. The band and the label were firing on all cylinders. Mac and Laura were not. The show was widely rumored to be Superchunk's last.

Wurster outside the *Late Night with Conan O'Brien* dressing room, 1994.

Superchunk at the Merge 10th anniversary show at the
Cat's Cradle, 1999.

Brandon Holley   Mac was getting a lot of
attention, which I think was a little hard for
them. Laura would get really annoyed at him.

Laura   Mac getting a lot of attention was not
the problem in our relationship.

Jim Wilbur   "Why are you driving like that?"
Or, "You forgot to brush your teeth!" Or,
"You're wearing that shirt again!" Or, "You're
being a dick to me!" And I'd just go, "No
fighting in the van!" When we'd practice, or
write songs together, it was like pulling teeth
with them.

Laura Cantrell   Mac was really entranced
by her. And as their relationship matured,
she shifted the dynamic, and started to feel
her power. It was obvious that the tables
were turned.

Jim Wilbur   There was a time when Laura
would let herself be bossed around. But she
changed quite a bit.

Mac   Laura didn't really convey her affection for me, which fed the jealousy of a young
guy going out with a hot girl. I probably
drove her batty, and vice versa.

Jonathan Neumann   They had this really
unhealthy jealous thing. Laura could be
really aloof, and seem unattached. And that
made Mac very uncomfortable. It would turn
into these little barbs and jabs.

Wendy Moore   Laura broke up with Mac
because he was a jerk. Because he was
self-centered, and just didn't care about
anybody else but himself. I don't think he's a
jerk. I think he's a great guy. But speaking as
a defender of Laura — he was a jerk.

Mac   I take umbrage at that description of
me. Even as a twenty-three-year-old!

Laura   I started going to see a therapist,
which I wouldn't have done if I wasn't sort
of waking up. I felt like Mac tried to talk me
out of it. And I remember thinking, "Oh god,
Mac hates that I'm going to see a therapist,
because it means that I'm not going to put
up with his crap anymore." But I really think
all these things that Mac "made" me do —
Merge, and being in the band — were very
therapeutic for me. It sort of dragged me out
of this shell I had been in for my whole life.
And I thank him for that.

Mac   I was looking at the therapy through
the narrow prism of our relationship, which
was still pretty raw, and had freshly ended.
I didn't really know what it was. We had
a pretty heavy conversation where it
became clear that she wasn't going to
therapy to talk about me, or us, but about
her whole life. I felt stupid that I was ever
worried about it.

Brandon Holley   She just reached a point
where working with him, playing with him,
and being his girlfriend was too much. And
she cut out the part that drove her crazy.

Mac   I had this stubborn idea that if we were
together for long enough, she would become
a different person. Happier, more affectionate. It's that dumb impulse to try and remake
your partner into someone more like yourself.
Which never works. There was lots of agonizing about breaking up. There were a couple
of conversations where we just knew that
it wasn't working, but literally weren't able
to call it a day. We'd sit there and say, "Let's
just not break up!" As though if we didn't, we
would just start getting along.

Jim Wilbur　Laura's not demonstrative. It's not a flaw, it's just a trait. Even just when I'd be driving the van and needed directions from her, she would never tell me the next turn until the last possible moment. I'd have to ask her at every step. She's just uncommunicative — she doesn't want to give it up. I can only imagine what that would be like in a relationship.

Jon Wurster　Mac called me the night before the touring started for *On the Mouth*, in the spring of 1993, and said, "Laura and I are breaking up."

Jonathan Neumann　Thank god! Guys, move on! You know?

Jim Wilbur　And then it was even worse! Their relationship was so bad that breaking up wasn't much different from what it was. It wasn't heartbreak. It was, "I couldn't stand you when we were going out, and I kind of can't stand you now."

Mac　One of the worst nights happened in South Carolina. We were winding up a tour with Unrest and th' Faith Healers, and we were playing a crappy show in Columbia. Something happened onstage — Laura's bass amp was on the fritz or something — and I was getting antsy to play the next song, and get the show over with. I made some comment to Laura and she snapped, "Fuck you!" And it turned into a little fight onstage. I remember thinking, "Is this really happening? We're arguing on stage? What's the point?" After the show, I had food poisoning and puked all night in the hotel bathroom. A night for the ages.

Laura　No, it was not a fun moment. I think it was as hard on Jim and Jon as much it was on us.

You guys can't break up! What are we gonna do?

— Phil Morrison

Mac　It seems pretty classic, looking back at it. Laura was incredibly quiet and withholding. Not deliberately; it's just who she was. I was outgoing, but in some ways I was just as noncommunicative and immature emotionally. It's easy to be outgoing and gregarious and get along with everyone if you never actually engage with people on a serious emotional level, which I had no idea how to do as a kid who was obsessed with music, and girls, and art, and hanging out, and having fun. So it was kind of a perfect storm for initially getting along great — because what's not fun about the first part of any relationship that starts with late nights hanging out and drinking beer, playing music, seeing bands and taking road trips? — and then really not getting along later when the reality set in that our personalities were not what the other person really needed in their life.

Peyton Reed (Director, *Bring It On* and *The Break-Up*)　I was in a state of shock. Camelot's over. They were living this indie-rock wet dream. Like, "Oh man, what if I could be in a really cool band, and my amazing, hot girlfriend is in that band with me and we start our own label!" So when they broke up it was like, "Are there going to be no more Superchunk records?"

Phil Morrison　I was definitely worried. The fact that both this band and this label seemed to be implicitly in jeopardy was really scary. Right or wrong, there's this feeling of, "You guys can't break up! What are *we* gonna do?" And there wasn't any sense of assurance from either Mac or Laura that everything was going to be okay.

Jon Wurster　Not to sound callous or anything, but I didn't allow it to impact me, or even matter to me. For better or worse, I was just always focused on the music. I loved them, but it was their thing. As long as the band keeps going, and it's not weird, then I'm fine with it. And it never got weird, as far as I was concerned. Obviously, Jim was more in tune to it.

Mac　What really brought it home for me was when, after we'd gotten back from Europe in 1993, Laura called me and said

I needed to come by her place to pick up a birthday present she had for me. So I dropped by the house on a summer morning, and Laura came out to the car to give me the present, which was an empty photo album she had made. It was hot out, and I asked if I could come in and get a glass of water, and she hesitated. And I realized that it was because her new guy was inside. Ouch.

Bob Lawton   I don't want to sound like a backward-thinking guy, but just to make the point: Wouldn't you just dump the chick bass player? There's a mindset of what usually happens in those instances — she'd be gone. And you'd just get a new bass player. I am astounded, even now, that these two people said, "We're not going to break up the band. We're going find a way to make it work. We're not going to break up our business relationship." I don't know how they did it. Who would even try?

Mac   We never seriously really considered stopping. In some ways it all made it harder to break up, because it's more complicated. That was one reason we dragged out our relationship. We had the band and the label. And my impulse is always, "On with the show." To a fault, maybe.

Josh Phillips   It was weird. There was certainly coolness between them, and there was some bitterness between them. There were even times where they weren't talking to each other. But on the other hand, they were working together every day, and playing in a band. They would talk professionally, but that was it. There was definitely a period where it looked like Laura was going to be out. Like she didn't want to be doing that.

Phil Morrison   Certainly it was always a question mark about how much Laura liked being in the band. So that was a reason to be concerned.

David Doernberg (Superchunk merch guy) I think the fact that it was all guys made it difficult for Laura being on the road. She really wanted a girl to go on tour with them, and I don't blame her. We were horrible. Horrible hygiene. You're out all night. Showering was the least priority. Hearing guys tell horrible gross stories – Laura would just shake her head. I think she just got tired of it, and I don't blame her at all.

Laura   There were times when I thought about leaving it all. At one point I remember thinking, "I should move to Chicago. I really like Chicago. I like the people there. What's keeping me here?" Well, Merge is. I can't take it with me. And I really felt like I had nurtured it, on my own, for the first few years. It was my baby, kind of. Mac was away at Columbia for the first year, and I did all the day-to-day operations. It was in my house. So it was obviously easier for me to stay up all night doing Merge stuff. But I think in a way, me keeping it in my house as long as I did, I may have been like hoarding control of it.

Josh Phillips   She developed a sense of herself as somebody who was actually doing this worthwhile thing, and was capable and intelligent. Once they broke up, that was part of what undergirded her new sense of self, and I think that she had an investment there. And obviously Mac had his own investments.

Laura   And there was still a lot about Superchunk that I found rewarding. There's something addictive about getting up in front of people and playing for them. Especially when you get something back. And I had a hard time with the idea of giving that up. And also the idea of, what if they replaced me? Like, would I always regret that? Would it make me angry?

Mac   Being in the band, we did have the feeling — and still do sometimes, actually — that Laura didn't really want to be doing it, but didn't *not* want to be doing it, either. Like it was a burden to her. Which puts the rest of the band in a position where we felt like we were forcing someone to do something they didn't want to do. But finding someone else is not an option that we ever considered.

Brandon Holley   They still kind of drove each other crazy for a while. Things didn't really settle down for a few years.

Mac   This was about the time that I started doing stuff with Portastatic. It just came out of stuff I was doing anyway – recording at home on a four-track – before Superchunk started. At some point in 1993, Tom Scharpling asked me about doing a 7-inch on his 18 Wheeler label, so I had to come up with a name for the stuff I was doing. My four-track was called the Portastudio, and there was certainly plenty of tape hiss and static in the recordings I was doing at home, so it made sense. Portastatic served a few purposes for me: I never felt like Superchunk was capable of making delicate music. We were good at what we did, but not terribly successful at branching out from that, which used to bug me. So Portastatic gave me a place to make music that was quiet, slow – whatever I wanted it to be – and to make records without too much pressure, whereas Superchunk records by that time had become such a big deal, with all kinds of expectations attached. It also allowed me to play with other people: Jennifer Barwick, Ash Bowie, Claire Ashby, Sarah Bell, Ben Barwick, and others. It was a great antidote to the Superchunk rock juggernaut. I did the first Portastatic full-length, *I Hope Your Heart Is Not Brittle*, in 1994. Laura and I had an argument about it that stayed with me a long time. She wasn't sure if Merge should release it – wasn't sure it would sell enough to make it worth it, as though her opinion was based strictly on Merge's well-being. I said, "I didn't start a record label so you could tell me I can't put out my own album on it."

In November 1993, Superchunk toured its way out to Cannon Falls, Minn., to record *Foolish* at Pachyderm. Nirvana had recorded *In Utero*, their follow-up to *Nevermind*, there in February with Steve Albini. To save money (this was Superchunk's first record without the benefit of an advance, however meager, from Matador), the band booked four days that had been previously reserved, and then released, by Smashing Orange, an unfortunately named Delaware band then on MCA Records. When Smashing Orange decided they needed another day after all, Superchunk was down to three days to record seventeen songs.

They hired Pachyderm's house engineer, Brian Paulson, a friend of Albini's who had recently produced Uncle Tupelo's *Anodyne* and Slint's *Spiderland*, to produce the record.

Jon Wurster   We just tried to do too much in too little time. The first song we did was "Why Do You Have to Put a Date on Everything?" And we went in and listened back to the first take. And the playback was so loud that I couldn't really hear anything, and the song speeds up so much, and I said, "I don't know. Can we hear it again?" And it was just like, "No. Let's move on." And we just kept rolling.

Jim Wilbur   There was an element of making the record about their breakup – which I think was kind of glorified – while that was going on. I think Mac was writing lyrics at that time based on the breakup, but I think a lot of it is also made up.

Laura   Brian and I got flirty while we were making that record. It was a difficult situation. It's not a good thing to be a rock chick who has recently become single, who also happens to be on tour with her ex. Actually, I'll say it was just not a good thing for me to be single, especially on tour. It may sound big-headed, but much to my annoyance, I was constantly having to deflect attention from men, though I felt flattered by it some of the time. Tricky territory. Mac and I had been broken up for a while at that point, but because we were around each other all the time, we hadn't really broken up, you know? We were still keeping an eye on each other constantly. It was awkward.

Mac   I was stewing, but we needed to finish a record, and I didn't want to make a big deal about it.

The cover art for *Foolish* was a self-portrait of Laura wearing a blue dress with red dots. Hanging in the background, over her right shoulder, is a dead rabbit strung up by its hind legs.

Laura   Mac just went ahead and did the covers for the first few records. And then I said, "I want to have a go." And so we

Laura's painting for the cover of *Foolish*, now hanging in Amy Ruth Buchanan's house.

I asked for Mac's vocals to be taken out of my monitor mix. Because the words were making me cry. I would be on stage, playing these songs, and I would be crying.

— Laura Ballance

started taking turns. Obviously, I felt like that record was a lot about me and Mac. So I painted me. Then I thought, "Shit. What do I put in the background?" And I'd recently seen *Pets or Meat: The Return to Flint*, and I thought, "That'd be something." On the one hand, the rabbit is me, kind of trapped and hurt and raw. But on the other hand, because I am so evil and bad, the rabbit is Mac. Look what I've done to him.

Amy Ruth Buchanan   She was painting it up in her room. And it is kind of a dark painting. And that was all I knew. It was sort of a solitary process of working on that painting, and it seemed — yeah, it seemed like a very dark, sad painting. She didn't talk to me about it.

Spin ranked *Foolish* as the eleventh-best album of the year, calling it a "consistently exquisite piece of work" and an "expansive, almost cinematic look at suburban mixed emotions" with guitars that "sound like ghostly orchestras arguing across dark dewy lawns."

Laura did an interview with a reporter from *Alternative Press* prior to the release of *Foolish*. He guessed, just from listening to an advance copy, that she and Mac had split. As with Superchunk's previous records, Mac's vocals are buried in the mix, lending the whole album the sense that he is struggling to shout over the crash of the guitars. But the lyrics, when discretely audible, repeatedly

return to themes of betrayal, obsession, and emotional exhaustion. On "Without Blinking," Mac asks, "Did you really do this without thinking / or was there some concentration at work? / 'cause when you said 'I'm sorry' you were not blinking / you can't pretend to not know how that hurt." And on the single "Driveway to Driveway": "From stage to stage we flew / A drink in every hand / My hand on your heart had been replaced / And I thought it was you that I had chased / Driveway to driveway drunk."

Phil Morrison   There was a "goodness gracious!" kind of moment, hearing it for the first time.

Josh Phillips   Laura felt that there were songs being written about her. And that made her feel creepy, being on stage while songs were being sung about her.

Jim Wilbur   Even before *Foolish*, just after I had moved down from Connecticut, Laura and I were at a party, sitting on the porch drinking beer and smoking cigarettes. And she said, "Every time we play a song, I feel like I have to say, 'I'm sorry.'"

Laura   Like it's all my fault. I felt like every song was about me in some way. But of course when I would say that to Mac, he would deny it. We wouldn't talk about it very often, and it usually wouldn't go well. It would annoy him and make him angry if I suggested that I knew what any of his lyrics were about.

Jim Wilbur   I think he used it as a springboard to get different imagery, but I don't think it's an autobiography of the breakup. With Mac's approach to writing lyrics, only very infrequently does he write something that's absolutely, "Holy shit! I know what you're talking about!"

Laura   When we started the tour for *Foolish*, I asked for Mac's vocals to be taken out of my monitor mix. Because the words were making me cry. I would be on stage, playing these songs, and I would be crying. It was terrible. It was a hard tour.

Phil Morrison   That sounds like a pretty good compromise. To have that record exist, but have Laura not have the vocals in her monitor. It doesn't sound easy. It sounds pretty tough, and no fun, and difficult.

Mac   It's just not true. If I could sit down and decide to write a song about a specific topic and do it well, I might have done that. But I couldn't, and I didn't try. I read a Sammy Hagar interview one time where he said that you could have one girlfriend when you were fifteen years old and if she broke up with you, you'd have enough material to write songs for the rest of your life. I never thought I'd be citing Sammy Hagar's wisdom, but he's onto something. If you're in the middle of a traumatic or tumultuous relationship, it may come out in your songwriting, and it certainly did on *Foolish*. But so will every other traumatic situation you've ever been in. Things get abstracted, details are pulled from every phase of your life, from fiction, from your friends' relationships, from all over the place. Some songs start off about one thing, and by the end of the last verse you're in a different country. Some things are completely made up, or a chorus is written around a certain word that rhymes with another word but that has no basis in any other kind of reality. But people just get convinced that they're about what they think they're about.

Laura   It's sort of hilarious. Because recently, Mac asked me, "Do you still have that boom box that 'My Noise' was about?" And I said, "Um, what are you talking about? Uh, what boom box? I didn't know it was about my boom box!"

In her *Alternative Press* interview, Laura caused a stir and stoked speculation that the band might not survive by complaining that Superchunk's songwriting process wasn't democratic enough. "[Mac] is the dominant creative force in the band," she said, "and unless more of us have creative input, I don't think we can continue for very long."

Josh Phillips   There was a little bit of a rebellion there, where she and Jim all of a sudden wanted more input into the band. They said, "We're sick of this just being all about you, and your songs, and your writing." And Mac was a little disgruntled over that. He said, "If they want to be more involved, then let them write songs, and bring stuff. I'm not holding them back in any way." It was definitely an issue.

Laura   Yeah. And then I realized: I'm not really a musician. What the fuck am I talking about? I tried to write songs, and did write some that we ended up recording, but they sounded really weird. One of my weird songs is "The Mine Has Been Returned to Its Original Owner." It's freaky. I didn't write the words, I just came up with the seed of the music. Jon and Jim wrote a couple songs, too. But Mac is generally better at writing the catchy songs. I never wrote any lyrics.

Phil Morrison   Laura, around *Foolish*, went through a period where she was really intense on stage. It wasn't so boppy. It was really kind of — almost scary. And she started singing backup around that same time, which she had never done before.

Josh Phillips   The longer she was in the band, and the more she felt like she could actually handle the things at Merge and run a record label, she just seemed to get more and more confident. And that was projected on stage. She didn't seem to be hiding so much anymore. And it was personal, too. She'd always been nice, and very welcoming to me and to other people, but she was always deflecting. She didn't want to talk about herself. But after a while, it just felt like she had a certain confidence and self-assurance that let her interact differently with people.

It wasn't all sturm and drang during the *Foolish* years. Mac recalls one particularly fun show on Halloween in 1994. Dressing up onstage for Halloween — which also happens to be Wurster's birthday — is a Superchunk tradition.

Mac   Halloween is also the birthday of former Guided by Voices frontman Bob Pollard, and we played a crazy show at Penn State

Halloween 1995 in Boulder, Colo.: Laura (Lemmy), Wurster (a priest), DeWitt Burton (Conehead), Mac (Satan), Wilbur ("an adult"), and Joe Hickey (Pope).

Superchunk tech Jim Norton and Mac onstage at the 9:30 Club in Washington, D.C., Halloween 1998. The band dressed as the Misfits.

Wurster as Fred Durst in Montreal, Halloween 1999.

with them. Guided by Voices went on first, and within seconds of their first song Pollard had done a leap and kick that propelled him backwards onto his ass and into my amp stack, toppling it backwards where it crashed to the floor with the speaker cable broken off at the jack. Somehow, our roadie DeWitt Burton had it fixed before we went on. When we did go on, I was wearing a nurse costume made for an eight-year old, complete with fishnet stockings, that I had somehow squeezed into. I spent a good portion of the show crowd-surfing in that outfit. Jim never dresses up for Halloween, but Laura does a good impersonation of Lemmy from Motörhead.

Laura   We had this running joke where we would ask Jim what he was going to be for Halloween, and he would say, "An adult."

A month before *Foolish* was released, Peyton Reed and Phil Morrison traveled to Chapel Hill to shoot videos for "Driveway to Driveway" and "The First Part." They called in favors and recruited friends who were willing to work for free as crew members. Superchunk had made seven music videos up to that point, all for little more than the cost of film and shot by friends.

  Reed came up with a concept for the "Driveway to Driveway" video: A black-and-white *Philadelphia Story* riff wherein Mac competes with a wealthy scion, played by Wurster, for the attentions of a Southern Belle, played by Laura. Laura was called upon to slap Mac in one scene. Wilbur played Jon's butler.

Peyton Reed   It was that classic Little Rascals thing of like, "Let's get all these things together and put on a show!" That was really the feeling of it, which was great. But Laura hated it. *Hated it*. There was all that stuff swirling around about how much of what's on this record is autobiographical, how much is about Mac and Laura? And we were shooting this video where they were playing opposite each other in this romantic comedy thing. And there's even the moment where she slaps him. Laura got really emotional at one point, and I think there were some tears involved. Something became too sort of meta about playing opposite Mac.

Laura   I can't believe I didn't just go, "No!" Because it was torture. I dreaded every minute of having to participate in that. I cried a lot. You can probably see it on my face in the video. It sucked. Mac and I were just barely talking then.

Phil Morrison   It was tough. I felt like she was really being a champion for art.

Amy Ruth Buchanan   Maybe that slap got a little bit too realistic. It seems weird to me that they did that video at that time, pitting them as a couple. You don't like people talking about you, you know? But it was such a silly video. Maybe they said, "What the hell? Why not?"

Mac   "Driveway to Driveway" is not about Laura and myself, but there was no point in explaining that to anyone, and I didn't really feel like I should have to. Let people think what they want, because they're going to anyway.

Laura   There were some bad years. There were a lot of years of very difficult times, and bad communication, and irrational reactions to things and whatnot. Fortunately that's all much better now. Each of us did certain things that just pushed the other one's buttons, whether we knew it or not. And we were hypersensitive to it. And being around each other as much as we were, it didn't allow us that distance that people are usually allowed when they break up and need to get over it. The strange thing about starting a band with people is that it never occurs to you that you are going to be in a very close relationship with those people for as long as that band lasts. I have spent more time together with Superchunk than with anyone.

Jim Wilbur   There was still nastiness. That's inevitable. But that changed. I've heard Laura say, "It's the most important relationship in my life. That's my family." You know, it's a dysfunctional family.

* * *

Next Two Pages: A 1996 benefit for North Carolina Senate candidate Harvey Gantt at the old Durham Bulls ballpark.

Chapter Seven

The Book of Love

Stephin Merritt and the Magnetic Fields

In late 1991, Mac picked up a new 7-inch that had just come into Schoolkids. It was a release from Harriet Records, a Boston label founded by Harvard University history professor Timothy Alborn two years earlier. The A-side was called "100,000 Fireflies," and it was a haunting, spare, and strange amalgam: An artificial tick-tock drum-machine beat beneath what sounded like a toy piano playing sugary melodies and a gorgeous, classic woman's voice singing desperately sad lyrics with a delivery reminiscent of Petula Clark. It reminded Mac of a lo-fi, Motown-inflected Yaz, featured one of the most memorable opening lines ever laid to tape — "I have a mandolin / I play it all night long / It makes me want to kill myself" — and sounded like pop music from the distant future as it might have been imagined in 1965.

The band was called the Magnetic Fields. Mac had never heard of them, but he loved "100,000 Fireflies" and played it so frequently in the van on the road that Wurster suggested that they cover it. Mac had been thinking the same thing, and they came up with a version that swapped out the original's delicate reserve for furious guitars and Mac's urgent, strained vocal delivery. It quickly became a crowd favorite at shows; Superchunk recorded its version during the *On the Mouth* sessions in Hollywood and eventually released it as a B-side on a single.

Word eventually got back to the Magnetic Fields, then located in Boston, that some punk-rock band was playing their song. On October 22, 1992, Stephin Merritt, who wrote "100,000 Fireflies," and his bandmate Claudia Gonson went to a Superchunk show at nearby Brandeis University.

Stephin Merritt **I was horrified. It's probably best if I don't go into the details of why I was horrified. But we thought of punk rock as reactionary. We thought of punk rock as . . . Stalin.**

Not that Mac himself is very Stalinesque.

Stephin Merritt **No. More like Emma Goldman, maybe.**

Thus began Merge Records' relationship with the Magnetic Fields, which would last nearly a decade and produce one of the most memorable and audacious albums that any label had ever gambled on.

Merritt did not glad-hand with Mac and Laura that night at Brandeis. That task would be left to Gonson, the Magnetic Fields' voluble drummer and sometime vocalist, who also doubles as Merritt's manager.

Stephin Merritt   **I'm not into meeting people and all that.**

Brandon Holley worked with Merritt when he was a copy editor at *Time Out New York* in the late '90s.

Brandon Holley   **That guy is such a morose motherfucker. I love him. We would bring trees around where he worked to sort of help the oxygen levels.**

Merritt was, as he told the *Village Voice* in 1999, "conceived by barefoot hippies on a houseboat in St. Thomas," and had a rather chaotic and unconventional upbringing. He never met his father, Scott Fagan, a folk singer from the Virgin Islands who recorded for RCA and ATCO in the '60s and '70s. His mother, a schoolteacher, raised him as a Buddhist and moved him around the Northeast; he likes to say that he lived in thirty-three different homes in his first twenty-three years. He started writing songs when he was four, having found the lyrical sophistication of Pete Seeger's "Little White Duck" wanting and becoming convinced that he could do better. By the time he was fifteen, his mother saw enough musical interest on his part to make him promise that he would never become a professional musician. He attended a bohemian, progressive prep school in Cambridge, Mass., where he was encouraged to indulge his eccentricities (the unusual spelling of his first name is artificial; he saw a television program that recommended misspelling your name as a way to track which junk mail lists you're on).

Merritt met Gonson when they were in high school in the mid-eighties. She was everything he was not — cheery, talkative, and interested in other people. They formed a band in high school with Merritt playing guitar and Gonson playing drums, called the Zinnias. When Gonson left Boston to attend Columbia, Merritt started a short-lived project called Buffalo Rome with Shirley Simms that resulted in a self-released cassette. In 1988, Gonson transferred to Harvard and tried to get Merritt to start up a new band with her. When he refused, she put together the Magnetic Fields and started playing all of his songs.

Claudia Gonson   **We were banging through the songs, like rock and roll, guitar strumming, just wrong on every level. And so Stephin instantly inserted himself into the band. He was like, "Okay, I have to do this because you guys suck and you're destroying my music." So he showed up and he took over.**

Stephin Merritt   **I didn't want to be in a live band. I don't even want to see live music, let alone make it. But I said, "You're not doing this well enough. You need my help."**

Merritt started playing guitar, and Claudia moved to drums. Merritt hated the sound of his own voice — an affectless baritone that recalls Beat Happening's Calvin Johnson, only more in tune — and brought in assorted female vocalists, including Susan Anway of the eighties Boston punk band V;, who sang on "100,000 Fireflies."

Merritt didn't care much about independent music. His lodestars were ABBA, which he regards as the purest formal distillation of the pop aesthetic, and the Brill Building songsmiths. He was interested in writing and recording clever and beautiful pop songs. He didn't care much whether they came out on an indie or a major, as long as they came out, and the process was convenient and at least somewhat remunerative. He had no particular love for indie rock or affinity for the burgeoning DIY community; Claudia, on the other hand, was an avid observer of the indie scene and seemed to know just about everyone in it.

In 1988, Claudia Stanton, an A&R rep for Capitol Records, offered the Magnetic Fields a demo deal, paying the band $2,000 to record some songs with the option of signing them if she liked them. Merritt recorded the songs that would become *The Charm of the Highway Strip*, a highly synthesized reimagination of country music. He sang the vocal melodies himself as a placeholder; when he gave Stanton the tape, he told her that the vocals would be sung by Anway in the actual recording. Stanton listened, and, in spite of his caveat, rejected it because she didn't like Merritt's deep voice. "I hate Johnny Cash," she said.

Over the next few years, Merritt did a brief stint at NYU Film School and took courses at the Harvard Extension School, and the Magnetic Fields perfected their denatured, processed pop sound. Merritt recorded the band's first proper album, *Distant Plastic Trees*, mostly by himself, in 1989. He couldn't find a label in the U.S. to release it, but RCA Victor put it out in Japan, and an indie label, Red Flame, released it in England.

Stephin Merritt   **The major in Japan paid the indie in England, and the guy who ran Red Flame disappeared. With our 9,000 pounds. So we can be forgiven for not romanticizing the indie experience.**

After *Distant Plastic Trees*, the Magnetic Fields entered what Gonson calls its "miasmal period," in which they cast about for a label. There were the 7-inches on Harriet. There was the self-released *The Wayward Bus*, which the band packaged with *Distant Plastic Trees* on one CD. There was the *House of Tomorrow* EP on Feel Good All Over — "Horrible name," Merritt says. "It makes me shudder just to think of it" — a Chicago indie run by John Henderson (who, with Peter Margasak, booked Superchunk's first show there, at the Czar Bar). Henderson was one of Gonson's indie-rock friends; his relationship with the Magnetic Fields was more a function of their shared love of the Raincoats than his prowess at selling records. By the time Gonson and Merritt saw Superchunk ruining their song at Brandeis, they had dealt with five labels in four years, and were ready to try another.

That wasn't the first time, coincidentally, that Mac and Gonson had met: Though he didn't put it together until that night, Gonson had approached Mac on the Columbia campus while they were both students there

and tried to recruit him to appear in a short film she was making.

Mac   **It was supposed to take place on an airplane. And it was going to be all black and white, except for I would be on a plane eating mac and cheese, and the mac and cheese would be really bright orange.**

* * *

The first Magnetic Fields record that Merge put out was a reworked version of *The Charm of the Highway Strip*, in April 1994. It came out almost simultaneously with *Holiday*, the band's third full-length, on Feel Good All Over. That wasn't supposed to happen: *Holiday* had been finished much earlier, but it took Henderson a long time to get it into stores. The twin releases meant that the records were reviewed in tandem, which irked Merritt, and that people were more likely to buy one or the other, but not both. Up to that point, both labels had been vying to put out Magnetic Fields records, but the delay in getting *Holiday* out clinched it. Feel Good All Over went out of business not long after.

Claudia Gonson   **The reason that Merge made sense was that it was an incredibly functional, stable, good business entity. We can talk about how we all liked music, and we were all in the same scene. But really, it's a miracle. There are like five billion trillion labels out there that started and ran themselves into the dirt instantly, and ripped everybody off. And three or four of them worked with me, and I can tell you that they owe me money. What's been amazing about Merge is this incredibly competent head that they have on their shoulders, combined with this sense of real friendliness. And a work ethic that says, If you treat people in a human way, we can come to understandings on almost anything.**

Charm is what the robot cowboy played by Yul Brynner in *Westworld* might have listened to when he was feeling lonesome. It was a concept record about the open road, with lyrics that seemed to belong in a Lee Hazlewood album ("I'm never going back to Jackson / I couldn't bear to show my face / I nearly killed you with my drinking / Wouldn't be caught dead in that place") swathed in clanking, metallic melodies. Merritt, who decided that he could live with his voice, after all, sang all the songs. He also designed the cover art, which featured a black background with yellow dashes in a line. Merritt was characteristically exacting about his designs, and the Merge logo—"Merge" in simple black lettering inside a box with "records" beneath — occasioned Mac and Laura's first run-in with Merritt's finicky side.

Stephin Merritt **I don't know who designed the Merge logo, but I refuse to apologize to them for saying that it's butt ugly. It would have completely ruined the artwork.**

He delivered the art for *Charm* with his own version that fit the record's theme: A yellow road sign reading MERGE. Mac and Laura balked.

Mac **We really wanted people to know that it was our record.**

Stephin Merritt **Right. Your name is a traffic sign. Your logo is a potato stamp. Someone designs a record cover in which your name is used as a traffic sign. You give them a hard time about it. That was my idea for a new Merge logo, which they should have kept.**

Merritt's unusual manner of speaking — pausing for awkward periods of time between thoughts — took some getting used to. Laura was convinced for a long time that Merritt hated her, but she came to admire his refusal to indulge in pleasantries.

Laura **I had conversations with him where I know I just said the wrong thing, and he responded in a certain way, and I was just like, "Okay. I'm never talking to him again." It intimidated me for a long time, but at a certain point I just realized, "No, it's funny. I like it. The more droll he is, the louder I'm going to laugh."**

Mac **A conference call with Claudia and Stephin is always pretty fun. Claudia and I will babble on, and then when it's time for**

Stephin to answer something directly there's usually a dramatic pause, and then a very concise answer. It's kind of a special thing.

Charm was the first Magnetic Fields record that was widely and readily available in the U.S. Mac and Laura asked Merritt to tour to support it, but he refused, both because he hated touring and because the only performers on the record were him and Sam Davol on cello (Gonson was a member of the band but didn't contribute to the recording) — a duo that wouldn't translate well to the stage. A year later, in 1995, Merritt was suddenly everywhere. Merge released a new Magnetic Fields record, *Get Lost*, and reissued *The Wayward Bus* and *Distant Plastic Trees*. Merritt also released a side project called the 6ths on a major, London Records. The 6ths was a supergroup of sorts; Merritt wrote and recorded the songs, which were indistinguishable from Magnetic Fields songs, and sent them to various vocalists to sing. The first 6ths record, *Wasps' Nests* (named for two of the most difficult words to pronounce in the English language) featured vocal turns by Mac, Lou Barlow, Yo La Tengo's Georgia Hubley, Luna's Dean Wareham, and other indie-rock luminaries.

Merritt liked keeping one foot, however tentatively, in the major-label world.

Claudia Gonson **It wasn't so much major versus indie. It was just catch-as-catch-can. It was a million little things, and they were all happening. And anybody who wanted to do it, we were like, "Yes! We'll do that! It'll be fun." It was sort of a throw-it-and-see-where-it-sticks ethic.**

But he also worried about being stuck in what he once called the "indie-rock ghetto." He had set out to make unadulterated commercial pop music, yet somehow found himself found himself on a label that was being hailed as ground zero of a newly-minted genre of music that he didn't care for in the least.

Claudia Gonson **Stephin Merritt does not own a record by Pavement, or Sebadoh. He used to get really, really upset at being associated with indie rock, especially words like "twee." He just really had his own specific**

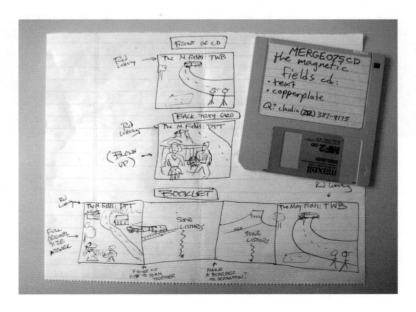

Artwork and instructions for *Get Lost* and *The Wayward Bus / Distant Plastic Trees*.

An Indie Rock painted by Gonson for the Merge fifth anniversary fest.

desire of how he wanted to be out there. And he felt controlled by me and, to a certain degree, I'm sure, Merge.

Daniel Handler (Author, under the name Lemony Snicket, of the *A Series of Unfortunate Events* books; accordion player for the Magnetic Fields)   There was a kind of cuddly camaraderie among so many bands back then. Everybody said that everyone else's band was incredible. But Stephin has always been the kind of person, where, if you ask him what he thinks of the Spinanes record, he's going to tell you. I think that it was kind of shocking to say, "Oh, Superchunk just sounds like a rock band." That was, like, heretical.

Stephin Merritt   I ridicule the ideology of the so-called indie-rock ethos. I have nothing to do with that, and I'm sorry that Mac and Laura do. No doubt they are completely insincere about it and are just using it to sell records. And I am not joking. Still, I could make only calypso music for the next hundred years, and win all of the calypso Grammys for the next hundred years, and still be found only in the indie-rock section of every store and online retailer. Probably if Claudia's friends were all metalheads, we would be considered an eccentric metal band.

Gonson had her own brief diversion from the indie-rock ethos. In 1996, Danny Goldberg took over Mercury Records, where he hoped to mine the same vein that he had worked while he was at Atlantic. And he hired Gonson as an A&R rep. She had relationships with just about everyone in the indie world, she was in a cool band on a cool label, and she had just helped Merritt organize *Wasps' Nests*, which was a veritable treasure trove of unsigned talent.

Claudia Gonson   Danny said, "I hired you in for four reasons: Sebadoh, Sleater-Kinney, and Ani DiFranco." There was a fourth band that I can't remember. "You're an indie-rock girl, you know how to get Lou Barlow on the phone. I want you to bring these people in."

Gonson was at Mercury for two years. The assignment was ludicrous: DiFranco had virtually staked her career on not signing to a major label, and by 1996, Sleater-Kinney and Sebadoh had been thoroughly courted by majors and made their intentions clear.

Claudia Gonson   My calls to them were very hard for both of us. They'd be like, "Hey, we know you! You're the girl from the Magnetic Fields." And I'd say, "Yeah, I work for Mercury." And then it would be this awkward silence. I think they felt betrayed in some way. It was just not a comfortable experience for me. I remember running into Lou Barlow on Avenue A, and I said, "Oh my god, it's so weird I ran into you! Because I just had this conversation with my boss, and he wants me to talk to you." And he was just like, "I gotta go." And he just sort of ran. It was a very creepy time.

The next Magnetic Fields record, *69 Love Songs*, would deliver Merritt from the indie-rock ghetto. There's a story that Gonson tells to help explain how *69 Love Songs* came into being: In 1994, Merge asked the Magnetic Fields to play at their fifth anniversary celebration at the Cat's Cradle. On the drive down from Boston, they stayed overnight in Washington, D.C. In the middle of the night, with the band members sprawled out across someone's living room, Merritt sat up in the dark and shouted, "Indie Rocks!" The rest of the band wearily humored him as he explained: In the late seventies, pet rocks were a fad. So why not Indie Rocks? Or Soft Rocks? Or Punk Rocks? He went back to sleep. The next day, when they got to Chapel Hill, Gonson collected rocks from the parking lot behind the Cat's Cradle, went to an art supply store, and painted up about twenty Merge Indie Rocks. She sold them for $1 apiece that night at the show.

Claudia Gonson   So that's exactly Stephin Merritt in a nutshell. He has these ideas, and he never thinks about executing them. For every idea he executes, he has three thousand that he doesn't.

69 Love Songs was the rare one that he did execute. It's the kind of record that has an origin myth: In January 1998, Merritt was drinking alone at a piano bar on the Upper

East Side, writing songs. He was listening to Stephen Sondheim, and thinking not about love but about the American composer Charles Ives and his book *114 Songs*, and — "Indie Rocks!" — decided that he would write a musical revue called *100 Love Songs*. It would feature various performers singing a vast and comprehensive survey of every kind of song there is to be written about love, from country to punk to krautrock to Irish folk ballad, all to be penned by him. The idea was quintessential Merritt: A taxonomic and clinical take on the most intimate and emotional of subjects. It quickly dawned on him that such a musical would be a challenge to finance, so he downgraded the idea to an album of 100 love songs. When that proved excessively long, he trimmed it down to 69: A suggestive number that had the virtue of being visually appealing on an album cover.

Daniel Handler   He got the idea at the same time I had the idea for *Lemony Snicket*. I said, "Oh, I just decided to write these thirteen books about terrible things happening over and over again." And he said, "I'm going to write and record sixty-nine love songs." So we both watched the other person's career-changing moment happen. It was all in his tiny, tiny apartment and he was just working on it all the time. I would stop by and hear stuff or play stuff, and I remember that he had this glass of orange juice that he had been drinking the night before. And he woke up in the morning and he had another sip of it, and he was surprised that the ice was still in there. But it turned out to be bugs.

Merritt constructed a massive chart on his wall listing the songs — he ended up writing well over 100 — delineating their genre, instrumentation, and variety of love they addressed. There were last-minute substitutions and additions, and it ended with a series of mad dashes to the finish line. One day, all of Merritt's friends would get an e-mail from him saying, "In ten minutes we're meeting at Dick's Bar because I've finished the album." Two days later, they'd get another: "In fifteen minutes, I'm having a party because I finally finished the album."

* * *

Ed Roche, Touch and Go's label manager, often found himself saying the same thing over and over about how Merge spent its money. Eventually, Mac came up with a handy time-saver: Anytime you want to tell us about how we're wasting money, he told Roche, just say, "Jiminy Cricket."

Roche said Jiminy Cricket a lot. A 1996 fax from Roche to "Laura, Spott, Mac, and Jiminy Cricket," for instance, patiently explained why the label shouldn't be responsible for providing free copies of CDs to booking agents. It opened with: "Laura should be holding a ruler so that she can smack both Mac and Spott when they turn this into a joke."

Roche was a stickler for numbers, armed with spreadsheets and formulas for projecting sales — an enforcer for Touch and Go's austere approach to the business. Mac and Laura, on the other hand — well, mostly Mac — were obsessed with making the records look cool and special, and were inclined to indulge their artists when it came to packaging.

Ed Roche   Their hearts were in the right place, but I can't say their heads were. If we were spending money on a five-color print job for a CD booklet when a four-color print job would get the same results, I would point it out to them in the hopes of saving us, them, and the band money. But Mac would be like, "Didn't you see how fucking great it looked?"

Many debates about costs played out between Mac and Laura first, with Mac usually advocating the more ambitious and riskier route and Laura in the bean-counter role.

Ed Roche   If you wanted a rational answer, you called Laura. If you wanted an enthusiastic answer, you called Mac. Eventually, I just stopped calling Mac for business questions because I knew what he'd say. Whereas I'd call Laura and say, "Hey, if you just change this one thing, it'll save you $150." And she'd say, "I'll talk to Mac; we'll change it."

One day in 1998, Gonson called Mac and Laura to tell them that the next Magnetic Fields record was going to be a sixty-nine-song, three-CD musical tour through American songcraft from Stephen Foster to the

Ramones, accompanied by a seventy-six-page full-color bound booklet (Merritt's idea) with photos and a lengthy interview.

Mac   I knew it was going to be good, and I really wanted to hear it.

Laura   I thought it was crazy! Crazy and backwards!

Ed Roche   I told them there's no such thing as a triple record.

Actually, Merritt had always assumed it would be a double album. It was Mac who told him that it would be physically impossible to encode that amount of music on to two CDs.

Stephin Merritt   I said, "What are you trying to do to me, you fascist!? It has to be two CDs!" The "69" was supposed to be a visual palindrome. But of course he was right. And it still works out numerologically, because of the three and the six and the nine.

Mac and Laura didn't think at first they would actually have to confront the unlikely prospect of trying to make money off of a three-disc set.

Stephin Merritt   Everyone in the world, including Claudia, including all of the other members of the Magnetic Fields, including Merge, including my mother, thought that I was going to come to my senses after making, oh, twenty-three songs. But once I wrote one hundred songs, it became clear to everybody that this was going to happen.

Sure, the Clash had *Sandinista!* and George Harrison had *All Things Must Pass*, but they had enormous audiences. *Get Lost*, the Magnetic Fields' previous release, had sold roughly 17,000 copies. There were plenty of people willing to part with $12 for a Magnetic Fields record, but how many would be willing pay $36? One of the reasons Merge didn't wind up like Feel Good All Over or any other number of failed indies is that Mac and Laura let the hard economics of each release guide their strategy. That's the only way you can make money when you're selling 5,000 to 10,000 records on most releases. The major-

label philosophy essentially amounts to gambling — you throw hundreds of thousands of dollars into a hundred different bands, in the hopes that one of them turns up Ace-King and covers the losses on the 99 others. The Merge philosophy was rational: Spend as little as possible on each release, and they're all more likely to be winners. An elaborately packaged triple-record with a list price of more than $30 ran precisely contrary to that philosophy.

Claudia Gonson   There was a general feeling at that point that Stephin had made a lot of records with them and they were doing fine. And he had this groundswell of energy behind him, and he made money for the label, so let's see where this goes. But how could we do it so we didn't take a bath? How the fuck are we going to do this record? That was a big worry.

Jim Wilbur   *69 Love Songs*? I just remember laughing. "You are going to be living under a bridge this time next year, my friend!"

Mac, Laura, and Touch and Go came up with a compromise, which Merritt accepted: They would release *69 Love Songs* as three separate, independently priced discs, with a limited-edition 2,500 copy run of the three-disc and booklet set, as a sort of collector's item.

Mac   We had a connection to our bands, and we wanted to be able to do this cool thing. And sometimes it's worth it to sacrifice the reality of the bottom line for art, just to have a cool thing. We'd print just enough of the limited edition so we could sell out of it, for the hardcore fans. And everybody else would just buy the single volumes.

69 Love Songs was released in September 1999. The sheer audacity of the project alone was a story in the music press; Merritt was featured on NPR, and made the cover of the *Village Voice*. *Spin* gave it a 10 out of 10. *Voice* critic Robert Christgau gave the record an A+. *The New York Times* hailed Merritt as a "contrarian pop genius"; it would eventually be ranked the best record of 1999 by *Magnet*, second best by the *Voice's* Pazz and Jop Critics' poll, fourth by *Spin*, sixth by the *Times*, and ninth by *Rolling Stone*. For a release party, the band performed the entire record, in order, over two nights to sellout crowds at the Knitting Factory. None of this surprised Mac and Laura. What did surprise them is that the limited edition sold out immediately, as did the individual volumes.

Trish Mesigian (Former Merge employee) Oh, it was a nightmare. I mean, it was a great nightmare. Everyone in the office was scrambling to get this record back out while it was still hot.

Stephin Merritt Nobody could buy it for six weeks. I was very happy that the initial run had sold out. I was obviously not happy with the amount of the initial run, or that it was taking so long to repress.

The problem wasn't just about rushing more copies into stores to meet the demand. It was figuring out what, exactly, the demand was. The smallest number of booklets that it made economic sense to order from the printer was 2,500. Which meant pressing 7,500 CDs. Sure, the first batch had sold out. But would a second? Or third?

Corey Rusk That was definitely a rough one. It's such a phenomenal story for the Magnetic Fields. How often in any band's career is a three-album box-set package with a big fat book their breakout record that sold seven times as many as any of their previous records? We weren't always right in trying to be the voice of reason. The limited edition was not the right call, because the box set instantly sold out and everybody was clamoring for more. And it took a while before we could get more box sets, because we had to figure out — yeah, these all disappeared; but what if we make 5,000 more, and there's a demand for 500 of them and then it just dies? We were talking about spending large amounts of money on packaging for something you're really not sure where it's going to go. So it was bumpy those first few months with that record.

It got smoother. To date, the box set of *69 Love Songs* has sold 62,500 copies; combined with the individual CDs, the record has sold more than 150,000 units. Sales spike each Valentine's Day. Within three years, the Magnetic Fields were performing it, recital-style, at the Hammersmith in London with Peter Gabriel, and at Lincoln Center's Alice Tully Hall as part of the American Songbook series. So much for the indie-rock ghetto.

* * *

Merge moved out of its one-room office over Armadillo Grill in 1996, and took up residence in a house along a divided highway in Chapel Hill (it happened to be next door to the house that Mac had lived in during his year off from college, nine years prior, where he and his friends had screen-printed boxes of *evil i do not to nod i live*). In 2001, Laura was riding her bike through downtown Durham, a formerly vibrant neighbor to Chapel Hill that had been devastated by the collapse of the tobacco industry, when she saw a FOR SALE sign on a yellow brick two-story storefront that had once been the Self-Help Credit Union. Flush with *Love Songs* cash, Merge purchased the building for $250,000, a transaction that was significant enough to merit stories announcing it in both the Durham *Herald-Sun* and the Raleigh *News & Observer*.

But the Magnetic Fields didn't stick around long enough for Merge to buy another building. Merritt released three more records with Merge: one 6ths full-length, one EP by a side project called the Future Bible Heroes, and one soundtrack under his own name. But in 2002, the Magnetic Fields signed to Nonesuch, a division of Warner Music Group. Major labels had approached the Magnetic Fields many times during the years they were on Merge; Merritt was always willing to hear them out, but Gonson was mistrustful. But Nonesuch was the home of Wilco, Laurie Anderson, *Nixon in China* composer John Adams, and Phillip Glass.

Claudia Gonson The idea that we could have been on Nonesuch, in my brain, was like the idea that I could have been the president of the United States. It wasn't a remotely realistic fantasy. And then suddenly

The Magnetic Fields performing *69 Love Songs* at the Lyric Hammersmith Theater in London, 2001.

Stephin Merritt's notes to the mastering studio for *69 Love Songs.*

there was just this strange moment of, Wow we can really do this. And I think Stephin was very excited by things about the Nonesuch catalog. It's been an important stamp for Stephin to feel that he's a Nonesuch artist as well as a Merge artist.

The story of the burgeoning star who abandons the indie that put him on the map is something of a cliché. But in the case of the Magnetic Fields, there is a rather cruel irony at play in the fact that Merge, with its scarce resources, undertook a relatively huge financial risk on behalf of *69 Love Songs*, one that the executives of Warner Music Group would almost certainly never have tolerated. And if there is any release that proved that Merge was just as capable as a major label of making a record happen, it was *69 Love Songs*. But there was no rancor in the departure.

Mac It made me sad, but they were very upfront about what they wanted to do, so we never felt betrayed when they moved on to Nonesuch.

Laura If a band wants to move on to a bigger label, they should do it. We don't want unhappy bands on our label.

Claudia Gonson **They were gracious as always. And I was pretty unhappy about having to sever a — it wasn't really severed. I really don't see it as an ending. It's just more like having to put on hold the immediate relationship. But there was nothing really to say. They understood. But they said, "We have to warn you. It's not what you think it is. You don't have as much freedom." So there was a sense of them kind of — sort of like talking to your older siblings. Like, "I know you want to fly and be free, but let me tell you, it's not all it's cracked up to be." Which is true. Nonesuch are much more involved in the creative process in a way that I think Stephin has found frustrating. They ask him to do re-records, they ask him to change titles. They ask him to change artwork. There's a whole different level of back-and-forth than we had with Merge.**

Phil Morrison **When the Magnetic Fields left, I told Mac and Laura, "Well, you have the greatest record they will ever make." And I think that, so far, I'm still right.**

Tom Scharpling **A major label is not going to say, "Let's put a three-disc set out of this thing." Mac and Laura made something happen that wouldn't have existed anywhere else. That's the beauty of what Merge became, is that things like that were a possibility if they believed in them enough.**

* * *

Facing Page: Misspelled marquee, New York City, 2001.   Next Page: Misspelled marquee, San Francisco, 1999.

THE
BOTTOM LINE
PRESENTS
MAGNETIC
FEILDS

NEIL GAIMAN

$20 00

GIFT CERTIFICATE AVAILABLE

The Great
AMERICAN
MUSIC HALL
FRI
THE MAGNETIC
EFIELDS
SNAKEFARM
THE FLY SEV
BOX OFFICE
815

Poster by Ron Liberti, 1996.

Polaroid of Polvo taped by producer Bob Weston onto the interior of the box containing the master reels of *Today's Active Lifestyles*.

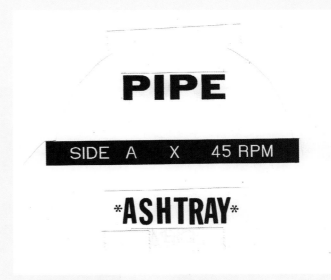

Original art for the label of Pipe's "Ashtray" b/w "Warsaw" 7-inch.

Pumpkin Wentzel and Charles Gansa of Guv'ner.

Polvo in Toronto, 1993.

Annie Hayden (Spent) and Sasha Bell (Ladybug Transistor; Essex Green) in New York.

Flyer from the 1992 "Noisy Christmas with Superchunk Japan Tour."

Wurster with dancers from the video for "The First Part," 1994.

Pipe in Chapel Hill, April 1992.

Ash Bowie playing drums with Portastatic, Princeton, N.J.

Spent.

Stephin Merritt outside the offices of *Spin* in 1994.

Jan 5, 1994

Frank,

    If it wasn't for John King telling
me about you I never would have
heard yr songs. I owe both of you
thanks.

    I picked "Firing Room" and "Make
a Deal w/ the City" at the Ajax store
in Chicago (right, as if it might be
somewhere else) So, anyhoo, I'd
like to get "My Life is Wrong" and
"Axl or Iggy"

    I wish you luck on getting a
band together for live performances
       Take Care
       Jim Wilbur
       201 D Barclay Rd.
       Chapel Hill, NC
           27516

A 1994 fan letter from Wilbur to Fred (F.M.) Cornog, addressed in error to "Frank."

Wilbur at the Wet Behind the Ears kickoff dance party
in Mac's kitchen, 1990.

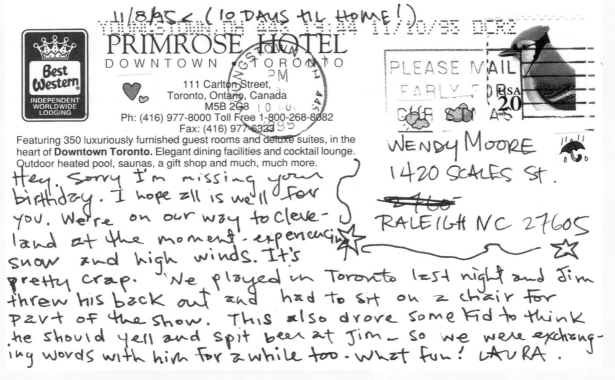

11/8/95 < (10 DAYS TiL HOME!)

PRIMROSE HOTEL
DOWNTOWN TORONTO

♥ ♡

111 Carlton Street,
Toronto, Ontario, Canada
M5B 2G3
Ph: (416) 977-8000 Toll Free 1-800-268-8082
Fax: (416) 977-6323

Featuring 350 luxuriously furnished guest rooms and deluxe suites, in the
heart of **Downtown Toronto.** Elegant dining facilities and cocktail lounge.
Outdoor heated pool, saunas, a gift shop and much, much more.

PLEASE MAIL
EARLY F
C E
USA 20

WENDY MOORE
1420 SCALES ST.
~~2760~~
RALEIGH NC 27605

Hey, Sorry I'm missing your
birthday. I hope all is well for
you. We're on our way to Cleveland at the moment - experiencing
snow and high winds. It's
pretty crap. We played in Toronto last night and Jim
threw his back out and had to sit on a chair for
part of the show. This also drove some kid to think
he should yell and spit beer at Jim — so we were exchang-
ing words with him for a while too. What fun! LAURA.

Postcard from Laura to Wendy Moore, 1995.

The Clientele in London during the making of *Suburban Light*.

Matthew McCaughan, Mac's brother, during the recording of Portastatic's *De Mel, de Melão* in Mac's house, 2000.

London, 1993.

Laura and Claire Ashby in England,
summer 1993.

Promo photo from *Here's Where the Strings Come In*, 1995.

Poster by Ron Liberti, 1995.

The window of Sounds, a record store on St. Marks Place in New York City, in 1995.

The Question Is How Fast

1995

When Laura saw Perry Farrell and Courtney Love hanging out backstage at the Whisky in 1992, she ran to hide behind the merch table. Three years later, on a July afternoon in Atlanta, she was sharing the stage with Hole again, at Lollapalooza, the mammoth summer concert tour organized by Farrell that came to symbolize the forced mainstreaming of alternative music (or was it the "alternification" of mainstream music?) for the MTV set. The festival was then in its fifth year; it had pulled in more than $26 million in 1994 with Smashing Pumpkins and the Beastie Boys leading the bill. The 1995 tour was known as the "indie-rock Lollapalooza" owing to the presence of Sonic Youth, Pavement, and the Jesus Lizard on the main stage.

Superchunk was booked to play eight dates, from Connecticut to North Carolina, on the smaller side stage, alongside Built to Spill, Mike Watt, and others. Despite the festival's fairly cheesy "modern rock" reputation — not to mention the imprudence of placing bands like Pavement in front of a crowd that was waiting to see Cypress Hill (a juxtaposition that resulted in a show-ending

Trying to stay cool with an icy towel on the head, Lollapalooza, 1995.

	⠀M	- 3:30 PM
BUILT TO SPILL	4:00 PM	- 4:40 PM
MIKE WATT	5:10 PM	- 5:50 PM
REDMAN	6:20 PM	- 7:00 PM
SUPERCHUNK	7:25 PM	- 8:05 PM

Lollapalooza stage schedule.

hail of dirt clods for Steve Malkmus and his bandmates in West Virginia) — they had a blast. The machine rolled like clockwork, and Superchunk's position as the last band before dark on the side stage (they called it the "kiddie stage," but Lollapalooza called it the "Mind Field") meant large and interested crowds and a good hour to play, whereas the Jesus Lizard, which had ostensibly better billing, had to play their dark and angry set under the noonday sun on the main stage as concert-goers strolled in.

The third slot on the main stage was practically cursed. It was initially Sinéad O'Connor, who backed out one week into the tour because she was pregnant; the promoters called in Elastica to replace her. When Elastica dropped out two weeks later after their bass player quit, the tour's promoters asked Superchunk to take over the newly vacated opening slot on the main stage. To a lot of bands, this would have been the equivalent of being called up to the majors. To Superchunk, it threatened to screw up the nice little thing they had going on the side stage each night, and they turned it down.

When an offer came back for an even better slot later in the day, they agreed.

Superchunk took the stage after Beck. They played "Slack Motherfucker," and Mac told the crowd that it was a relief to play it for an audience, he could safely assume, that had never heard it before. He signed off with, "Thank you, we were Sinéad O'Connor, and we really like the big stage."

They liked the side stage better. The next show was Raleigh, Superchunk's last date on the tour, and the band was back on the Mind Field. They played to a welcoming hometown crowd at dusk, and it's that show, on the kiddie stage, that Jon Wurster cites as among his favorites of all time. They felt like they were where they belonged.

Mac and Laura bristled at the misperception that Superchunk, and Merge for that matter, didn't really want to sell a lot of records; that they relished presiding over an exclusive and willfully obscure club. The truth was that they wanted to sell as many records as they could without wasting a lot of money, dealing with people they didn't want to deal with, or ceding control of the band or label. They did want to be on the main stage, but they didn't want to give up a great slot on the side stage in order to get there. And after the success of *Foolish*, they occasionally found themselves caught between what they wanted to do and what they needed to do in order to succeed.

In April 1995, Belly asked Superchunk to join them as opening act for a U.S. tour. Belly was fronted by Tanya Donelly, formerly of the Throwing Muses. They were on Sire Records at the time, and touring in support of *King*, the follow-up to their debut record *Star*, which went gold with the success of the single "Feed the Tree." *King* was highly anticipated, and Belly was featured on the cover of *Rolling Stone* in April. Superchunk was skeptical of joining a "buzz band" tour, but they decided it was a way to expand their audience.

Bob Lawton   The long support tour. Labels always say, "Get on a big support tour! It's a big platform, it's all good." No, it could be the biggest waste of time in your life. Why did the Pixies break up? Because they got on this stupid U2 tour, and got treated like shit. And they were just like, "We're miserable, this sucks, we're done."

Laura   We were just trying to push it a little further. Obviously, doing a tour with Belly, we were trying to reach an audience that we hadn't before. They asked us to do it, and I was like, "This doesn't feel right to me. But if you guys want to do it, I'll do it." And they wanted to do it. And it sucked. I'm always right. And Mac will tell you that in various song lyrics.

Jon Wurster   We'd met Tanya before, and she was nice. And all those tours look great on paper. But then when you get there, it's different.

Jim Romeo   They were just used to touring with friends, and the hospitality that goes with that. Maybe they had a more innocent view of things, but they felt like, if a band liked you enough to invite you on tour, then they would treat you with respect. But often when bands get big, or are on major labels, they disassociate themselves, and the crew takes over.

Bob Lawton   They were asking Superchunk to set up in front of them. And anytime that you have to set up in front, especially with someone like Mac, jumping around all crazy, it puts a real crimp in the show. When they played New York, I went up to the drummer, Chris Gorman, in Roseland and said, "Hey Chris. Can you move the drums?"

Jon Wurster   And they said, "We're not going to move anything. You get this amount of space. You get three-quarters of volume on the PA, you're not as loud as everybody else." We didn't think they would do that, because Tanya was sort of cut from the same cloth as we were. But she had no idea any of this was going on. It was all tour-manager decisions.

DeWitt Burton   The microphone stand for Jon's drums was almost up Mac's butt. But he was still doing his windmills, and his Pete-Townsend-as-a-young-boy imitation. He tried not to let it affect their show.

Mac   We were worried about doing a tour with a big band like Belly, because we were predicting all these things that could happen. And so ahead of time, we got assurances that they'd strike the drums, we'd get our own monitor mixes, it's all good. So then literally the first night, they're like, "We're not striking the drums."

Jon Wurster   Their production manager was this guy they hired from like the Joffrey Ballet or something. Total douche. We were lucky to be there in his eyes. But at that point, their record was not really killing. And it seemed like as many people were coming to see us as them. And it just wasn't fun. You're in this little, scrunched-together first spot.

Bob Lawton   This is the whole difference between doing it yourself, and being on a major label with a bus and a road crew: It's really taken out of your hands. How you want to be presented and how you want to present yourself, even to the opening act. Who are, allegedly, people you asked to come play with you.

Jim Wilbur   So we said, "If there's no change by Denver, we're going to leave the tour." And we played the show, and afterwards, we went and sat down. And Tanya and the guitar player came in. And she looked at us and she was like, "You're leaving, aren't you?" And the guitar player, he just couldn't believe it. "This is bullshit!" But they had numerous opportunities. We're weren't fucking around.

Jon Wurster   So the next morning, we just drove straight back to North Carolina. That was a lesson in being — if you are at that level — aware of what's going on in your name.

Bob Lawton   For a band to leave a tour, that's a big deal. If they had been on a label, there would've been huge amounts of pressure to stay.

Jim Romeo   They didn't have to answer to anyone but themselves when they did that. They didn't have a manager, or a label. They had said, "Let's try to play to bigger audiences, and let's try to do this." And then they realized what they would have to sacrifice in order to do that. And when they saw the more unsavory aspects of it, they sort of just said, "We don't want to be part of this."

They drove straight back to North Carolina on April 20, the day after Timothy McVeigh bombed the Alfred P. Murrah Federal Building. Their route took them past Oklahoma City, and they could see the smoldering ruins from the highway.

One month later, they headed back to the studio, this time to Fort Apache in Boston, to record *Here's Where the Strings Come In* with Wally Gagel, a producer who has worked with Lou Barlow's Folk Implosion, the Rolling Stones, Jessica Simpson, Lindsay Lohan, and the Backstreet Boys. They had written most of the songs for *Strings* in a tiny cinderblock room they rented as a practice space from Stacy Guess, the trumpet player for the Squirrel Nut Zippers. The songs were the most collaborative the band had seen yet, with everybody bringing in parts and constructing them as a group.

They took a leisurely eleven days to record and mix *Strings*, an eternity by Superchunk standards. The band stretched out a bit on some songs, adding subtle keyboard parts and recording an impromptu, live-to-one-microphone acoustic version of "Detroit Has a Skyline," transforming a propulsive barn-burner into a mournful heartbreaker.

Strings was Superchunk's most accessible record to date. It was still a wash of frantic, overdriven guitars, but the songs were brighter, and Mac's vocals were more audible above the din. The opener, "Hyper Enough," was a bouncing anthem with a sing-along chorus and an indelible guitar hook that, in its way, was a self-penned answer to "Slack Motherfucker." Where "Slack" was a proclamation of Mac's compulsive industry, "Hyper Enough" was a sardonic examination of its limits. The chorus is a curt response to an offer of a pulse-quickening pharmaceutical: "I think I'm hyper enough as it is."

It sounded like something you might hear on the radio. For the first time, and at the suggestion of Corey Rusk, Merge pulled the traditional music-industry levers and hired Karen Glauber, an independent radio promoter, to engineer a hit.

Jon Wurster   That one just clicked in terms of sound, just because Wally's production style was so good. We knew "Hyper Enough" was going to be the one that could be a "hit" of some sort. I look back on that time, the mid-nineties, as some weird golden age of music, when stuff like that could become a hit. There were so many one-hit wonders back then — like the Breeders, with "Cannonball." Things seemed relatively possible. So the consensus between Karen and Corey was that "Hyper Enough" could maybe do something.

Jim Wilbur   It wasn't like a direction that we would talk about. "Like, we need to make it sound more like this." Jokingly, we would say, "We need really popular music. We should get a picture of Tiffany on the wall and we should ask her, 'Is that good?'" We always wanted to sell more records. We never intended to *not* be successful. But we didn't have talks about how to try and make that happen.

Superchunk and crew in Denver on the morning they left the Belly tour, April 1995.

I always tell a band, You've got to write me a prom song and a rock anthem that can be played in sports arenas. That's all I ask.

— Karen Glauber

○———————●

Corey Rusk   This was the post-*Nevermind* world. A lot of mainstream music listeners and people at radio stations who never paid any attention to the music we were involved with all of a sudden had a desire to be involved with "the next big thing." We had worked with Karen on Urge Overkill, and when I heard *Strings*, I thought, "Damn, this is fucking great. There's no reason on earth that it shouldn't be huge."

Karen Glauber   I flew to North Carolina to meet with Mac. I said, "Are you up for this? If I asked you to do a radio show, are you up for visiting radio stations? Are you up for the idea of hearing your songs played next to some of the worst music you've ever heard in your life?" I think every artist wants their songs to be heard as much as possible, but occasionally, in context, it's kind of like, "Wow, they just segued the Red Hot Chili Peppers into me and then into Metallica." But Mac said, "Yeah."

Jon Wurster   So you've got to remix it for radio. Because that's what you do. And you listen to it, and the drums are louder and vocals are louder. That's kind of it. And of course it was expensive.

Karen Glauber   Just to make it a little more commercial. Because the sound of it at the time was a little too indie-rock-y. It has to be just mixed a certain way so that it pops on the radio, that the vocals are up enough, that the guitar's up enough, so that when it's subjected to compression, it doesn't sound muddled and muddy.

Jon Wurster   We also did a radio mix of "Yeah It's Beautiful Here Too," which has "yeah yeahs" before the chorus. Because, and I quote: "KROQ is going to like a song that has the word 'yeah' in it." Something the kids can chant along with. That was actually the thought that went into that. I think we all got taken in a little bit.

Karen Glauber   Of course. Hand claps and "yeah, yeahs," for sure. You can't argue with it. I also like a nice pause right before the final chorus. There are certain manipulative things that work. I always tell a band, You've got to write me a prom song and a rock anthem that can be played in sports arenas. That's all I ask.

Jon Wurster   During that period, they were trying to get us added to the big alternative-rock station in Seattle at the time. Someone at the station said, "If Superchunk is so good, why aren't they on a major label?"

Corey Rusk   We were used to the mainstream not being interested in us, and us not being interested in them. So even as we were trying to get commercial radio to play Superchunk, there was a lot of moral discussion going on: *This feels like something we don't want to be involved in.* At the same time, our job is to sell as many records as possible without crossing any moral or ethical boundaries. It was a tricky process and a tricky era. I do think the radio helped that record, but we never got far enough for it to make a huge difference.

Phil Morrison   The idea of, "We're going to try to have some sales on this one" — that was a very self-conscious choice. As opposed to it being self-evident. It's just funny to think that that was such a self-conscious decision to make.

Laura   It felt weird. Corey was behind that. In some way, it was like natural progression: OK, Nirvana did well. And Danny Goldberg wanted to meet with us. So why couldn't we be on commercial radio? But I guess it wasn't quite time yet for that kind of thing to be able to happen, like it can now. We can have something happen like Arcade Fire, and Spoon.

Ed Roche   We all put a lot more into that record, more bullshit promo material and stuff like that. So *Here's Where the Strings Come In* probably sold a little better; but it probably made less money.

Jon Wurster   That was sort of the high point of the band, at least in terms of presence, or exposure.

Ron Liberti   Dude, they had coffee cups and stuff. "Hyper Enough" coffee cups. I could tell that they were trying, you know?

Strings shipped more than 50,000 copies, more than any other Merge record had. It ended up selling 37,000 copies, according to SoundScan (though it surely sold more through independent stores that weren't yet providing data to SoundScan). It topped out at 37 on the *Billboard* Heatseekers Chart, which is devoted to high-selling records from acts that have never cracked the *Billboard* 100, and spent twenty weeks on *CMJ*'s college charts. On tour that fall, Superchunk played to sellout crowds in Los Angeles, Chicago, New York, Boston, San Diego, and Cleveland.

Despite the effort, "Hyper Enough" never did become a commercial radio hit. By 1995, much of the promise of the alternative-rock explosion had begun to dissipate. Kurt Cobain had shot himself in 1994. Sonic Youth and Pavement weren't packing them in at Lollapalooza like Smashing Pumpkins had. *Spanaway*, Seaweed's 1995 debut on Disney's Hollywood Records, sold roughly the same as *Strings*, the marketing muscle of the Disney Corporation notwithstanding. The window that had been opened in 1991 was closing.

* * *

It wasn't until around the release of *Strings*, after they'd rented an office and hired three full-time staffers at Merge and Superchunk had sold more than 150,000 records, that Mac and Laura quit their day jobs — Mac at Schoolkids, and Laura at Kinko's. It wasn't

because they were making so much money that they could afford to quit; it was that the label was keeping them too busy. (It would be years before they paid themselves any kind of regular salary.)

Superchunk's attempt to engage the mainstream with *Strings* was deliberate and clear-eyed, but Merge's early forays into the wider world beyond Chapel Hill were occasionally less graceful. For its first five or so years, Merge was a tiny operation compared to the money, and sales, generated by Superchunk. The band's success subsidized the label — Laura was forced to borrow from Superchunk's cash reserves at times in order to keep Merge afloat. It took Mac and Laura a while to learn the ropes of keeping a record label flush.

Laura Cantrell   Mac called me once and said, "Bricks has made a little money. We're going to send you a check." And I got a check for like $1,000. I thought, how is it possible that Bricks made that much money? And then I talked to Josh Phillips and he said, "Don't tell Mac I told you this, but Laura made an accounting error and we shouldn't have gotten any of that." They never said, "Sorry, we need it back." They took it as a loss. I'm sure it was an enormous amount for a little record company at the time.

Laura   I was so excited to pay Bricks! We'd gotten our first statement from Touch and Go after the Bricks record had come out, and I was happy that we owed them money. What I didn't realize was that I needed to be holding a return reserve.

Mac   When distributors buy records from a label, they'll pay for them. And then hopefully the distributors sell them to record stores, and the record stores sell them to people. But if that doesn't happen, they'll sit in boxes in a warehouse somewhere for a couple months until the distributor returns them to us. And then you have to pay the distributor back. So you're supposed to keep a reserve in case that happens.

Laura   I just paid everybody on the records that had been shipped, but most of them were returned. And we couldn't ask for the money back. To this day, Bricks is in the red because of that. I did the same thing with Angels of Epistemology.

Mac   It's just one of those learning-curve things.

Another learning curve came in 1993, when Polvo's second full-length, *Today's Active Lifestyles*, came out.

Mac   They had found this image of a bunch of lion heads with horns on them from a Jehovah's Witnesses religious pamphlet, and clipped it out, and put it on their record cover. And the cover is really simple other than that. There was just a stripe across the bottom, and these lion heads. We had no idea where the image came from when Polvo gave us the cover art. And then we got a cease-and-desist from the Jehovah's Witnesses saying that they were going to sue us. We actually recalled all the copies that we could, and made new covers that were just blank, basically. What are you going to do? You don't want to go up against the Jehovah's Witnesses.

Laura   We had to eat the expense of making new record covers. From that point forward, I decided, Okay, we don't have a contract, but I'm going to write up this list of things, including a promise that what you give us, musically and artwork-wise, needs to be something that we can release without getting into trouble. And if you have any copyright issues, you're responsible for dealing with them. But it was a cool cover. I think they were just upset because Polvo sounds like the devil.

Mac   The Polvo thing was the first reminder that we were operating in this real world that other people are paying attention to. You never really think about that, for the most part, because people outside of the indie music world generally weren't paying attention. At that point, even if Polvo had asked us if they could clip something, we probably would have said yes.

Two years later, another Polvo matter taught Mac and Laura that, even in the indie world, business was business. In 1994, Merge released Polvo's *Celebrate the New Dark Age* EP. It was the band's fifth release on Merge; Polvo had done more projects with Mac and Laura than any artist aside from Superchunk. Polvo's Ash Bowie had helped mind the store at Merge while Superchunk was touring. Bowie also played drums in Mac's side project, Portastatic.

Mac   We were on tour and I got a message to call Corey. I called him from a pay phone in Salt Lake City. He asked if we would mind if Touch and Go signed Polvo directly. It wasn't Corey's idea. The band had come to him. They wanted a bigger advance and more money to spend on promotion than Merge had — even though they never asked us for it — and they knew that by signing to Touch and Go, they were cutting out the middleman, which was us.

Corey Rusk   It was very awkward. I would never approach one of our label's bands. With Polvo, it was weird, because we put out their records in Europe. What happened was, Polvo did want a larger advance than Merge was comfortable giving them, and they had been talking to Caroline Records. And Caroline was going to give it to them. But Caroline wanted to sign them world-wide. So Polvo came to us, and I said, "Why don't you just come to Touch and Go?" I called Mac and Laura and said, "They can either leave both of us and go to Caroline, or I can give them what they're asking for." They said, "We understand. If they're going to take the money somewhere, we'd rather it be you."

Laura   It bothered both of us. Because Polvo was one of our first bands besides Superchunk that actually did something. It seemed weirdly predatory. For Corey of all people to step in there, it was really weird.

Mac   We were put in an untenable position. Do we somehow block this from happening and make our friends in Polvo mad at us by preventing them from doing what they

Fax for Polvo's Ash Bowie with questions from a Japanese zine.

want? And it wasn't like we had a contract. That was a real bummer.

Laura   We just sort of let it go.

Mac   We didn't really have a choice. But it did mean that in the back of our minds from then on we had to worry about bands just wanting to sign directly to Touch and Go in order to increase their profit share. And so we had to make Merge into something that was valuable in and of itself to the artists we work for.

Laura   I think maybe they felt second fiddle to Superchunk. And of course, Superchunk was always going to be this high priority, and it didn't make sense to them to be on this label where the big band, which also ran the label, was always on tour. But I still think of Polvo as a Merge band.

* * *

It wasn't long before major labels were looking at the Merge roster as a poaching ground, too.

One target was F. M. Cornog, the hermit-like New Jersey antitroubadour who home-records sparkling pop songs under the name East River Pipe. Merge started releasing his records in 1994; Wilbur turned them on to him. Cornog had been selling homemade cassettes through Ajax and released a 7-inch on Sarah Records in England. His songs had garnered enough praise from the British press and American zines in the post-Nirvana heyday that Mark Kates, Nirvana's A&R rep at Geffen, was wooing him. Cornog had a salable story: He was a four-tracking alcoholic and drug addict bouncing around the flophouses of New Jersey who was rescued by his wife and manager, Barbara Powers, after she fell in love with his songs. But he refuses to perform or record in a studio, and knew enough even then to insist on retaining ownership of his master recordings. Those would be deal-killers for most major labels in a rational business environment, but in 1994, the sky was the limit when it came to potential indie stars, and Kates flew out to New York to take Cornog and Powers to dinner. They were thinking about doing a deal when a package of free CDs arrived from Kates on the same day that Kurt Cobain's body was discovered in Seattle.

F.M. Cornog **It was almost like an omen. We were like, you know what? We've got to pull back. Yeah, this is fucked up. I'm a drug addict. I'm a fucking alcoholic up the ass. I kind of knew that was my future, if I took that fork in the road. It was like a hamburger machine ready to kind of churn me up. That closed the door for me on that possibility.**

Wilbur had sent them a fan letter mentioning that he was in Superchunk, so Cornog and Powers figured Mac and Laura might like East River Pipe and gave them a call. They did. Powers, who dove into her managerial role by reading books about the music industry and attending music business seminars, insisted on a rudimentary one-page contract that she wrote.

F. M. Cornog **Laura and Mac were like, "Look, we don't do contracts, but we'll sign this stupid thing if you want. It's more informal than that. But if you guys want to be uptight, and have us sign this piece of paper, we'll do it. Jeez, you know?"**

Merge released a 7-inch and two full-lengths by East River Pipe, including 1996's *Mel*, which caught the ear of two executives at EMI America, the U.S. arm of EMI, a British label.

F. M. Cornog **So we have breakfast with these guys, and they almost wanted to hand me some cash right there at the table.**

They offered him five "firm" records for orders-of-magnitude more money than Merge could ever pay. ("Firm" means EMI was obligated to pay for them under the contract, as opposed to more traditional deals, in which the label retains an option to do the next record if it chooses to.) No touring, no interference, plenty of promotion.

Barbara Powers **They said all he had to do was come into the building once a year, in the middle of the night, and slip a DAT through the mail slot. So we thought, "Finally, here are some people at a big label who were**

going to give us money and leave us alone. So we decided to do it. But the snag was, EMI loved *Mel*. And they wanted to rerelease it, but it had already come out on Merge. That was probably the only time we ever had any real friction with Mac and Laura. Merge was still pretty small. How much could they really do with *Mel*? And why not just let us have it back and let the record have the life that it could have? We talked about a corelease with EMI, and I have to say, I respect those guys. Because that was even a bigger turnoff to them. They didn't ever want to be perceived as a fake indie needing a handout from the big guys. So there was absolutely no way Merge was going to do that.**

Mac **We were not into that. That's not about Fred and Barbara. That's about someone at EMI just thinking he can do whatever he wants. We wouldn't really begrudge him going to EMI for future records. But we didn't want to give them a record that we had already done.**

Powers, Cornog, and EMI America were in the midst of trying to figure out how much money to offer Merge to just buy *Mel* back from them when EMI abruptly shut down its American operations.

F. M. Cornog **They probably looked at my deal: "These guys are totally out of control — we gotta close this down!"**

Because the deal was firm, EMI paid out Cornog for the full amount of the contract. He and Powers used the money to buy a house in New Jersey. East River Pipe has continued to release its records on Merge.

Ironically, it was Powers's insistence on a contract that gave Merge the leverage to say "no" to EMI America taking over *Mel*. An oral agreement doesn't hold much sway against major-label lawyers, something they learned from . . . And You Will Know Us By the Trail of Dead. When Merge started working with Trail of Dead in 1999, it was with the understanding they would get the band's next two records. The Austin art-rock quartet had a vicious live show that usually involved the destruction of some or all of their instruments, and they combined a self-consciously reckless

F. M. Cornog in his "studio"—a corner of his Queens apartment—in 1999.

and hard-drinking rock'n'roll lifestyle with a cheeky, college-boy intellectualism (frontman Conrad Keely explained one record by way of reference to *War and Peace*). *Madonna*, their first and only record for Merge, was named one of the year's best by England's *New Musical Express*. Words like "savior of rock'n'roll" and comparisons to Nirvana were being tossed around. They were even written up in *Vanity Fair*, of all places, as a band to watch. And then they signed to Interscope.

Laura   They had everything Superchunk lacked. They were bad boys. They did drugs, got blind drunk, got in fights, broke things, dyed their hair, and wore all black. The press ate them up.

Mac   When Interscope was trying to steal them from us, Jimmy Iovine invited them over to his house, and they told me about it. They were impressed with the trappings. One of them said, "The piano that John Lennon played on 'Imagine' is in his house!" I thought, I'd like to see that piano, too. But so what? It's like a gimmick he uses to entice bands.

Laura   They had agreed that they were going to do two records with us.

Brian McPherson   I called their lawyer. He's alright. He's just a typical L.A. lawyer, kind of a blowhard. I said, "Look, they owe us another record." But it never went anywhere. We ultimately decided just to leave it, because those guys were just bad vibes at a certain point. That was kind of shitty. I felt personally affronted even though it had nothing to do with me. The innocence is over, you know? What if this band ends up being really huge? This can't happen again. So at that point they kind of got it. They're not stupid. They have a staff, they have families, they have a business. They work hard. And it would be nice to make sure that, even if the deal terms are not egregious or long-reaching, they get what they bargained for. You know, they got f'ed in the ass. It's the cost of an education.

Trail of Dead's next record, *Source Tags and Codes*, released on Interscope, garnered ecstatic critical praise, notching a rare perfect 10 rating on *Pitchfork*. It sold 123,000 copies, a number that failed to impress Interscope, which back-burnered the band's subsequent two — critically unheralded — releases. They split from Interscope in 2007 with an angry screed on their Web site: "At the expense of a massive debt to them of half a million dollars, [Interscope] really helped us to grow. They've taught us about the worthlessness of A&R people, how to yell at idiots running an art department, and how to shake hands with smiling retailers who have no idea who you are. . . . [T]heir idea of marketing [was] keeping it a secret that we'd released a record." (The band has since launched its own imprint on Justice Records, which is distributed by Universal Music Group — Interscope's parent company.)

* * *

Next Two Pages: Publicity photo for *Here's Where the Strings Come In*.

Facing page: Mike McCarthy, Britt Daniel, and Jim Eno at Eno's Public Hi-Fi studio in Austin, Texas, during the recording of *Ga Ga Ga Ga Ga*, September 2006.
Previous page: Daniel with tambourine at Public Hi-Fi, September 2006.

Chapter Nine

The Underdog

Spoon

Much of Britt Daniel's life before Spoon consisted of Britt Daniel searching for people to start Spoon with. Daniel, a tall, gangly blond from Temple, Texas, grew up listening to Julian Cope, the Cure, and That Petrol Emotion. And he caught hell for it from most of the shit-kicking rockers at his high school. He knew he wanted to make music and always figured that once he got to college, he'd find like-minded musicians to play with who were desperate to sound like Wire or Gang of Four. It didn't happen.

Britt Daniel **I was struggling to find people who were like me. My best friend has a story about when I met him. It was our first week of college at the University of Texas, and he walked into a party, and I came right up to him and said, "Do you play an instrument?" And he said, "No." And I was like, "OK, never mind." And I went back and sat on the couch.**

In Austin, Daniel started working at KVRX, the college radio station, and managed to cobble together a three-piece called Skellington that self-released three cassettes. But it didn't go anywhere.

Britt Daniel **They were the two guys that I could convince to be in a band. I taught the bass player from scratch. He was really into the Red Hot Chili Peppers. And the drummer was really into metal. Just trying to get everybody on the same wavelength, or even to learn the songs, was a struggle.**

In 1993, Brad Shenfeld, a colleague of Daniel's at KVRX, asked him to play bass in a country-rockabilly band he was starting called the Alien Beats. He declined, but reconsidered after realizing that he was in no position to turn down a chance to at least be in a band with a guy he liked. The Alien Beats recorded one 7-inch at the University of Texas's student studio; when their regular drummer couldn't make it, Shenfeld asked another drummer he knew, Jim Eno, to fill in for the session.

Britt Daniel **He just came right in and learned the songs. I wasn't used to dealing**

with musicians like that, who could remember that there's a stop after this part, and that this part is a chorus, and this is a verse. It was very impressive.

Eno, a soft-spoken electrical engineer, wasn't much of a rocker. He had gone to North Carolina State University and lived in Raleigh during the late eighties, but the roiling scene that Mac and Laura were navigating never made it onto his radar. While he'd played with friends, his first experience in a regularly convened band was as the drummer for the official jazz band of Compaq Computer Corporation, where he worked after he graduated.

Jim Eno   The first time I ever played with them was also really the first time I played jazz. So I showed up in a conference room, which is where they would practice. And it's a fifteen-piece jazz band, and there were charts, but I couldn't read music at all. So they said, "Oh here's a shuffle song. Go ahead and sit down. You can play this." So I'm behind the drums and the horns are playing, and it sounds great. We get through to the end of the song, and all the horns stop. So I get up and I put my sticks in my bag, and I'm starting to walk away, and then the band starts playing again! I'm like, "My god, that was weird." So I sit back down and start playing again, and then the band stops again. I'm like, "Okay, is everyone *really* going to stop this time?" And someone taps me on the shoulder and says, "Uh, Jim, you missed your solo." The twelve-bar drum solo where I got up and all I did was pack my sticks up. They were like, "This is the most avant-garde drum shit I have ever seen in my life!"

Daniel and Shenfeld invited Eno to join the Alien Beats, which lasted a year before

People were feeding us lines about how great we were going to be.

— Jim Eno

Shenfeld graduated and went to Los Angeles to attend law school (he is now Spoon's lawyer). With Shenfeld gone, Daniel was once again in a position of trying to find musically like-minded people to play with; he begged Greg Wilson, whose insistent guitar playing in the band Sincola he admired, to start a side project with him. They called it Spoon, after a Top Ten hit in the seventies in Germany by the experimental band Can. Daniel wanted to play guitar and found a bass player, a woman named Andy Maguire, through an ad in the paper. They just needed a drummer.

Jim Eno   Britt always calls it "the audition." But he just called me and said, "Hey, I'm writing these songs. I was wondering if you wanted to come over and try them out and see if you like them." And they freaking blew me away.

Daniel had only written a few songs for the Alien Beats, and they were sort of New Wave country. But his Spoon songs were angular, astringent, erratic and fierce, full of unusual time signatures and song structures, sudden pauses and bursts of atonal guitar noise.

Spoon recorded a few songs to give to clubs, which they self-released as a 7-inch called *The Nefarious EP* in 1994. *Nefarious* got some play on KVRX, and Spoon started building a local audience. Austin has always been a music town — it bills itself, after all, as the Live Music Capital of the World — but it was lousy with "next-big-thing" bands in the early nineties, owing largely to the success of Richard Linklater's generational anti-manifesto *Slacker*, which was set there, and the rising prominence of the South by Southwest music festival as a showcase opportunity for unknowns to get the attention of major labels. Spoon was one band among many in Austin, and while their sound — which drew a lot of Pixies comparisons — attracted fans, they didn't particularly stand out.

In 1994, South by Southwest rejected Spoon's application for a showcase, so the band joined the bill at an antifestival show that March at the Blue Flamingo. They were up against Beck, who was playing at Emo's on the same night, but Gerard Cosloy happened to catch Spoon's set. Daniel didn't pay too much attention to the music business. He had learned about Matador Records not from reading about Cosloy's exploits in zines, or asking folks at the record store what the cool labels were, but from noticing that his favorite records — Liz Phair, Guided by Voices, Pavement — all had the same logo on the back.

They met Cosloy that night, and kept in touch with him. There was no talk of Spoon joining Matador's roster at first; it was just friendly encouragement, with Cosloy helping Daniel set up shows in New York and Boston. A year later, Cosloy invited Spoon to play at Matador's South by Southwest showcase as a "special guest" of the label.

Britt Daniel   **He was unbelievably helpful, and supportive. It meant a great deal to me mentally, in terms of believing in myself.**

Wilson soon quit Spoon to spend more time with Sincola, and Daniel, Eno, and Maguire started working on a proper record as a three-piece in 1994, with Austin producer John Croslin. Croslin had been in the Reivers, a much-beloved but little-heard local roots-pop band that was signed to Capitol Records in the late eighties. Croslin had an eight-track in his garage, and Daniel persuaded him to record *Telephono* free of charge over the course of a few months in the spring of 1995, working nights after Croslin got off work from his job at a bookstore.

Early on, Daniel wore sunglasses onstage because he thought it was cool, and it's a pose you can hear on *Telephono*. It was jittery and detached and shot through with hipster noir; the band's goal was simply to capture the sound of a Spoon live show, but Daniel's vocals were often treated with distortion and sung in an occasionally awkward drawl that drew attention to the artifice of studio production. It was self-consciously cool, and for better or worse, it *did* sound like the Pixies, and a little bit like Nirvana, and it had some of the ironic swagger of the Jon Spencer Blues Explosion. But every rock record is an exercise in accommodating and stretching the strictures of genre. And where *Telephono* hits all the indie-rock buttons, its songs have a discipline and a restlessness that take nothing in the rock songbook for granted. "Nefarious,"

for instance, reaches an infectious chorus within its first thirty seconds, only to swap it out for different lyrics and a different melody over the same chord changes on the second and third go-rounds, before returning to the original chorus on the last repetition. It sounded like a band struggling to figure out what a great record is supposed to be.

Putting a band together had been a constant struggle, but with *Telephono* in hand, getting a record deal was almost laughably easy. Daniel sent tapes to a bunch of labels, and the next thing he knew, Spoon was getting flown out to Los Angeles to meet with A&R reps from Interscope, Warner Bros., and Geffen. Daniel also sent a copy to Matador. Cosloy said he loved it, but didn't make an offer. So Spoon heard out the majors.

Jim Eno   **People were feeding us lines about how great we were going to be.**

Britt Daniel   **I knew there was something not to be trusted about the major-label system, but I wasn't really sure what. They just seemed to either make a band really huge in a really cheesy way, or else not be able to succeed. And I didn't really want to come out huge with our first record. It kind of scared me. And I wanted to be able to make records the way I wanted to, and not have someone come in and say, "This is great, we just need to have it mixed by" whoever the hot producer is at the time. And there were people who thought that was a great way of doing it. We talked to people who said, "This record is great, it just needs another $50,000 for the mix, and then it's ready to go." People would literally say that. And those were the people we couldn't work with.**

In the end, it was Geffen that made Spoon an offer. Under the guise of seeking his advice, Daniel made one more pass at Cosloy.

Britt Daniel   **I mentioned it to Gerard, like, "Do you know this guy at Geffen? He wants to put our record out."**

Cosloy finally bit, Spoon passed on Geffen, and Matador ended up releasing *Telephono* in 1996. It was in many ways an ideal situation: The record was already done, so Matador knew exactly what it was getting. And they were licensing it as a one-off deal, meaning Spoon would still own the master and wasn't obligated to do its next record with Matador.

Telephono disappointed.

Britt Daniel   It didn't do so hot. It certainly sold a lot less than Matador was hoping. They lost a lot of money on it.

It sold fewer than 3,000 copies. *Rolling Stone* gave it two stars and said it should have been called *Smells Like Doolittle*. Spoon was dismissed as a Pixies knock-off.

The Pixies problem — those familiar boy-girl harmonies — had, ironically, already been solved in the least pleasant way imaginable: Maguire left the band before *Telephono*'s release and sued Daniel and Eno, claiming she cowrote most of the songs on the record and was entitled to royalties. The suit dragged on for nine months before it was settled, with Maguire getting a cut of royalties from radio play or other public performances of the record. Daniel and Eno recruited Croslin to fill in on the tour to support *Telephono*, and Spoon, bedeviled by legal troubles and dismal sales, hit the road.

Britt Daniel   It was brutal. We kept going out, and going out, all year long. We'd play in Fargo to maybe three people, and one of them was pacing the floor like he had cabin fever and didn't know that there was a band on stage. That was a real thing that happened. We played New York in front of sixty people, most of whom were there as guests of Matador. We were losing money. It was a grumpy and stressful mood on the road.

Jim Eno   It was a pretty miserable experience. John was going through a divorce. And we would play a show in, say, Chicago, and there would be twenty people there. And the next time we'd come through, there would be forty. And the next time there would be ten. So it's the third time you hit a city, and your audience is going down.

Daniel and Eno loved working with the people at Matador, but their dreams of a soft launch

Spoon in the Elektra era: Jim Eno, Britt Daniel, Josh Zarbo.

at a cool label weren't panning out. It was closer to a nonlaunch. Matador's publicity people couldn't find a way to convince the press to write about Spoon, and when they did, it was usually to accuse them of being derivative, a tag that the label's publicists couldn't help Spoon shake. And the records weren't getting into stores.

Jim Eno   So here we are touring our asses off, and there's no press about us, and no one can get our records in the stores. No one knows we're playing, which is why ten people show up. And if those ten people decide they want to buy our record tomorrow, they can't.

Eno's final straw with Matador came in St. Louis, when, "to try not to have a nervous breakdown," he took a walk before the show and wandered into a record store. He found a record by labelmate Tobin Sprout in the store's listening booth — a coveted spot that labels can land for their artists either through persuasion, discounts, or cash payments — and no Spoon records anywhere in the store.

Jim Eno   **Tobin Sprout had never toured. So why didn't Spoon have a listening booth in St. Louis?**

Daniel and Eno regrouped after *Telephono*, releasing the five-song *Soft Effects* EP—a loose, classic-rock-inspired departure from *Telephono*'s rigidity featuring "Waiting for the Kid to Come Out," which *The New Yorker* would later call "the first great Spoon song"— through Matador in 1997. The same year, they brought in Josh Zarbo as a permanent bass player, from the Denton, Texas, band Maxine's Radiator. When they began work on their next full-length, *A Series of Sneaks*, their options were wide open. They did it the same way they did *Telephono*, funding the recording themselves and working with Croslin, this time at various professional studios around Austin.

    For a band that was somewhat demoralized by a less than stellar debut, Ron Laffitte, the general manager of the West Coast office of Elektra Records, seemed like a godsend. Elektra sat out the flurry of major-label attention paid to Spoon before *Telephono*, and after looking at the record's sales figures, the other labels that had been so convinced that Spoon was going to be huge quickly changed their minds. When Laffitte heard *Telephono,* he fell in love, and became convinced that Elektra could — with an investment of time, patience, and money — make them stars. The label had a long history of finding and developing bands who were outside the mainstream, like 10,000 Maniacs, Stereolab, and, appropriately enough, the Pixies. And what's the point of working at a major label if you can't find bands that you love and make them stars? Laffitte romanced Spoon. He went to shows, and called their manager and lawyer on a weekly basis to demonstrate his commitment. He literally wouldn't leave them alone.

Ron Laffitte   **They were too good not to be signed.**

Britt Daniel   **He really came after us hard. Which played well.**

Daniel and Eno knew that Matador wasn't working, but they still feared working with a major. They were worried about getting dropped if the record didn't do any better than *Telephono.* They were worried about getting the support they needed to push them to radio stations. They were worried about working with people who didn't really care about the music that they loved. They didn't know what to do, and entered into agonized negotiations with Laffitte. He understood their hesitations, and he promised them that he would get them what they needed. He called Daniel every day to talk it through.

Britt Daniel   **We weren't babes in the woods. We knew what the risks were. And he was very aware of that, and tried to soothe those concerns. And he seemed to genuinely like Spoon. And I bought it.**

Ron Laffitte   **Britt was a lot more sophisticated than I anticipated. He had a very good understanding of the pitfalls of signing. Frankly, I think he had a better view of it than I did. My view of Elektra at the time was unrealistic, and a little romantic about how much time and energy the label would invest in a band like Spoon.**

Spoon signed to Elektra for a "firm" three-record deal. It seemed remarkably low-risk from the band's perspective: *A Series of Sneaks* was already in the can, so the label wasn't going to meddle with it. They'd put Laffitte through the wringer and he answered every question the right way. They even made Elektra chief Sylvia Rhone — the one who said Lou Barlow didn't "have what it takes" — offer her assurances that she would stick with them if *A Series of Sneaks* went south.

Britt Daniel   **We said, "If the record doesn't do so well at the beginning, then what do we do?" And she talked about working it long-term and going back and doing that second record and getting you on opening tours and making it work at radio or press. All this record-biz talk.**

Daniel, Eno, and Zarbo didn't indulge in their major-label status, earning them a reputation at Elektra as charmingly naïve penny-pinchers.

Britt Daniel   We were really rational about it. We did things like take a bus home instead of a flight so that we would save money for them. When we laid out our budget for the tour, we said, "We don't need per diems. Never had them before. Those are for people who make money." Elektra said we had to take them. But there was a lot of goodwill there. They couldn't believe we were such team players. At least that's how it was presented to me. They were probably thinking, "These guys are boneheads. They're doing it small-time."

Eno first got a sense that something was amiss when the label picked the minute-and-a-half song "Car Radio" as the single, and asked the band to make it longer.

Jim Eno   I think it's probably the first time in the history of music that a band was asked to do a radio edit to make a song longer. We didn't want to seem like a bunch of assholes, so we sat in front of a digital editing system for a couple days and did it. We were going to just take thirty seconds from the chorus of a Third Eye Blind song and pop it in. That would have sounded good.

The length didn't matter. *A Series of Sneaks* was released in May of 1998. It got excellent reviews compared to *Telephono*; its wiry, compressed, antic songs — only two of which made it to the three-minute mark — earned it 9.4 stars out of 10 from *Pitchfork*. Elektra waited months, while Spoon toured all summer, to push "Car Radio" to radio stations. Major labels select specific time frames to push songs to radio by calling program directors and hyping the song. If it picks up some steam, they keep pushing it. If it doesn't, they move on to the next release. Elektra decided to push "Car Radio" during the week that the radio promoter responsible for Spoon was on vacation. It made it into rotation on one station.

At the time, Elektra was in the midst of a remarkable string of hits, with Third Eye Blind, Busta Rhymes, and several other bands on the label hitting the charts. Spoon and its off-kilter, decidedly noncommercial record suddenly looked like small ball to the people in Elektra's New York headquarters, and Laffitte, in L.A.,

found himself unable to get the company to devote much attention to it. He stopped returning Daniel's calls. He didn't come to any of Spoon's shows. Elektra didn't pony up for the promotional budget Laffitte had promised. He was ashamed that he couldn't live up to his word, and was busy engineering his exit from Elektra.

Ron Laffitte   I made a lot of promises to the guys in Spoon that were based on what I believed would be my ability to dig in and stay the course with a band that would eventually be able to break down the walls. I thought I could keep those promises, and as it unfolded, I realized I wasn't getting it done. I went underground a bit. I did a disappearing act.

Sneaks sold about as well — or as poorly — as *Telephono*. Laffitte left in September for an A&R job at Capitol Records. Elektra dropped Spoon the same week.

Jim Eno   Our manager called us and said, "You're dropped." I said, "They can't drop us! We have another firm record in the contract." Well, one thing you learn is that a firm record doesn't mean shit. They can do whatever they want. It's ridiculous. When you sign to a major, you're really worried about getting dropped, because all your friends have been dropped. So what do you do? You talk to your lawyer and negotiate for six months to get two firm records. That's how you can guarantee you won't get dropped. Well, no. Not really.

Britt Daniel   I felt like a fool. The very things that I had been striving to not let happen to the band happened, and they happened in a worse way than I could ever have imagined.

After he got fired, Laffitte called Daniel to apologize for not living up to his end of the bargain, and to express his desire to support Spoon in any way he could going forward. Daniel told him, "You can fucking forget that. We're never going to work together again."

Ron Laffitte   It didn't go well. It was a bummer. I blame myself.

It was during the tour for *Sneaks* that Mac first saw Spoon, when they played at the Lizard and Snake in Chapel Hill. Mac wasn't a huge fan of *Telephono*; the songs didn't grab him, and the cover art, which featured a black-and-mustard photo of a guy in Jackie O. shades, had an "asshole quality" that put him off. But at the Lizard and Snake, they were great.

Mac   Britt was playing an acoustic guitar, but plugged in and fuzzed out. There weren't a lot of people there, but they sounded like a power trio, way beyond *Telephono* already. That turned me around on Spoon in a big way.

Jim Eno   Britt and I recognized Mac in the crowd. We were excited that he showed up, but he was right up front, alone, and he left after three songs. We thought he hated us!

The *Sneaks* tour included a leg opening for Harvey Danger, a Portland band that was at the time enjoying its briefly ubiquitous Top 40 hit, "Flagpole Sitta." But after getting dropped, the band was unsure whether to carry on with the tour, now that, without support from the label, they were likely to end up losing money. They decided they couldn't pass up an opportunity to open for an act that, at the time, was selling 20,000 records a week based on the strength of their single's radio play. Shocked to find that Harvey Danger was, however, drawing just two hundred people a night, they bailed out three-fourths of the way through the tour, exhausted and embittered.

Daniel thought the band, and his music career, was over. He moved to New York and got a job as an administrative assistant at Citibank.

Britt Daniel   I didn't think I'd ever be able to make records. Getting dropped as a baby band on a major was like the kiss of death. It felt like things could not get any lower.

One day, he suffered the ultimate indie-rock humiliation when he ran into Janet Weiss, the drummer for Sleater-Kinney, on his lunch break while wearing his work coat and tie.

Jim Eno   I thought it was just a bump in the road. Britt's a great songwriter. It was a huge

Getting dropped as a baby band on a major label was like the kiss of death. It felt like things could not get any lower.

— Britt Daniel

hit to our ego, but we never had the discussion where we were just going to hang it up.

Daniel has described the post-*Sneaks* years as a "lost period." His uncertain future had a dramatic effect on his songwriting. There was no new record to write for, no career to think about, no more idea of what Spoon was supposed to sound like. He expanded his musical tastes beyond Wire and Gang of Four to Elvis Costello, and Motown, and soul.

Britt Daniel   The pressure was off. I was just writing them for myself. I doubted we'd ever record them. Maybe we'd play them live or something. So I stopped trying to be indie-rock cool, or play by the rules of what I thought good bands did, or post-punk bands were supposed to do. I felt vulnerable, and that was starting to come out. And I was doing things that I hadn't had the guts to do before. I just felt like, well, if I want to have a piano on a song I can have a piano on a song. Fuck it. Nobody's going to hear it anyway.

It was an off-hand exchange that turned things around for Spoon. They were playing a few shows with the Archers of Loaf and At the Drive-In, and brought along their friend Hunter Darby for the ride and to serve as tour manager. Musing about the Elektra situation, Darby said, "Ah, the agony of Laffitte." Britt decided that had to be a song title, and another friend came up with the companion title of "Laffitte Don't Fail Me Now."

Britt Daniel   And there we had it, you know? These songs had to happen. They were too funny not to.

In June 2000, Spoon released "The Agony of Laffitte" b/w "Laffitte Don't Fail Me Now" as a 7-inch on Saddle Creek Records. The songs were not novelty tunes. Eno describes them as "two of the most bruising, emotional songs I've ever heard." They dissect Laffitte with the icy bitterness of a jilted lover, playing on Laffitte's sense of himself as a good-guy defender of artists at a label run by Rhone, whose loyalties lay elsewhere. "All I want to know is / Are you ever honest with anyone?" Daniel asks on "Laffitte Don't Fail Me Now." On "The Agony of Laffitte," he sings, "It's like I knew two of you, man / One before and after we shook hands." Musically, the songs were a far cry from the intense angularity of Spoon's previous records; they were closer to Lindsey Buckingham than Black Francis.

The spectacle of a great, and wronged, band issuing a kiss-off to a major label was what it took for the press to finally show a serious interest in Spoon, and the single sparked a round of stories about the failings of the major-label system. "Something went wrong, terribly wrong, with Spoon," wrote Camden Joy in the *Village Voice*. "Before their imminent classic *Sneaks* ever had its chance to be 'worked,' some god gave them the finger. . . . Of course, it's not just Spoon; [e]veryone who looked or sounded 'alternative' suddenly couldn't summon up enough sales to make big the eyes of the bigwigs. Spoon, for one, were not surprised, but that doesn't mean they weren't hurt." Laffitte became a symbol of the avarice and short-sightedness of the music business and was beset by questions about the songs from colleagues.

Ron Laffitte **I guess it was fair. What happened to them was not fair, and I was responsible. I made a mistake that affected these people's lives. Spoon is one of my favorite bands, but I didn't spend a lot of time listening to those songs. I wish they hadn't been written.**

It took a while for Spoon to get back in the studio. Daniel was still unsure about his future, and Eno set about building a studio in his garage in Austin so they could record cheaply and at will.

Jim Eno **It was difficult. I had a job, but Britt had a lot rougher times than I did when it comes to financials. I was using the money to help the band. He was trying to eat. I was trying to figure out how we could do it at my place and make it cheap, and trying to get Britt excited about recording his songs.**

Buoyed by the press and antiestablishment goodwill attending the release of "The Agony of Laffitte," they set about recording *Girls Can Tell* over several months in 2000.

Britt Daniel **I didn't know what would happen. I figured I was out of the record-making club at that point, but I was going to try anyway.**

Girls Can Tell is a record by a band that has figured something important out. Daniel's new unselfconscious approach to songwriting was matched by a drastically different sound, swathed in reverb, pianos, Mellotrons, and vibraphones. Gone were the onstage sunglasses, the antsy rock guitars, and the affected vocals. They were replaced by patient grooves, Motown hooks, and Daniel's studied crooning and laid-back falsetto. Eno's forceful and restrained drumming came dramatically to the fore; with *Girls Can Tell*, Spoon became masters of artfully delayed satisfaction, constantly walking the songs up to and back from the brink of indulgence. They made the record with the help of Austin producer Mike McCarthy, who likes to wear business attire in the studio, a habit that the band picked up. You can hear it on *Girls Can Tell*; it's a record made by people dressed for work.

Mac **There's something about that record that's so classic-sounding. Not as in classic rock, but literally classic: I've been in bars when that record comes on, and for the first millisecond before I realize it's Spoon, my brain flashes through the Rolling Stones, Elvis Costello, the Psychedelic Furs. It's so stripped down and elemental that it sounds like it could be almost from any rock era. It's really the perfect album.**

Superchunk soundman Jason Ward and Britt Daniel
on tour, 2001.

Jim Eno with a fan in Florida, 2001.

No one wanted it. Spoon still had a manager and lawyer in L.A. who were shopping it around, and Daniel would sneak out of work to the pay phone of the Marriott Hotel in Times Square for status updates, because it was the closest quiet place to conduct conference calls.

Britt Daniel **Every month it would be the same thing. Nothing was happening. I thought it was the best thing we'd ever done, and no one was interested.**

Daniel had had high hopes for Merge — he knew that Mac had been at that show in Chapel Hill — and sent him an early version of the record, but never heard back. But Jim Romeo, Spoon's booking agent, also booked Superchunk, and made sure Mac listened to the final version. He loved it. Laura took convincing.

Laura **I had never really listened to Spoon before *Girls Can Tell*. When I first heard it, the working title was *French Lessons*. I actually got pretty attached to that title. But my immediate reaction was, "This is too catchy for Merge." I could see frat boys wearing their hats backward digging that record. For some reason, that freaked me out. I had not**

yet come to accept and appreciate the back-hatters of the world. But it sounded great, and the songs were catchy as hell, and once they got in my head, there was no escape. So I came around. Once word got out that Merge was putting it out, people started coming out of the woodwork to tell us how excited they were.

Finally, Mac called Daniel in the summer of 2000 and, apologizing for taking so long, told him Merge wanted *Girls Can Tell*. Merge was the only label that expressed real interest. It released *Girls Can Tell* in February 2001, and sold an astonishing 20,000 copies, more than *Telephono* and *Sneaks* combined. NPR did a feature on Spoon, its major-label travails, and its indie rebirth.

Britt Daniel **For the first time, we put a record out and our expectations were not completely crushed. Things were working. Press was happening, the records were in stores, it was on college radio. And we were dealing with people at the label that didn't make you want to take a shower after hanging up. It was a dream come true.**

Merge was able to sell four times as many copies of *Girls Can Tell* in the first six weeks after its release than Elektra was able to sell of *Sneaks* in a year. The tour for *Girls Can Tell* was Spoon's best yet.

Jim Romeo   They played Maxwell's in Hoboken in 1999 or 2000, and they drew four people. And then literally a year and a half later they sold it out in advance.

At one point on the tour, Eno recalls, they were making their way toward New York, where they had a show booked at the Bowery Ballroom. The day after that show was scheduled as a day off, but they'd kept a hold on the Bowery so that, in the unlikely event the first show sold out, they could add another.

Jim Eno   Every day, as we moved closer to New York, we would wake up and look at the presale numbers. And this tension was building as we made our way. We ended up selling both nights out.

Eno got a lesson in indie-label accounting when he received his first profit-split statement from Merge. Given the sales of *Girls Can Tell*, he was expecting a good-sized check, but it was for $6. What he didn't understand was that a $6 check meant that the record had already earned out — Merge had made back all the money it spent on the advance and on producing and promoting the record, plus $6. On every statement thereafter, Spoon would get half the money made on every record they sold. The checks got significantly bigger.

Jim Eno   I was talking to this guy in a major-label band, and he was telling me about how they had to audit their label's books, and

○———————●

I thought that it would do really well, even though it had horns. And modern rock doesn't have horns.

— Karen Glauber

they found a $1-million math error. I was like, "Well, we just got our first statement from Merge, for $6."

After *Girls Can Tell*, Spoon went on an unrestrained tear of great records and good luck. In 2002, Merge released *Kill the Moonlight*, a piano-and-drums-heavy masterpiece that made dozens of year-end best-of lists and was named one of the Top 100 indie records by *Blender*. The single, "The Way We Get By," a propulsive and infectious ode to living poorly — "You sweet-talk like a cop and you know it / You bought a new bag of pot / So let's make a new start / That's the way to my heart" — was featured on the soundtrack to *The O.C.*, which had at the time captured the minds, hearts, and ears of the fourteen-and-up set nationwide. Daniel was featured in *Time* under the headline, "These Guys Just Might Be Your New Favorite Band." It was the first time Merge had penetrated so deeply into the mainstream — it's also the sort of placement major labels used to have a lock on — and it pushed *Kill the Moonlight* to 143,000 in sales.

Three years later, *Gimme Fiction* debuted at number 44 on *Billboard*, Merge's first entrance into the Top 100, with 160,000 copies sold. *Entertainment Weekly* described it as brimming with "classics-to-be." The single was a booty-shaking vamp worthy of Prince called "I Turn My Camera On" that sounded almost nothing like anything Spoon had done before, and it became their calling card. Merge hired Karen Glauber to work it to radio, and it began to get enough commercial play to make a crucial jump.

Karen Glauber   The difference with "I Turn My Camera On" getting radio play was, at Spoon shows you'd all of a sudden see these mainstream girls start doing sorority-girl stripper dances to it instead of the indie-rock head-nod. It's a totally different level. The beer-up-in-the-air kind of thing. You just know when something's a hit.

"I Turn My Camera On" also found listeners through a lucrative and decidedly nonindie side business: It was the soundtrack to a Jaguar commercial. There was a time when the notion of even classic, major-label rock being used to hawk cars or shoes was considered unconscionable. When Nike licensed the Beatles' "Revolution" from Michael Jackson, who owned the copyright, for use in a 1987 advertising campaign, it caused an uproar. The Beatles sued, furious that their song was being used to sell shoes. Bruce Springsteen turned down an offer from Chrysler of $12 million for the rights to use "Born in the U.S.A.," and Neil Young decried the practice in "This Note's for You." So there's no small irony in the fact that the past decade has seen a boom in using indie-rock songs in commercials. Eager to find something that sounds new to help their products cut through the televised clutter, advertisers have turned to bands, like Spoon, that haven't been played to death on commercial radio. And indie labels and bands have come to rely on the business as an acceptable and almost integral stream of revenue.

When Superchunk was approached by British Knights, a sneaker company, in 1991, it was different. A friend of theirs in the advertising business was working on a commercial for British Knights, and explained to them that if they declined to license a song, the company would just find a soundalike. So they agreed, but found the notion of allowing one of their existing songs to be used to sell shoes so distasteful that they actually went into the studio to record a new "Superchunk-sounding" instrumental, called "Tasty Shoes, Tasty Shoes." They were paid $1,000, a couple British Knights baseball caps, and a pair of sneakers for each member, and earned the ire of the few fans who actually saw the ad. Today the pay is much, much better, and the ire is almost nonexistent.

Laura   Now *I* want a Jaguar commercial.

Matt Suggs   One way a lot of bands are able to make a living doing what they do is selling their shit to advertising. I never would blame a band for doing something like that. It's like a happy medium; you could stay on an indie and have complete control of what you're doing, and maybe sell a song to a big advertiser. On the flip side, I can see why it's kind of lame.

Jim Eno   We're paying the bills, you know?

I know artists who are on smaller labels than Merge that get licensing, so it does seem like the mentality is changing. They're embracing smaller artists. You don't have to sell 250,000 records and have a Top 10 hit to get in ads. I know bands that sell 5,000 records and get some pretty good placements.

Aside from the Jaguar ad, Spoon has licensed "My Mathematical Mind" for use in an Acura ad, though they've turned down many offers, including one from Hummer. Those two car ads, which were in heavy rotation, served as the best exposure Spoon has ever had.

Corey Rusk   Repetition is what gets people used to something. Music that might have sounded too far left of field to your average person fifteen years ago, now you start hearing that sort of thing in music on TV or commercials, and it becomes more familiar and acceptable to them, and they're more interested in buying it. And that leads to bands that fifteen years ago wouldn't have sold these quantities of records being able to now.

Karen Glauber   It has opened up the consumer's brain. It's a lot easier to hear something, and they can Google it and figure out what it is and just buy it on iTunes.

Of course, once Spoon became a phenomenon (in spite of, rather than because of, their decision to work with Elektra), major labels came calling again. The band rebuffed all offers, including one from Elektra — the band's manager suggested that the A&R rep who made the call check their corporate history.

Karen Glauber   I think their decision-making process is informed by the situation they went through before. There's a level of confidence in working with Merge. They've put out consistently great records and they're making consistently great music. So for them to start over on a major would've been, I think, a great mistake. They've done great by Merge, and Merge has done great by them.

Corey Rusk   Bands who had the major-label experience that didn't work out are far more likely to stay out of the major-label system if they get a second chance later on and are making music that people are reacting to. They know they can make it work outside of it, and they know how volatile it is within it. I would contend that Spoon wouldn't be selling any more records on a major, and would probably be making less money.

And their next record, released in 2007, almost certainly wouldn't have been named *Ga Ga Ga Ga Ga*. You can almost hear the label executive objecting, "DJs aren't going to say it!" The title, which came from Daniel's onomatopoeic mimicking of a piano riff on its second song, was among a list of titles Daniel e-mailed to Mac for his input. "He said that was the one he liked the best," Daniel says. "That is literally what happened." *Ga Ga Ga Ga Ga*, a rollicking record full of joyful horns and blue-eyed soul, debuted at number 10 on the *Billboard* Top 100 in July 2007, and has sold 300,000 copies. *Rolling Stone* gave it four stars and included it in its Top Ten records of the year. Spoon — which now included Robbie Pope, who joined the band in 2006 after Zarbo quit — appeared on *Saturday Night Live, Late Night with David Letterman*, and *The Tonight Show with Jay Leno*. In terms of sales and promotional reach, it was in no way appreciably different from a major-label release.

The single, "The Underdog," a danceable Van Morrison–esque tune, perfectly sums up Spoon's relationship to the major label system: "You have no fear of the underdog / That's why you will not survive." Daniel initially didn't want it on the record, but Glauber convinced him that it was the best shot for a single.

Karen Glauber   I give Britt credit for trusting me enough. I was like, "Dude, I'm going to be the one in the trenches working your record." I thought that it would do really well, even though it had horns. And modern rock doesn't have horns. In modern rock, we've gotten to the Top 20, which is ginormous because we haven't really spent money. You have to spend money at a certain point to get a record to the Top 20, and we weren't willing to do that.

Spoon's story — two overlooked records followed by a series of breakthroughs that built from release to release — was unremarkable twenty years ago. It was how the major label system was supposed to work. *Greetings From Asbury Park, N.J.* and *The Wild, the Innocent and the E Street Shuffle* were not commercial successes, but they were the records that Bruce Springsteen made on his way to making *Born to Run*. They were investments that his label made in the hope of an artistic and commercial payoff, and they worked. Spoon was on the verge of their *Born to Run* when shortsightedness almost killed the band. Daniel and Eno took Mac and Laura's faith in them just as personally as they took Elektra's scorn.

Jim Eno   It's just so nice after a tour to get an e-mail from them asking if it went well. They're just really sweet. It's so rare in the music business to get that.

Eno finally quit his day job just a few months before *Ga Ga Ga Ga Ga* came out — in other words, two years after *Gimme Fiction* cracked the *Billboard* charts.

Britt Daniel   Whenever I thank Mac and Laura for taking a chance with us, which has completely changed my life, they always say, "You did all the work. You made the records, and you did all the touring."

Daniel has never spoken to Laffitte about the songs that he inspired. But he was happy to hear that, around 2002, his friends in a fellow Austin band called the Faint were being courted by Capitol Records, and Laffitte was the one doing the courting. They agreed to meet him for lunch in Brooklyn, and Andy Slater, the president of the label and Laffitte's boss, joined them. They showed up carrying a copy of "The Agony of Laffitte" and handed it to him across the table. The Faint didn't sign to Capitol.

Jim Eno   They got a good lunch out of it, though.

* * *

Facing page: Spoon: Britt Daniel, Eric Harvey, Jim Eno, Robbie Pope.   Next page: Daniel, Pope, and recording assistant Matthew Colecchi at Public Hi-Fi, September 2006.

Wurster sleeping in the van during Superchunk's
1998 tour of Brazil.

Poster for Butterglory's 1996 European tour
with Guv'ner and Cat Power.

Backstage Polaroid of Superchunk and Lambchop by Annie Hayden.

Superchunk at the Great American Music Hall,
San Francisco, 1999.

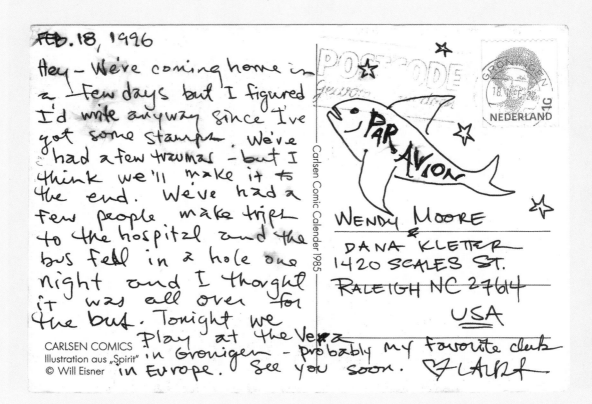

Laura's postcards from the road.

Wurster in Australia, October 1994.

Neutral Milk Hotel, Columbus, Ohio, 1996.

Laura with Neutral Milk Hotel, 1998. From left: (Unknown), Scott Spillane, John D'Azzo, Laura, Jeff Mangum, Jeremy Barnes.

John Woo and Claudia Gonson of the Magnetic Fields, 1996.

From left: Tom Scharpling, Mac, Jonathan Marx (Lambchop), Laura Cantrell (Bricks), Kurt Wagner (Lambchop), and Paul Niehaus (Lambchop), Merge office, 1994.

Butterglory video shoot, 1995: Roman Coppola, Matt Suggs,
Debby Vander Wall, Stephen Naron, Mark Fay.

Aggi Wright (The Pastels), Mac's wife Andrea Reusing,
and Wurster in Mallorca, Spain, 1997.

Merge meeting agenda. Item VII: "Mirla [Merge's accountant] says we don't have any $."

The video shoot for "Watery Hands," directed by Phil Morrison and featuring
Janeane Garofalo and David Cross, 1997.

"Watery Hands" video treatment by Phil Morrison.

Superchunk
"Watery Hands"
Scene Breakdown
(inc. scenes not in treatment)
(also note: anything marked "band" includes instruments)

1. Prologue on stage

D & J & Band: handheld coverage
*Art: directors chairs, harlequin masks
*Sound: sync-sound

2. Epilogue in room

D & J & Band: handheld coverage (inc. cutaways of watching
video)
TV Monitor: lockoff
*Art: TV and VCR, chairs or couch
*Sound: sync-sound

*3. Jon plays in a medium shot. Cut to a closeup of the floor
tom. It is beaten by Janeane's hand. On the drumhead is
written "Hate" with a bar struck through it.*

J: arm beating drum
Band: Jon playing
*Art: drum head

*4. Mac plays in a medium shot. Cut to a closeup. The guitar
and clothes are slightly different and David's hand hammers
ala Van Halen.*

D: MCU torso wailing on guitar
Band: LS and MS Mac / LS and MS Jim
*Wardrobe: David in Mac's clothes

*5. Laura plays in a medium shot. Cut to a closeup of David's
torso in a similar shirt. The torso plays bass and gyrates
suggestively.*

D: MCU torso in Laura's shirt
Band: LS and MS Laura
*Wardrobe: David in Laura's clothes?

*6. In individual shots of each band member, Janeane and
David enter frame with the help of a bad bluescreen video
key. They perform conceptual movements.*

D & J: conceptual movements
Band: indvidual performance shots

MORE:

Handwritten notes:
BQE North
McGuinness Humboldt Exit
Left B.QT. Ramp. ont McGuinness
Go over Polaski Bridge
Go straight Across Jackson
Go straight onto 11th St.
Make Right when you reach
Queens Plaza South.
Go three blocks to 22nd St.
Turn Right
Silver Lug on Right
Parking on left of Bldg

Roger Williams
2128 708 8816 202 1621

Pier Platters co-owner Bill Ryan
handling Superchunk merch.

Wilbur at the "Watery Hands" shoot, being wheeled by Damon Chessé (left) and David Doernberg (right).

Claire Ashby, Corey Rusk, and Laura in the photobooth at Lounge Ax in Chicago, Ill., on Laura's birthday in 1998.

Sasha Bell (playing flute) and Gary Olson (playing trumpet) of Lady-bug Transistor at the Cat's Cradle during Merge's 10th anniversary festival, 1999. Deanna Varagona (Lambchop) in glasses.

Party for Merge's 10th anniversary fest. Clockwise from bottom left: Richard Harrison (Spaceheads), Matt Suggs, Brian Paulson, Patrick Buchanan (in baseball cap), Jonathan Marx (Lambchop), Chad Nelson (Touch and Go), David Doernberg behind him, Meg Fleischel (Touch and Go), Paul Niehaus (Lambchop, blurry at very back), Jaime Fleischel (short hair, in T-shirt facing right), Tom Reardon (baseball sleeves), Geoff Abel (Capsize 7, striped shirt against door), Martin Hall (Merge), Sasha Bell (Ladybug Transistor), Marisa Anne Brickman ('Sup magazine, turning to camera), Mike Wolf (Flying Nun U.S., wearing flashlight T-shirt).

Lambchop's Kurt Wagner and Mark Nevers with NPR's Renée Montagne, Los Angeles, 2000.

Members of Lambchop dash through the rain to Mac's house during the Merge 10th anniversary festivities.

Merge's 10th anniversary cake.

Stephin Merritt on tour, 1998.

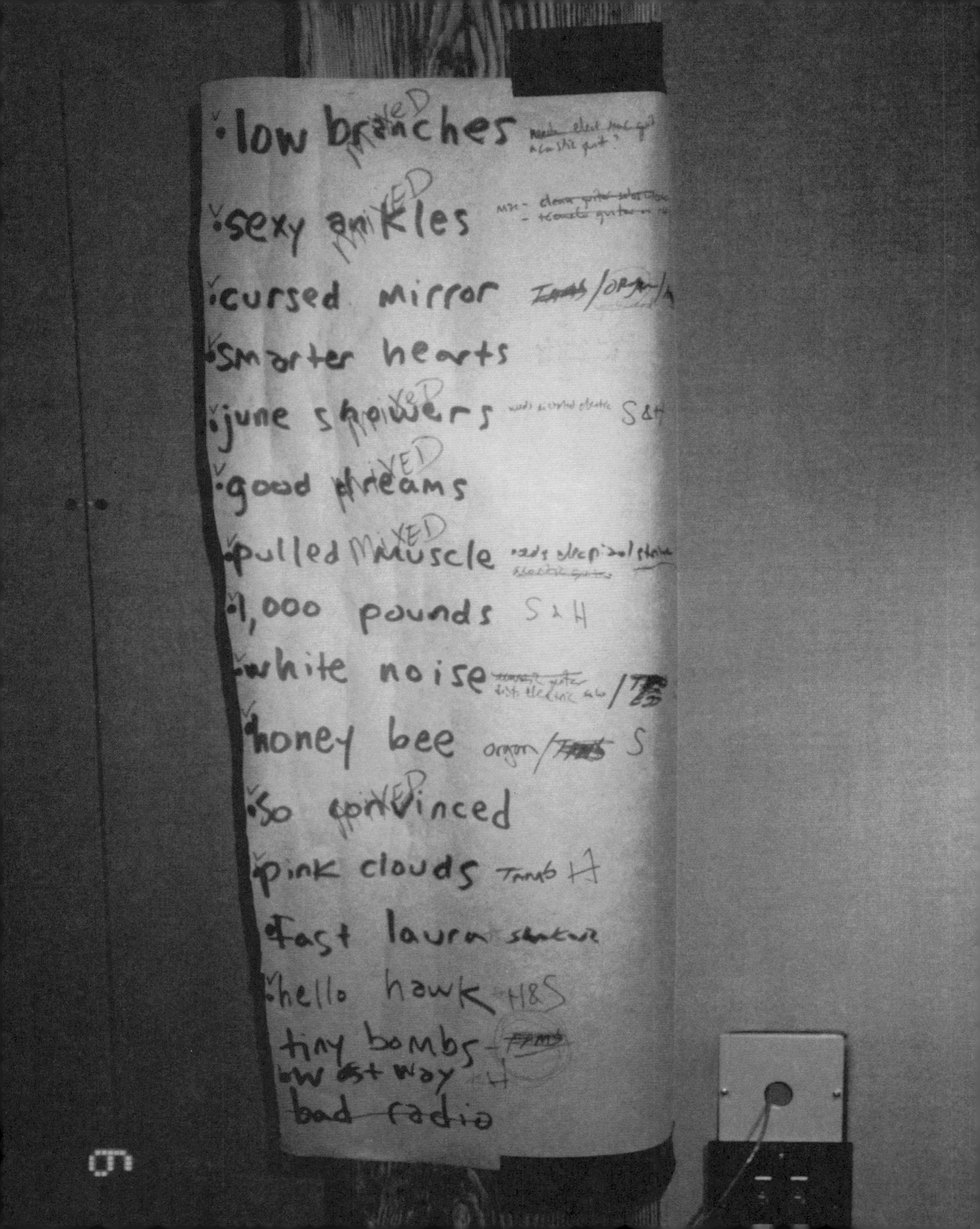

low branches
MIXED
sexy ankles
MIXED
cursed mirror
smarter hearts
june showers
MIXED
S&H
good dreams
MIXED
pulled muscle
MIXED
1,000 pounds
S & H
white noise
honey bee
organ/
S
so convinced
MIXED
pink clouds
H
fast laura
hello hawk
H&S
tiny bombs
lowest way
H
bad radio

Chapter Ten

Tiny Bombs

1996 to 1999

For its first six or so years of existence, Superchunk galloped at a furious pace. By the time *Strings* came out, they'd released seven full-length records, including two collections of singles, and seventeen 7-inches. In 1996, after pushing *Strings* harder than any previous record, they eased off the accelerator. They would wait an unheard-of-in-Superchunkland two years to put out their next full-length, *Indoor Living*. They played shows, including a year-end trip to Australia, but for the first time since 1991, the band's calendar featured months-long swaths of blank space. They spent just two days out of the entire year in the studio, recording four songs for the *Laughter Guns* EP, which they released in a limited edition of 5,000 in October to hold fans over.

Superchunk was in a strange place. There were established vectors that bands were obliged to follow. A 1991 story in the Chapel Hill–area *Independent Weekly* championing Superchunk and bemoaning the local hype surrounding Lollapalooza, which had started that year, summed up the expectations: "The local scene deserves as much attention, anticipation, and adulation as [Lollapalooza]. When Superchunk draws 20,000 or 30,000 people around here that'll be more like it." The trajectory was supposed to go from passionate obscurity to jaded celebrity. Bands either break through, or they break up. Superchunk had steadily sold more records with each release, and after *Strings* were at the peak of their career. Their name had become synonymous with indie credibility. But their efforts to translate that into broader commercial success — the Belly tour, the "Hyper Enough" radio push — had failed. They were no longer perceived as having insurgent momentum, and they never did draw 20,000 people. So they got coverage like this, from a 1996 *Rip* magazine profile: "Truth be known, I'm pretty much up on most indie rock, but Superchunk just never made it to my CD player. I'd heard them at friends' houses and thought they were cool, but I owned none of their records." The writer made much of that fact that the friend she brought with her to see a Superchunk show before the interview was surprised to find out that they weren't Supergrass.

And indie credibility wasn't quite as profitable as some had hoped. In January 1996, Atlantic dissolved its relationship with Matador; *Billboard* speculated that Superchunk's decision not to stay with the label was a factor. Nor was Superchunk so young anymore. "We're all almost thirty years old, and our audience is still twenty," Wilbur told an Australian newspaper in 1996. "You see yourself getting older, and you wonder what you could possibly be doing that is still relevant to these people. It's scary to think about it. It's not youthful rebellion any more. It's an idiom I can exploit for artistic means."

Matt Gentling   There was a sense even back then that people would remember Merge, and that it would leave its mark on music. But they were kind of financially strapped a lot of the time. They were operating just right around the line, and even just under the line, quite a bit.

Claire Ashby   Superchunk supported that label for the first ten years or so. I'm sure they were outselling everybody else on the label. Merge was paying something to Mac and Laura, but I don't think they were making a ton of money off it.

Laura   Superchunk loaned Merge money a couple of times, to help keep things rolling. But I always paid Superchunk back. It was a little matter of cashflow.

Liz Sloan (Former Merge finance director)   At one point we explored taking on some bank debt just to have more comfort from a cash perspective. And they were not interested in leverage. They didn't want to go that route. And that's why I think they'll be celebrating their twentieth anniversary.

Laura   It's not in my nature. I don't gamble. I don't like giving money away. I don't like paying interest. But I actually do love paying the bands. There's nothing better than finishing a profit-sharing statement and realizing that we owe a band a big chunk of money.

Jim Wilbur   **Superchunk was so much more of a thing than Merge for a while. And then the balance shifted.**

Jason Ward   **They were aware that they were not going to blow up. They sort of locked in their core audience. When I'd tell people that I toured with Superchunk, they'd say, "Oh, I loved them when I was in college. They're still around?"**

Tom Scharpling   **It seemed like they hit a ceiling with things. Is that wrong to say? Am I being insulting by saying that? It kind of leveled off. And it's a frustrating thing, I'm sure.**

Jim Romeo   **In the last ten years, Superchunk has probably played fewer shows than they did in all of 1994.**

Jim Wilbur   **Jon would have expectations. He would get upset if no one came to the show. I'd get upset, but I wouldn't cry about it. You know, there were times when we'd play in Athens, a place where we used to always sell out, and there'd be 150 people. And he would take that personally. And I'd be like, "Well, R.E.M. are playing tonight."**

Phil Morrison   **There was a period of time where every Superchunk show I saw, I thought it could be the last one. Not because there would be some kind of tumult, but that maybe they would just stop. And end.**

Bob Lawton   **They kind of flattened out, or waned, whatever you want to call it. They started touring less, and recording less.**

Phil Morrison   **It went from being the thing that everyone was expected to put first, and drop anything else for, to becoming a thing where, if everybody agreed, Oh sure, I'm free for that, that they could do it. But anyone was allowed to veto for some other priority.**

Jim Wilbur   **When we'd do interviews – I remember at one point, Jon and I said, "If they ask anything about Merge, we're going to walk away." Because we didn't have anything to do with Merge. And Mac had to tell a guy, "Could we just stop the interview?**

Can we just talk about Superchunk?" Which was a bit churlish in retrospect. But it came up in every interview.

Mac   I thought they were such babies about that. What's the big deal? It helps the Superchunk story, but you don't feel like sitting there for two minutes while I talk about it?

Bob Lawton   I used to say, "Can't you do something? Maybe get arrested?" They were so unassuming. They didn't want to bring extra attention to themselves. Wilbur might take one hit of pot after a show — *maybe*. They had a couple beers. They barely touched hard liquor.

Jim Wilbur   No drug abuse, no fashion. There was nothing really to hang a tag on this band except that we looked like your neighbors. Most indie kids had the skinny, glasses, unshaven look. They're from central casting, a lot of times. We're the most unrock rock band. We didn't wear scarves. We don't have funny hair. I guess Laura and Mac did kind of have funny hair in the beginning. I didn't have funny hair.

Laura   Jim was *losing* his hair. The break-up was over, so the press didn't even have that to latch onto. After we played with the Supersuckers a couple times, I started joking that we needed a gimmick like their cowboy hats to keep people interested. Man or Astroman? was doing real well with their space suits at the time.

Lou Barlow   When I first met Mac and Laura, I felt like a completely sarcastic asshole. They were just incredibly friendly. My experience of being in hardcore bands was that things were always just sort of edgy. If you met another band, you never knew if they were going to be really nice, or just so cool that they were completely pricks. The question was always really up in the air. Back then, you were kind of supposed to be angry. But with Superchunk, they were from the South and a lot nicer, and they weren't pretentious.

Amy Ruth Buchanan   I think Laura had a retirement account before I knew what one was.

Lou Barlow   I was doing reviews with a friend of mine for this fanzine called *Popwatch*, and I was pretty opinionated about what I liked and what I didn't like. I was a little bit divisive, I would say, in my opinions about things. And I wrote something about Superchunk — like, "Oh, they're okay, they're too poppy, or they aren't heavy enough for me." Something like that. And Mac sent me a letter saying, "Wait a minute! I thought we were kind of friends." I just had to say something dismissive about him, and he totally busted me on it. I mean, he got me. He totally got me. And I remember thinking it was pretty sweet, because it obviously meant he cared. I thought that was great, and that I should probably watch what I type.

* * *

In the winter of 1996, Superchunk went on a lengthy tour of Europe with the coheadliners Seam that was attended by a rare showing of outright rancor, and ranks as legendary among Superchunk's many ill-fated tours of the continent.

Jon Wurster   That was probably the worst tour I've ever been on. It was so bad that Jim still carries the itinerary in his wallet, so whenever things go badly in his own life, he'll take it out and he'll know that it can get worse.

Mac   There was definitely some friction. I got along with everybody, including the Seam guys. But I think any time you're put in a bus for six weeks, there's going to be some personality traits that conflict. And the stronger personalities, like DeWitt, and some of the guys in Seam, kind of clashed.

I used to say, "Can't you do something? Maybe get arrested?"

—Bob Lawton

DeWitt Burton was Superchunk's roadie for the tour.

Jon Wurster   For some reason, the drummer for Seam, Chris Manfrin, didn't really bring anything. He didn't bring cymbals or anything. So he was using all my stuff.

DeWitt Burton   That guy was as prepared to play a rock show as Custer was to fight Indians at the Little Big Horn. I think he showed up with like a pair of sticks. The whole thing was, I felt like I was getting taken advantage of, because I was the only roadie there. And the Superchunk guys are just so great about helping you pack up and stuff at the end of the night. They would never let me pack the van by myself. And I told the Seam and the Superchunk guys that I would work for everybody, but, come on – you guys have to pitch in. So on nights when Seam headlined, I'd always have to say to Chris, "You've got to help bust down these drums and put them away." One night in Sweden, after the show, everybody was having a good time with all the beautiful people. Chris had just started taking down the drums and left the cymbals on the ground – it was people just spilling beer on them and stepping on them. And this is my friend Jon's drum kit, so I'm extremely

DeWitt Burton.

protective of it. So I'd seen this going on, and it just kind of came to a head.

Jon Wurster   After the show, I went to bed on the bus. I slept the entire drive overnight. And the next morning I wake up to find that the drummer for Seam is in the hospital. I was like, "What happened?"

DeWitt Burton   I said to Chris, "Get your fucking ass out there and pack those drums." And he got mad at me and suggested that he was going to beat my ass or something. He's got this Midwestern, Chicago tough-guy thing – but he's not. And I'm not a little fella. I'm a lot bigger than Jon, Mac, Laura, or Jim. I was like, Yeah right, on your best day, you redneck. He flew off into this volatile, explosive rage, screamed, jumped up and down like a small child, and then proceeded to turn around and smash his hand into a brick wall. Which reduced several of the bones in his hands to a powdery form. He sure showed me. And the rest of the tour, Mac was once again playing the drums for Seam.

Jon Wurster   Mac was the original drummer in Seam. So we figured out this way where, for Seam's set, Mac would play some songs, and I'll play some songs, and the sound guy will play some songs. Show goes on.

DeWitt Burton   I guess it was a good thing he was in Sweden where they have fine hospitals and everything, because they put his hand back together, put him in a cast and then he flew home. But as you might guess, that did cause a little dissent and a little aggravation among people cramped in a living space together.

Joe Hickey was Superchunk's soundman on the tour.

Mac   My wife Andrea came to visit for a few days on that tour. On her last night we were in Munich, and we skipped the bus and got a hotel room. I dropped her off at the subway to the airport in the morning, and walked back to the venue where the bus was parked. And I get back there, and everyone's freaking out, because DeWitt and Joe had — basically, DeWitt had punched Joe, and Joe's face was a big shiner. And one of them was going home, but no one knew which one. And I was like, "What!? I only left for like six hours."

Jim Wilbur   On the same tour, Jon dove off the stage during a song in Copenhagen when a guy reached up and touched Laura's bass. You're playing, you're in the moment, and all of a sudden the drums stop. And I look and see Jon flying through the air, grabbing this guy going, "What are you doing? You don't touch people!"

Laura   It was in Christiania, a weird, druggie enclave in Copenhagen. The place we were playing was a combination rock club, restaurant, and hostel. This guy started messing with me, and I started to see drum sticks flying through the air at him, and I realized Jon was trying to defend me! So sweet. He tried more subtle methods before tackling the guy, he really did.

Jon Wurster   He got thrown out. But at the end of the night — which is ruined at this point — we're loading up stuff, and I look over and he's there again. I'm like, "What's going on? Why is this guy here?" And the club owner says, "Uh, we could not really throw him out, because he lives here." He lived in the building!

Mac   I understand why Jim hated that tour. It was very grueling. Bus tours are hard, because you're trapped wherever the bus is. It's pretty much like the bus is leaving at this time, you go to sleep, and you wake up in a parking lot somewhere. And if you want to go somewhere, you have to walk or take a cab. And we're just so used to having control over our own movement. It's especially bad in Europe because the clubs are all outside the town in some industrial park in Germany. You can't really get around. And Jim couldn't sleep, and he couldn't relax, so he would spend long hours sitting in the jump seat next to the driver. One thing about the bus is that you can't take a shit on the bus. That's the rule. So the driver would literally pull over for Jim in the middle of the night. I remember

Jim one time saying he had to take a shit on a frozen river, under a bridge, in like Sweden somewhere, because that was the only place to pull over. And Jim's like, "No, don't worry, you don't need to pull into a truck stop. Just like pull over to the side of the road."

Jim Wilbur   I had health issues. I was a vegetarian, and unknowingly lactose intolerant. So I just felt bad all the time because I was eating cheese, and just having horrible gastrointestinal problems. But I cared about the band. I hated touring. I hated it. But I did it, because I'm a New England masochist. You know, Protestant work ethic and all that.

Laura   We had a code name for diarrhea in the band — Perlman. As in Rhea Perlman. It comes in very handy when you have Jim Wilbur in the van.

Tour antics aside, responsible young adults make responsible young adult music. Superchunk's next two records, 1997's *Indoor Living* and 1999's *Come Pick Me Up*, were calculated departures from the brash and salty-sweet guitar heroics that the band was known for.

For *Indoor Living,* the band tapped their friend John Plymale, who had produced the *Laughter Guns* EP. They headed out to Echo Park in Bloomington, Ind., a studio owned by Mike Wanchic, the guitar player for John Mellencamp.

Mac   Plymale is great in the studio. He never gave us an ounce of weariness, or the "Are you sure you want to do that?" look. He also introduced us to the greatest game you can play after spending twelve hours in an airless and artificial studio environment: A basketball variant called Tip It In, which we played on the court behind Echo Park. I think it's the only time the whole band participated in a sport of any kind.

Jason Ward   *Indoor Living* was the beginning of them changing a lot. They started to stretch out more musically. There were fewer chords and more of back and forth — almost like a Television kind of thing — these little interplays of guitar melodies instead of

Writing *Indoor Living* in Wurster's basement, 1997.

Writing *Here's Where the Strings Come In*, 1995.

unison power chords. And the tempos came down and the songs were a little longer. I really liked it a lot. And Mac also started developing more of an interest with keyboard parts and other textures that weren't just two distorted guitars and distorted bass.

Laura   When we were writing songs for *Indoor Living*, I started playing the bass parts in a higher range, because all of the boom-boom was getting a little dull for me. At some point, I wondered if Mac was thinking, "Oh shit, now she's playing like the bass players we used to have in the Slushpuppies!" Of course, I couldn't play a bass solo if you paid me to. In fact, we started covering Elvis Costello's "Lipstick Vogue," which has a break with this crazy bass part, and every time we played it, I thought, "I am a failure as a bass player." I can't solo my way out of a wet paper bag.

John Plymale   I think one of the reasons they picked Echo Park was that Mac looked at their list of equipment and they had a whole bunch of cool synthesizers. I definitely remember him wanting to experiment a lot with the synthesizers, playing around and trying to come up with ideas.

Ron Liberti   Mac was kind of feeling differently about how he was being represented. And I was coming to the point then, too, where I was kind of sick of screaming my head off. Not that I was ever really angry, but when I was younger, it came out in a certain way. And when I got to thirty years old or so, I didn't really want to scream anymore. I didn't really have anything to scream about.

John Plymale   Mac was making the vocals a little bit more part of the plan. He's an interesting guy, because the things he really likes musically are very different from the type of music that he makes. He's a really big jazz fan, and he's also a really big Bruce Springsteen fan. And I don't personally hear much of either of those really in his music. But obviously they're influences on him, in a big way. So you've got Bruce Springsteen, who's all about having a big, loud lead vocal in the mix. And then you've got jazz and bebop, where it's all about being obscure

and really to the left of everything. And Mac is somewhere in the middle of that.

Jason Ward   He started singing more sing-songy stuff, and singing falsetto, and backing harmonies. It was like watching him learn that he was actually a singer, and that he can hit notes.

Mac   I used to never want the rest of the band in the studio when I was recording vocals, because it's humiliating. But this time we came up with a nice little system with me in a glass booth facing Jim and John in the control room. Jim would weigh in after each take, which was a huge help, because he knows me and knows the songs better than anyone. A lot of the time in Superchunk, there's a sort of "every man for himself" vibe, with everyone just focused on taking care of their own stuff. So in the studio, everyone sort of has their heads down to a certain extent, concentrating on their own little world and their own parts. Having Jim out there made me feel like there was someone on my team.

Jon Wurster   I was kind of hoping that we'd branch out a little earlier than we did. Because I remember — and this is a completely polarizing band — but the Afghan Whigs, they had put out *Gentlemen* around the time of *On the Mouth*. And to me, that was a really advanced kind of record for a band that was coming from where they had come from. They were obviously thinking about it. And they were throwing in things that I kind of was hoping we would throw in. But we just weren't there yet. So the ones that came later are the ones where we were experimenting a little bit.

Indoor Living had its traditional Superchunk barnburners, like "Nu Bruises" and "European Medicine." But many of the songs were awash in organ and burbling keyboard noises, and peppered with carefully orchestrated oohs and ahs. Mac's deliberate falsetto was striking. "Like a Fool," the opener to *Foolish* three years earlier, had also featured Mac straining the upper ranges, but it was rough-hewn and raw. On *Indoor Living*, it was crafted.

Mac Christof Ellinghaus, who ran our European label, City Slang, asked me who the girl was singing backup vocals. There was no girl.

The record also found Mac taking a more concrete direction lyrically. "Song for Marion Brown" was an ode to the jazz composer and a meditation on art and commerce: "While the Capricorn Moon gathers dust / Now the box sets are moving in the malls . . . / They're charging admission now . . . / For your baby teeth and a lock of hair." Before Mac completed the lyrics, it was given the temporary title of "Baba O'Really?" by Wurster, because its chorus blatantly echoes the iconic guitar riff from the Who's "Baba O'Riley."

DeWitt Burton When they were writing that song, Laura said, "We should do this right here," and she played the chorus part on her bass. Jon and Mac and Jim look at each other and go, "Hey Laura, have you ever listened to the Who? Have you ever heard 'Baba O'Riley?'" And she says, "No." And they all looked at each other: "Then it stays." When they play it live, at the end, Jim screams into the microphone, "We're all wasted!"

Laura I don't recall that, and I'm a huge fan of the Who. Somehow, when I did it, it just didn't occur to me that it sounded like the Who. But hey.

The 1996 Seam tour also served as inspiration for *Indoor Living,* turning up in "European Medicine":

> Old faxes, torn in two
> One drummer turning blue
> He's alright, you know
> Drinking kills both parasite and host
> Continental clowns
> Buying francs with pounds
> Passed out on the ground . . .
> Smashed and shattered now
> One more hand, they'll have to put me down

DeWitt Burton William Shin, who was in Seam and now is a businessman in the Washington, D.C. area, called me on the phone one day and said, "Man I was just sitting in my cubicle at work, and I heard this Superchunk song that is obviously about that tour." If I'm

fodder for a song from the Superchunk band, whether it makes me look like a fool or a great guy, I'm honored nonetheless.

Indoor Living's final track, "Martinis on the Roof," was another rare lyrically direct Superchunk song; it was a musical eulogy of sorts for Gibson Smith, a friend of the band who had been killed in a car accident near Chapel Hill a few months before they went into the studio. Smith's apartment, above Cliff's Meat Market on Main St. in Carrboro, N.C., had access to the roof, where he used to throw parties: "Cheetos and 100 proof / Martinis on the roof / And you were leaving too soon." While the lyrics were mournful, the song itself was upbeat, with an almost Caribbean feel.

Laura I came up with the bassline that was the seed of that song, because I decided I at least had to write one song for *Indoor Living.* I thought it sounded like the Supremes combined with Soft Cell, and I assumed the guys would reject it. But they didn't. The words to that song have made me cry many times on stage.

Mac The last thing we did at Echo Park was the marimba part on that song. I kept hearing a marimba in unison with the guitars on the chorus, and the studio found one somewhere in Bloomington. On our last day there, we went and grabbed it, brought it to the studio, recorded that part, and split town.

Indoor Living sold 23,000 copies. It was generally well received, but most of the reviews cast a nostalgic eye back on the days of "Slack Motherfucker" as Superchunk's heyday. The *Chicago Tribune*'s Greg Kot, one of their earliest champions, wrote: "As the decade starts to wind down, they have become indie-rock elders, an established band with a long string of albums, singles and side projects, as well as a successful record label, the Chapel Hill–based Merge. At Lounge Ax on Sunday, the band and a club full of fans celebrated bassist Laura Ballance's 30th birthday. . . . It was a reminder that tunes such as 'Sick to Move' now qualify as nostalgia."

Superchunk toured heavily behind *Indoor Living*: The states in October 1997, Europe in December, the South and Midwest in February 1998, and Brazil in September.

Jason Ward   It was definitely kind of static in terms of their audience. People that were there were generally pretty into it. Of course, people would always get real psyched when they would play some raucous old song.

Jim Wilbur   We felt that people were going to come see us even if we put out a shitty record. Because we have a back catalog that they do like. So we can try to do things differently.

In 1999 — after taking another leisurely two-year break between recording projects — Superchunk went back into the studio to make their strangest record yet. They reserved a full two weeks, the longest they had ever spent in a studio, at Steve Albini's Electrical Audio in Chicago. Albini had come a long way since the band mixed *Foolish* in his cramped attic: He had built Electrical to his exacting specifications, including dorms upstairs for the bands, a pool table, an espresso machine, a live room lined with imported clay bricks, and studio techs who wore green-gray jumpsuits that made them look like mechanics from the 1950s.

They band asked Jim O'Rourke, who was known both for his work with experimental noise bands like Nurse with Wound and for his facility for writing horn and string arrangements for Stereolab and others, to produce. The result was *Come Pick Me Up*, a record of some of Superchunk's most classically pop-oriented songs cut with odd song structures, weird time-signature changes, dance beats filtered through noiseboxes, "doobie doobie bop bop" backing vocals, lilting string melodies, and a brass section featuring Jeb Bishop, who had become a major figure in Chicago's improvisational jazz scene; saxophonist Ken Vandermark; and former Volcano Suns bass player Bob Weston.

Mac   I wanted an artier Superchunk record. A record with some surprising stuff going on.

Jeb Bishop   Jim was really good at arranging and was good at thinking up expanded orchestration and instrumentation for things, and taking it out of just being a rock band into something more. And Mac was interested in trying to get some of that on a Superchunk record.

Wilbur, Jim O'Rourke, and Wurster during the recording of *Come Pick Me Up*.

Horn charts written by Jim O'Rourke for *Come Pick Me Up.*

Mac There was a snowstorm that hit right when we arrived in Chicago, and I literally didn't leave the studio for the first seven days we were there. Jim and I slept on the floor of the control room for a couple nights. You just go to bed and wake up in the same windowless room with little blinking gear lights, and keep working.

Jim Wilbur We just went over the top with strings and handclaps and whatever. But it was fun. It didn't change the way we wrote it. It was just when we recorded it, we asked O'Rourke to make up parts: "What would fit?" It was very off-the-cuff. He'd come in and be like, "I wrote this." And we'd get the string players, they'd look at it, they'd record it. *Boom* — it was done. There were no long, drawn-out discussions. Mac would say, "Well, I want to do this. Anybody object?" No. What's to object to?

Mac Jeb did a solo on the end of "Pink Clouds" during what O'Rourke told him was just a mic check to get levels. It was probably the first time he'd ever heard the song after maybe a playback in the control room or something, and it was amazing, and we kept it. We also kept Ken Vandermark's solo on the same spot, so there was like horn mania for the first time on a Superchunk record, and Laura said something like, "It sounds like Bruce Springsteen!" Jim and I were like *"Yes!"*

Laura Jim O'Rourke brought in a modular synthesizer when it came time to mix the record. It was a big silver box with a bunch of holes in it, like a telephone switchboard. He would put on this big fuzzy plush-suit and plug away. He looked like a demented stuffed-animal telephone operator patching through calls. He got some crazy sounds out of that thing.

Jim Wilbur I kind of think that it was necessary to do what we did. But I think some of the ideas were — not necessarily ill conceived, but ill realized. Or maybe they shouldn't have been realized. If you could go back, would you do it differently? Yeah. But you can't go back, and you've got to stand by

it. There were issues of Mac singing falsetto. But he was doing that because he was ruining his throat and he was trying to figure out a way to sing in a different way, that wouldn't tear it to pieces.

Mac A lot of critics hated the falsetto. But I was writing melodies that I thought were really cool, and that was the only way I could sing them. And frankly, I was sick of belting out the tunes.

Come Pick Me Up was a divisive record. *The Washington Post* called it "the most engaging album of the band's decade-long career." London's *Guardian* accused Superchunk of "stretching and striving to become a pop-folk band, but hesitating to leave their feedback-saturated roots behind, [leaving] their punk songs spindly and their low-key laments half-formed and immature."

Mac Sales kind of dropped off for us with *Come Pick Me Up* and plateaued around 20,000. But our live shows were still as big as ever, if not bigger. We definitely had people who were not as into the records, but were still coming to the shows and loved them. We'd hear a lot of, "Even the new songs rocked live" from fans. Well, yeah. We're not in a studio laying down cello parts, we're playing live rock'n'roll at the Cat's Cradle!

Laura The funny thing about the waning of Superchunk is that it seemed like once we started to branch out into things that weren't just fast and loud, some people lost interest because they wanted to hear "Precision Auto" again. But I'd also hear people say, "Oh yeah, they just do the same thing all the time, so I lost interest." It was confusing. Such a disconnect.

Ron Liberti I respected that they could go out on top. Not that they were going out, but they could do other things. They had the freedom to do other things because of Merge. And it wasn't like, Superchunk's done, now we're all going to go get a job at the Kwik-E-Mart.

* * *

O'Rourke at the controls.

Next two pages: Montreal, 1999.

20 Cigarettes

$\mathcal{L}$ambchop

Chapter Eleven

The Decline of Country and Western Civilization

Lambchop

If there is a quintessential Merge band aside from Superchunk, it is Lambchop. Based more on friendship than ambition, and more on music than careers, Lambchop has been plugging away for two decades, making records that defy categorization.

When Mac went to college, he left behind a rich and supportive underground music community for a big city that wasn't conducive to playing in bands. He missed Chapel Hill and the music scene badly enough to delay his studies and stay home for a year, and when he came back to stay, he and Laura set about building a burgeoning indie network. His Columbia classmate Jonathan Marx had the opposite experience.

Marx was raised in Nashville, where the major-label music machinery is as thoroughly entrenched, and as banal a part of the local economy, as steel in Pittsburgh. In the 1980s, it drew thousands of talented musicians, but for someone who wasn't interested in pumping out prefabricated radio-ready country, or writing patriotic songs on a production line, it was a backwater. Nashville's Jason and the Scorchers shook things up in the early 1980s, undermining

country clichés and filtering them through a punk aesthetic a full decade before alt country became a genre. But locally, the Scorchers were more bad-boy outlier than leaders of a movement. There was nowhere to buy the records that Marx wanted to buy, and aside from the occasional band coming through town, there were no shows that he wanted to go to. Marx grew up with a sense that good music, and like-minded fans, were elsewhere.

Jonathan Marx   **I had this sense of the music world being incredibly big, remote, and "cooler" than I could possibly hope to be.**

But New York was an awakening. He became friends with Mac, and through him, Laura, and met a host of people from Boston, D.C., Seattle, and other cities that were full of kids making noise. The record stores were overflowing with obscure 7-inches, and he could see any band he wanted. He went to see Antietam and Big Dipper at CBGB's one night, and came home blown away by the former's Crazy Horse–inspired rock. Two days later, he walked into the elevator of the Columbia library on his way to French class, and found himself standing next to two of them. They worked in the library.

Jonathan Marx   **Seeing Antietam in the elevator was a perfect emblem of my experience. My friends were in bands and putting out records, and I was suddenly in close proximity to all these things I had wanted to be a part of. I was really awed by it all.**

Marx didn't play an instrument, or write songs; he was content to sit back and be a fan of what his friends were doing. When he moved back to Nashville after school, he found himself back in nowhere land. All his friends were in D.C. or North Carolina or New York making music and putting out records that he couldn't even find in Nashville record stores. He would send letters with cash to Mac, who would buy whatever sounded cool at Schoolkids and send them back. He'd visit Chapel Hill whenever he could, and contemplated moving there.

Jonathan Marx   **It just seemed so fun. I remember mentioning to Laura that I was thinking about it, and she was like, "Why would you want to do that?"**

So he stayed in Nashville and landed an internship at *Nashville Scene*, the local alternative newspaper, waited for records to arrive in the mail from Mac, and searched for ways to find some sort of local connection to music that was worth caring about. One August night in 1990, his friend Jeremy Tepper was in town for a conference, and Marx was showing him around. They stopped in at a bar called Springwater in the West End district, and a band was playing that sounded different. Nashville is lousy with songwriters, and on any given night you can walk into a bar and hear familiar voices singing formulaic songs — "people trying to shop around their cut that they hope to sell to John Michael Montgomery, or whoever the fuck it is, and make $50 to pay the rent," as Marx puts it. But this band had nothing to do with that. They seemed to be there because they were enjoying themselves. They were tuneful and unconventional, and reminded Marx of the

New Zealand pop that was coming out on Flying Nun at the time. It was the first time he'd seen a local band that was doing something that sounded exciting to him. He fell in love with them. They were called Posterchild.

Posterchild was led by Kurt Wagner, a gentle, quiet, and sincere art school graduate ten years Marx's senior who had moved to Nashville from Chicago in 1986. Wagner's attitude toward making music was as casual and informal as Mac's was focused; he's likely to answer any question about his musical endeavors with some variant of, "it seemed like it would be fun." For Wagner, Posterchild was as much a social exercise as a musical one. He just liked to get together with friends and do stuff, and music seemed like a better time than poker.

Kurt Wagner   **We definitely didn't have any aspirations other than getting together every week and having a good time and playing these songs we made up.**

Those songs were a sort of genre-free distillation of the AM radio hits that Wagner grew up on in the 1970s, a fusion of folk, soul, and classic rock into a sort of elemental pop music overlaid with Wagner's curious singing voice, which sounded like a tired but dedicated father reading a bedtime story at the end of a long workday.

As per Wagner's freeform vision of what a band should be, Posterchild's lineup was in constant flux. Anyone could come to the party, but the original core was formed out of the flooring company Wagner worked for: His boss, Bill Killebrew, played guitar, and coworker Marc Trovillion played bass. They occasionally made four-track recordings, more as a lark or a pantomime of being in a band than as an avenue to get their music out.

Kurt Wagner   **Anybody could be in the band so long as they behaved themselves. That was really my only criteria. And believe it or not, it was enough. People would come and hang out and either say, "These guys are nuts," and leave, or they'd find some like-mindedness and stick around. It was sort of like a fantasy idea of having a band, without all the officialness of actually doing it.**

Early self-released Posterchild cassette.

Posterchild, 1992.

Posterchild played every third Saturday at Springwater in what the club called the Working Stiffs Jamboree, a recurring evening of music by and for the few people who weren't trying to network their way into the industry. Marx started going compulsively, and introduced himself to the band. He begged them for tapes, so they started recording practices on a boom box just to have something to give him.

Jonathan Marx   **There was no scene. There was just nothing to connect to in Nashville, and then suddenly I found this band. And they were all ten years older than me. It was like being introduced to this other world. It felt very much like they were artists — bordering on folk artists.**

Marx and Wagner became friends, and started going to shows and "whatever kind of vaguely halfway worthwhile shit was going on in Nashville." Marx had stumbled into the community he'd been looking for, but he was still just an observer until one night in 1992, when he and Wagner were talking about their childhood musical experiences. Wagner mentioned that he'd played cello as a kid, and Marx replied that he'd played the saxophone in his high school marching band, and his sister had played clarinet. "I always thought a clarinet would sound kind of cool in Posterchild," Wagner told him. Marx went to his parents' house, rooted around in their basement, dug up his sister's old clarinet, and started playing in his favorite band.

Jonathan Marx   **It was completely loose and unstructured at that point. I just basically started hanging out with them every week. They were these crazy, free-form sessions where we'd get completely baked and, for lack of a better word, jam. It was unhinged.**

But Marx was hell-bent on recreating in Nashville the kind of creative, and productive, indie culture he'd seen in New York and Chapel Hill, and he set about harnessing Posterchild's freeform, lackadaisical fantasy-band energy into an actual band with actual records. He convinced them to go into a studio, and in the fall of 1992 they recorded

"An Open Fresca" and "A Moist Towelette" in a makeshift studio run by a friend of theirs that was housed in a U-Store-It rental space. They were rough-hewn, and sounded like two guitar players, a bass player, a drummer, and a clarinetist who were not trying to sound like anything else. Marx hoped Merge would put it out and sent a tape to Mac, but didn't hear anything back. He didn't want to press the issue and make his friend say something he didn't want to say, so they decided to put it out themselves as a split 7-inch with a local band called Crop Circle Hoax.

Mac   **Jonathan would write letters talking about this band he was in, Posterchild. Not that I didn't trust Jonathan's judgment, but this friend, who I've never known to play music outside of a Government Issue cover band he sang in at Columbia, is all of a sudden telling me about this weird country band he's in, and he plays clarinet — I was worried about what that was going to sound like! And it was strange, but in the best way. The early Lambchop stuff had this spazzy, almost aggressive nervous energy. Even the quiet songs sounded off the rails and beautiful.**

Kurt Wagner   **Jonathan was a big revelation. He brought a lot of interesting ideas to us, like the idea that you can actually make a record yourself. And he proudly sent that 7-inch to Mac and said, "Look, I've got a band, and I made a record."**

Jonathan Marx   **At the time, it hadn't really occurred to Kurt that we could make this a thing. That we could be a band that puts out records. But I was just so obsessively interested in doing just that, because all my friends were doing it, that Kurt was like, "Hell yeah. Let's run with it."**

They sent "An Open Fresca" to Ajax, which picked it up, and this made enough money for them to buy more studio time. They recorded another batch of songs in 1993, which Marx again sent to Mac. By this time, Wagner had begun to work his powers of persuasion: When Superchunk played Nashville the previous October, he brought them a fruit basket. But rather than hand it to them in the dressing room at the Pantheon, he simply placed it onstage as they were playing.

Kurt Wagner   **It just got torn to pieces by the audience, and Mac slipped on a banana peel and fell on his ass. That was sort of my way of trying to get on Merge. I still recommend a fruit basket; I'm sure it will do the trick.**

Merge did agree to put out the single, "Nine" b/w "Moody Fucker," as the label's forty-fifth release. But it wasn't by Posterchild. Their first single got enough attention and positive reviews in zines to cross the radar of lawyers at Warner Brothers, which had recently signed the Champaign, Ill., power-pop band the Poster Children. The label sent Wagner a cease-and-desist letter claiming ownership over the singular variant of the name as well. Figuring he was in no position to face down a threat, Wagner considered changing the name to REN — the typographical difference between the two names — but decided that would just inflame the label, since R.E.M. was also on Warner Brothers.

Kurt Wagner   **We were thinking about Turd Goes Back. Laura *really* didn't like that one.**

One day, while reading a newspaper item about Shari Lewis, Trovillion started talking about her puppet sidekick, Lamb Chop. "Hmmm, that's stupid enough," Wagner said. "Nobody would call their band that, so nobody will threaten to sue us again."

Mac   **I was sure the puppet's people were going to come after us.**

Merge released the single in 1993 and followed it up with *I Hope You're Sitting Down*, Lambchop's first full-length, in September 1994. The sleeve for "Nine" was printed by Hatch Show Prints, a Nashville print shop whose block-letter, two- and three-color show posters for everyone from Hank Williams to Bill Monroe to Roy Acuff virtually invented the visual language of country music. It bore the message "written, recorded, printed, pressed, assembled in Nashville" and began Lambchop's two-decade attempt to reclaim its hometown

We called ourselves country partly to be funny, but it ended up getting taken seriously, which blew my mind. I didn't realize people took what you said seriously.

— Kurt Wagner

and musical heritage. Wagner gleefully and publicly described Lambchop as a "country" band, a moniker that stuck despite the fact that the description is, in some ways, patently false. While they employed the tools of country music — pedal-steel guitar, acoustic guitars, mandolin, banjo — they don't sound anything like country music in its contemporary or classical definitions. The songs are infused with elements of soul, jazz, and Burt Bacharach radio pop, but devoid of any twangy tropes. Wagner's lyrics are often inscrutable — "The Man Who Loved Beer," from their second record, *How I Quit Smoking*, is based on a 4,000-year-old Egyptian poem — or detailed sketches of quotidian domestic scenes. There are no witty or corny epigrams about heartache.

Kurt Wagner   **We were taking some of the notions about that Nashville sound, using the instruments of Nashville, and the recording facilities of Nashville, and just looking at what is country, conceptually. Everything but the actual sound. I mean, I grew up here. Jonathan grew up here. We had as much right as anybody to say, "This is what Nashville music sounds like." We called ourselves country partly to be funny, but it ended up getting taken seriously, which blew my mind. I didn't realize people took what you said seriously. I thought that everyone made up their own mind about stuff and didn't rely on you to tell them what you are.**

Deanna Varagona and Kurt Wagner,
making the setlist.

Mac   I'm still absorbing *I Hope You're Sitting Down* — or *Jack's Tulips*, depending on which spine you're looking at — to this day. It's layered, and some of the layers are so quiet or obscured that you don't hear them the first fifty times you listen to the record. The lyrics are almost spoken at times, but then Deanna Varagona will come in, doubling Kurt's vocals in a higher octave, or the horns and lap steel will swell under a surprise chorus, and the miniature sounds suddenly add up to something really affecting and heavy. The music is hard to place in time; it's really unto its own little world. It didn't fit into any kind of "indie rock" category — it was literary, it strolled rather than charged, it was delicate. It certainly didn't sound like anything else we had released on Merge.

Wagner's loose definition of what constituted membership in the band meant that it was constantly metastasizing, picking up stray musicians and continuing to expand the musical kinship Marx was looking for. *I Hope You're Sitting Down* lists no fewer than eleven musicians playing fourteen instruments, from ukulele to pedal steel to "open-ended wrenches." Shows in Nashville quickly became legendary for the crowd onstage rivaling the audience in number. Wagner viewed proficiency almost as a liability.

Kurt Wagner   I was a little self-conscious about our lack of true musical abilities. So if any actual musicians wanted to play, I'd say, "Come by. But can you bring something else?" Paul Niehaus is a great example of this. He's a great guitar player. And I said, "I've got this old lap steel. Can you play that?" It just so happened he was wanting to try the lap steel out anyway. So he was handicapped because he actually knew how to play music. It was more about the things that people could bring to the music other than their musical adeptness. Their ideas. Their sensitivity. Their inability.

Jonathan Marx   Kurt thought like an artist. He made Lambchop an art project without being pretentious. And as it became more of an endeavor, and he had less time to paint, it became, "I don't paint anymore. This is what I do for art."

They stumbled into some early breaks: In 1993, Lollapalooza was inviting select local bands to the play the side stage on each stop, and one of the promoters happened to have heard one of the 7-inches. He gave them a slot after Tool. The crowd loved it, and Lambchop was asked to do a whole leg of Lollapalooza the next year. It was their first tour.

Kurt Wagner   It was insane. We didn't have any concept of touring. We brought a Hammond organ that died during the first show, and we dragged it around for two weeks. We'd be playing and George Clinton would be on the main stage, and you wouldn't be able to hear us at all.

Mac   I went to see them when Lollapalooza came through Raleigh. They were on the side stage with Stereolab, playing at noon. It was a great bill, but even with thirteen people on stage they were so quiet that it felt like they were getting swallowed up by the wind and the dust and the sound from the main stage. But they built their set up to a rocker like "Nine" at the end, and their size and the stubborn novelty of the music they were playing really won people over.

But serious touring was a tough proposition for a thirteen-or-so member band, most of whom had day jobs that they weren't prepared to give up. (Marx eventually became the *Nashville Scene*'s managing editor and went on to cover arts for *The Tennessean*, Nashville's daily newspaper.) Aside from the obvious scheduling difficulties, the expense of moving and housing a baker's dozen of musicians around the country made it virtually impossible to book a profitable tour. Bob Lawton, their booking agent, tried to get Wagner to pare the touring band down to a more manageable size.

Bob Lawton   It was always, "Kurt, can we get this down to a smaller thing, so you can do it more?" And he'd say, "OK — six people." And in New York, there would be nine onstage! They'd just show up!

And bands with clarinets and horns and strings tended not to go over too well in rock clubs; Lambchop usually played quietly, with Wagner sitting down. They were the sort of band you'd expect to see at a place with seats. Lambchop's failure to hit the road was frustrating to Mac and Laura, and it placed a ceiling on their record sales. Merge didn't have the resources to offer enough tour support to make it worthwhile for the band, but they loved the music, so they kept putting out their records.

Europe was a different story. Christof Ellinghaus's City Slang put out *I Hope You're Sitting Down* there, and for reasons that even Wagner can't quite articulate — perhaps a misguided sense that Lambchop was a part of the "Americana" movement that was taking off in the mid-nineties — it sold well.

Mac   We sent Christof *I Hope You're Sitting Down* before it came out, and he initially passed on it. But like Lambchop records do, it grew on him. Even though he knew it was a strange record and an unwieldy band, he really felt strongly that he needed to follow his love of the record and put it out. He called us after it was already out over here and was like, "I need to do this record, I can't stop listening to it!"

When Ellinghaus asked Lambchop to tour Europe as a full band, and offered to underwrite the travel, the band looked at it as more of a vacation than a tour. It didn't go great.

Kurt Wagner   On the last night of the tour, I walked off stage, and the rest of the band was still playing, and Christof and I were both sitting there watching. And he told me that he lost $40,000 on the tour. And I said, "Well, I guess we're done then." He goes, "No. Maybe next time we lose $20,000."

Indeed, after *How I Quit Smoking*, Ellinghaus brought them over again, and lost less money. The investments paid off, and Lambchop's European audience grew to the point where the band could take off for a couple weeks every year or so to profitably tour European concert halls with Austin's Tosca String Quartet and elaborate stage decorations, playing to thousands of people. And then they'd come back home and go back to work in relative anonymity.

Kurt Wagner   We'd get offered a show at Royal Albert Hall, and then I'd come home and sand floors. And I thought that was beautiful. I was convinced that you could make records and balance it with a normal life.

That dream evaporated in 2000, when he had to quit the flooring business because his knees and lungs were giving out from all the kneeling and sawdust, and the band took up too much of his time to find another job.

Lambchop is an almost maddeningly prolific band, with a total of sixteen releases over their fifteen-year relationship with Merge. Their 1997 release *Thriller* was named the tenth best record of the year by the London *Independent*, and 2000's *Nixon* was described as a "near-masterpiece" by both *Spin* and *The Onion*. But none of them ever broke through in the states, and sales peaked at 20,000. The action was in Europe.

Jonathan Marx   Merge certainly doesn't reap any kind of great financial gain from being involved with us. But that's not what Mac and Laura set out to do in the first place.

Kurt Wagner   Mac and Laura were just so sweet. Laura would say, "We're happy to put out anything, anytime you want." And for someone to say that was all we needed. We

didn't need a contract. Just the understanding that they believed in the art we were making, and were happy enough if that's all we could do for them. They just wanted to hear another record.

Mac   Kurt is making art. Sometimes it's difficult, sometimes it's crowd-pleasing, and sometimes it's just incredibly quiet, but it's his art and he's constantly refining it and expanding it at the same time. It's a beautiful thing to watch, and I feel lucky to be a part of it. It's true that we work hard at Merge, and are sometimes frustrated by our inability to grow Lambchop in the U.S. in the way that they have exploded overseas, but it's also true that we just want to hear a new record.

Ed Roche   Nobody would admit it, but I think there are some labels that probably would have given up on Lambchop because they weren't able to tour the states. But Merge has stuck with them the whole time. It's not just business with the band, because they are friends, and Mac and Laura have a very strong relationship with Lambchop.

Of course, by the same token, if Lambchop hadn't stuck with Merge, and migrated to a label that could underwrite U.S. tours the way City Slang could in Europe, their story might have been different.

Bob Lawton   It was so frustrating for us all, because we all just felt that they were so great. And they can't get arrested here. Was it Merge? If they were on Lost Highway, would they have more profile here? Are they actually impeded by being on Merge who can't spend oodles of money? It's a fair question, and I'm not going to answer it. Because they're the same records, right? It's not a different record that goes to Europe. It's the same people, it's the same songs.

Jonathan Marx   Our relationship with Merge is part of who we are. Maybe someone would have thrown more money at us at the front end, but they also might have just given up at some point because we didn't sell enough records. And then where would we be?

In 2006, with the release of Lambchop's eleventh full-length, *Damaged*, Lambchop and Merge finally decided to try to mount a U.S. tour done right. Part of the frustration with their failure to catch fire in the states the way they did in Europe was that American audiences rarely got a chance to see Lambchop the way they were meant to be seen: In a quiet concert hall, with the full band and the help of the Tosca String Quartet.

Mac   For the Lambchop show at the Merge 15th anniversary festival, we had put them in the Carolina Theatre instead of the rock club. We got a string quartet to play with them. People were in *tears* by the end of their set. It was just incredibly moving, and after the show Kurt said, "Well, that's basically what it's like every night in Europe." So we wanted to try that here on a larger scale.

Kurt Wagner   Mac and I, after years of trying to do things budget-y here, we decided to invest in that notion. A U.S. tour with the full band, and the strings, in nice venues. Nobody came. The shows were great, but it was mildly attended. It was proof, I guess, that both of us were wrong. Overall, it was astonishing just how little interest there seemed to be in us at that point.

The only people who need to be interested, of course, are Mac and Laura. The answer to Lawton's question — did Merge help or hinder Lambchop? — is unknowable. But what is certain is that without Merge, Lambchop wouldn't have become what it is.

Jonathan Marx   I'm glad to still be part of Lambchop, and part of Merge. There's part of me that feels like we must be hoary, or outdated, especially when you look at Spoon or Arcade Fire and go, "Wow, those guys are actually popular." Us? Well, we do what we do, and maybe there's a certain amount of pride in just being ourselves.

* * *

Facing Page: Kurt Wagner.   Next Page: Paul Niehaus during a Lambchop performance on KCRW's "Morning Becomes Eclectic."

Shutting Up

2000 to 2009

Superchunk's last full-length album — that's "last" as in "most recent," not "final" — was provocatively titled, at least to some observers, *Here's to Shutting Up*. The implication being that the band, after a dozen years and as many records, was trying to say with a wink that it had recorded its swan song. *Here's to Shutting Up* may well end up being the last Superchunk full-length, but it wasn't planned that way. The band had settled into a slower-paced rhythm of a record every other year. Mac and Laura obviously had plenty to occupy them during the downtime, and Wurster had started a comedy duo with Scharpling based on characters Wurster would play while calling in to Scharpling's WFMU radio show.

They wrote *Shutting Up* in the fall of 2000 and winter of 2001 at Wilbur's house, a remote outpost deep in the woods west of Chapel Hill that he shared with Brian Paulson and George Nicholas, who was Merge's attorney before McPherson. It was known as the Hurlyburly House, after the play and movie by David Rabe, owing to many a late drunken night passed there. They spent three-hour sessions

there, three days a week, building songs from the ground up. For the first time, they employed acoustic guitars and keyboards in the writing process, and planned an even more drastic step away from the "classic" Superchunk sound than *Indoor Living* and *Come Pick Me Up*.

Mac I wanted to make a record that blew out people's expectations of Superchunk. One thing, however, is that people don't especially *want* their expectations blown.

They systematically wrote and recorded snippets of songs and riffs to be later combined into full compositions, coming up with about thirty in total, most of which Wilbur concocted a nonsensical name for — "Something About Marvin," "Frank's Bath," "Ford's Lobsters," etc.

They recorded *Shutting Up* in March 2001 with Brian Paulson, who was working with Superchunk again for the first time since *Foolish*, at Zero Return, an emptied-out warehouse with a control room consisting of two shipping containers fused together

Recording *Here's to Shutting Up* in Atlanta, March 2001.
Clockwise from top left: Exterior of Zero Return Studios; Mac; Brian Paulson; Wilbur.

and set up on cinderblocks. It was built by the members of Man or Astro-Man? in Cabbagetown, a transitional neighborhood in Atlanta, and it had rooms to sleep in, so the band rarely left the confines of the studio and started slipping into an all-night schedule that kept them recording until 4 a.m. Breakfast was carryout from the Long John Silver's down the street.

Shutting Up did indeed blow expectations. The record's defining moment was the "who-put-peanut-butter-in-my-indie-rock" shock of hearing the whine of a pedal-steel guitar on a Superchunk album in "Phone Sex" ("I like to think that our invite for *Austin City Limits* got lost in the mail," Wurster would later write). While it had its rockers — "Rainy Streets," "Art Class," and "Out on the Wing" — it was for the most part a layered, lazy, acoustic-driven record, and featured Superchunk's longest-ever song, "What Do You Look Forward To?" which weighed in at more than seven-and-a-half minutes. It was a tough record to make.

Mac   Doing anything new and different with Superchunk is like pulling teeth, and sometimes it shows. But sometimes it's great. We were using more effects, loops, and delays and stuff. But it's hard for a band that has done things one way for twelve years to start doing things differently.

Here's to Shutting Up was released one week after the September 11 attacks. Superchunk was scheduled to play the Merge CMJ showcase at the Bowery Ballroom in lower Manhattan on September 15, after which they had a worldwide tour of Europe, Japan, and the states booked. It was the worst possible time to mount a tour.

Mac   We sort of didn't know what to do. We didn't know if there was going to be a show, or if CMJ would be cancelled.

Jon Wurster   Mac wanted to go. I didn't really want to. It was just, "Oh my god." Jim didn't want to go, I don't think Laura wanted to go. It just didn't seem appropriate. I know there's the whole thing about "rock'n'roll can get us through," but I wasn't feeling that at all.

Laura   I could not believe Mac wanted to go there. I guess it's part of his personality: He wants to be where things are happening.

Phil Morrison   Mac and our friend Dave Doernberg and I drove up to New York from North Carolina on September 13. We'd all been at our friend Joe Ventura's wedding the weekend before.

Mac   The Clean was scheduled to play that same night as Superchunk. Those poor guys had arrived from New Zealand on the 10th to wake up to that on the 11th. They wanted to leave the U.S. immediately, but of course they couldn't.

Bob Lawton   We didn't even know if the Bowery Ballroom was going to be open on Saturday night. We didn't find out until the end of the day on Friday that they were actually going to have electricity. It was supposed to be a Merge showcase. And Mac could get there, and maybe one or two other bands.

Mac   We had to construct a show from bands from other labels that had already made it to New York before 9/11. So we had Ladybug Transistor for Merge, and the Faint and another Saddle Creek band because their showcase was cancelled, and we got Laura Cantrell because she lived in New York, and the Clean. And I played solo.

Bob Lawton   We just cobbled this thing together and made it a benefit, and gave all the money to the local fire station closest to the Bowery Ballroom. It was cathartic to see bands coming together and playing. Take a bad thing and try to make it good. We're rocking and we're going to go on, just like everything else is going to go on, eventually.

Mac   It was a really emotional night. People were in tears during Laura Cantrell's set, and the Clean did a really powerful version of this old song of theirs called "No More Violence." The air still smelled burnt. I was really glad we made it happen in a way that seemed to make anyone who came feel a bit better. Or at least gave some people a place to be around other people.

A trip to the movies, the celluloid cave, offers escape; theater provides the ritual of repetition. But live music at its best absorbs the listener in every next step. The most successful artists at the Bowery Ballroom concentrated on tangibles, not transcendence. In a time of isolation, their art connected people modestly, at just the right scale for spinning heads to grasp.

— *New York Times* review of the CMJ show, September 2001.

* * *

Jon Wurster   So then we did this tour, and it was so tough. We wanted to just hit everything — bam bam bam. So we flew from Raleigh to Tokyo. And then we were going from Japan to Europe, but it was cheaper to fly back to Raleigh and then to Europe. So we went home for one night and then we flew to Europe the next day.

The Archers of Loaf's Matt Gentling came along for the Japan leg of the tour as a guitar tech.

Matt Gentling   We landed, and Jim drove me in the van from the airport to my truck. And he was going to go home, do some laundry, catch a couple hours of sleep, and then the next morning they were going to get up and go to Europe. Like, immediately. I could see how tired they were. There was just this overall pall of fatigue.

Jim Wilbur   It was a bad time to try and promote a rock record. Just took the wind right out of everybody's sails. That tour was brutal.

Jon Wurster   And because of what was going on in the world, nobody was coming out to shows. So we did Europe, and that sucked, and we played in England and that sucked. Our final show was in Dublin. No money. Promoter didn't have the money, because our agent had done some deal with him where he didn't have to pay us. It was so fucked up.

Jason Ward   That tour was remarkable for the incredibly poor attendance in all places

save for London, Paris, Rotterdam, and Amsterdam. Everywhere else it was just insane — an 800-person room with, like, 40 people in it.

Laura   Everything went wrong. The van kept breaking down, no one was coming out, and those that did seemed to be in a daze.

Jon Wurster   We flew back to the states, had four days off, and then toured the entire U.S. It was tough. Turnouts were not great; nobody was really going out. The last show of the tour was in D.C. with Aereogramme and Rilo Kiley. I consider that the final real Superchunk show, in a way. That was our final show as a full-time touring concern slash real band. I think at that point, I had made my mind up that this is not going to be my full-time thing anymore. And I think Laura felt that way too. When we were rehearsing for that tour, she was just not really in a great place. I remember just hugging her, at one point, and she was just not feeling good about the band. She wasn't sure if she wanted to do it anymore. When we got home, Lawton e-mailed about some more dates for maybe March or February or something. I just looked at these dates, and my stomach sort of started to churn. I just didn't want to do it. Same places. Same songs. It just wasn't interesting anymore. It wasn't fun. I mean, it was fun to be around the guys, because I still had fun with them. But it felt like a treadmill.

Phil Morrison   There was a point where Jon started thinking about just removing from his life the things that caused him anxiety. It was kind of a conscious choice. You get to a certain age, and you think, "Wait: Do I even still want this? Or has it just become habit?"

Bob Lawton   I remember just being on pins and needles. Like, "Whoa." It was huge.

Jason Ward   We were all sitting there going, "Maybe this era is kind of over." Especially in terms of the expense of touring.

Matt Gentling   Stuff was going wrong. And another thing is, Merge had some great

Superchunk on tour in Japan, 2001.
Clockwise from top left: Wilbur; Mac and Laura; Wilbur, Japanese soundman Hiro Kanazawa, and Mac; Wurster.

It was kind of like a dream come true, because your favorite band from high school is actually opening up for you. Which is also a little odd.

— Robbie Pope

○────────●

bands coming up like Arcade Fire and Spoon, and those guys were starting to make them money, on one hand, so they didn't have to tour. You know, I could tell they were tired and kind of burned out on what they were doing.

Jim Wilbur   It was just kind of like a depression. Jon was really upset. And then we did a tour with the Get Up Kids.

The Get Up Kids were early standard-bearers for the emo scene (as well as huge Superchunk fans — they named their debut record, *Four Minute Mile*, after a line in "Yeah, It's Beautiful Here Too"). Their 1999 sophomore record *Something to Write Home About* helped put Vagrant Records on the map as a label that knew what fourteen-year-old kids wanted to hear. In 2001, Interscope bought a minority share in Vagrant, in part on the strength of the Get Up Kids' sales. Scott Litt, who had worked with R.E.M. and Nirvana, produced their 2002 record *On a Wire.*

Robbie Pope   We put together a huge list of bands that we wanted to take out, and we all were kind of like brainstorming and somebody threw out Superchunk. At that point, it didn't seem like they were up to a whole lot. When I was in high school, I listened to Superchunk all of the time. And so did all of my bandmates. *Foolish* was a big record for all of us. So we were like, fuck it, let's have our booking agent ask them, and see what happens. It was like kind of like a dream come true, because your favorite band from high school is actually opening up for you. Which is also a little odd.

Bob Lawton   It was almost as if they were afraid to ask. I didn't know what the Get Up Kids' crowd was, per se. I just knew they were playing these big gigs, and that the Superchunk thing was a little on the wane. It was a time when you were thought of negatively if you've just been around forever. Everyone wants the new thing. And this was a lot of young people who wouldn't normally go see Superchunk.

Mac   *Here's to Shutting Up* was a really up and down tour, and we really didn't plan on doing much more touring for that record. But they weren't treating us like an opening band. They were paying us well, and we'd be able to play a normal-length set. So why not try to play for a completely different group of people than we would normally play for? We had a great time. We all love opening for other bands. You get there last, because the main band's soundchecking, so you can show up late, soundcheck, play early, and then just hang out.

Robbie Pope   It was kind of awkward at first. The tour started in Florida somewhere, and we had soundchecked, and we were all kind of nervously excited because Superchunk is going to show up and play. So they show up, and we do the "Hey, we're going on tour together, yay!" thing. And right before Superchunk goes on stage, we're all kind of standing there, chatting, drinking a beer, saying, "Have a good show." And as Jim walks by to go on stage, he just turns and says, "Watch and learn, boys." It was hilarious.

Mac   The Get Up Kids were super professional. They were on a bus, we were in a van. They had the light show, they had a whole thing. I don't think any of us felt like, "I wish we had done that," or "I wish we were doing that." To me it was more, "I'm glad we're doing what we're doing."

Jim Wilbur   That was a demoralizing tour, to a degree. Nobody cared about us. But the idea was that we'd be putting ourselves in front of a different audience on purpose.

Laura   I would look down from the stage and see all these kids in the front row who had clearly rushed in to grab a spot as close as possible to the Get Up Kids, and they would make a show of looking as bored as possible during our set. Some would even have their head down on the barrier in front of the stage, trying to catch a nap before their favorite band came on. I found it hard to muster much enthusiasm most nights.

Mac   Certainly there were nights when you feel like nobody cares. Like they're all thirteen years old and literally just like waiting for the Get Up Kids. But that's cool. I thought it was really fun. After we'd play, we'd go hang out at their T-shirt table, and we were talking to kids who were like twelve, thirteen, fourteen, and were with their moms and dads. It was so funny.

Robbie Pope   Everybody in the Get Up Kids had a girl-in-the-band crush on Laura when we were growing up. And now Laura is on tour with us, and at one point we're all drinking and hanging out. And Laura was chatting just like one of the guys, and talking about some toe fungus she had. And I remember thinking, if you had told me when I was sixteen that one day I would be sitting with Laura Ballance talking about her toe fungus!

Laura   I never had a toe fungus. I was probably talking about my bunions. Robbie probably still thinks that bunions are a form of toe fungus!

The Get Up Kids shows were mostly sold out, and most of them were in venues larger than Superchunk usually played. But the audiences were largely uninterested in Superchunk, and any hopes of kindling a Superchunk revival among a younger audience didn't pan out. *Shutting Up* sold 17,000 copies, their worst-selling record since their self-titled debut.

Jim Wilbur   I wasn't ready to give up. But everyone was tired and kind of demoralized. And Laura got married. And Mac had a baby. I was like, let's not work on a new record right away. Let's just sit back.

Jon Wurster   We had a meeting at Laura's place. And at that point I was ready for it to

be over, so I could move on. And Mac said, "That's fine if you don't want to do it anymore. But let's not break up. Because bands that break up don't keep selling catalog records." On the one hand, I understood that. And on the other hand I almost wanted some finality to it.

Jim Wilbur   I was upset. Mac and I both didn't want to stop. And Jon was like, "I want to say that I never want to play some of these songs again. I want to say that." I said, "It's a trick in your mind that says that you know more now than you're going to know in two years. And for you to say that means you're sort of desperate. Why don't we just see how things lie and see how we feel?" And then Jon was like, "Could we just say that we'll only do something if we're all a hundred percent into it?" And I was like, "Of course. Nobody's going to force you to do something you don't want to do. But that doesn't mean you have to underline it quite so hard."

Mac   Bands that break up always get back together, and I didn't want to get on the reunion train in a year. Mainly I just thought, "Why not just take a break?" We also had a show already booked, a benefit for Alejandro Escovedo at a club in Raleigh. And I didn't want Superchunk's last show ever to be at some crappy nightclub in Raleigh.

Jon Wurster   In retrospect, it was a smart thing to do. Because we play a couple times a year, and it's not like every time we play again, it's like, "They're getting back together again," you know? Because technically we didn't break up. And we've managed to record a song a year probably. So it all kind of worked out. And I'm glad that Mac sort of pushed for it to not be completely over.

Superchunk went on one more tour after the Get Up Kids, a brief East Coast swing in 2003 to support the release of *Cup of Sand*, their third collection of B-sides and rarities. They've released two limited-edition live CDs as part of the Clambake Series ("clam" is musicianspeak for a mistake); one of acoustic record-store shows and one of an original soundtrack they performed live for a screening of the Japanese silent film *A Page of Madness* during the San Francisco International Film Festival in 2002. They've gone into the studio to contribute tracks to compilation CDs here and there, and released one 7-inch-only single of "Misfits and Mistakes," for the soundtrack to the *Aqua Teen Hunger Force* movie. In 2009, they released *Leaves in the Gutter,* a five-song EP. Live, they've reconvened for various benefits — a show in Chicago to raise funds for the Ulman Cancer Fund for Young Adults in memory of fan Sean Silver; a couple of shows in North Carolina to boost voter registration for Barack Obama — and other special occasions, like *The Daily Show's* 10th anniversary party in 2006.

Of the latter show, the *Village Voice* wrote:

> They're still around, and they're still closing shows with the first single they ever released, and somehow that's not really the least bit depressing. Their charged-up fuzzcore felt deliriously warm and comforting even when it was new, and they still take a visible child-like glee in guitar windmills and peals of feed-back . . . I hated seeing the Circle Jerks last month; it seemed like such a cynical ploy for these middle-aged guys to keep pounding out the same angry tantrums they wrote when they were teenagers. But Superchunk wasn't anything like that, maybe because their songs deal with emotions and ideas [that] could be considered adult. I didn't really get "Slack Motherfucker" when I was 13; I'd never had to work a shit job. I get it now.

Jim Wilbur   We were doing well right up to when we stopped. And we do well when we come out of retirement.

Jon Wurster   I think to this day, Superchunk will always be remembered more for how we did it than what we did. At this point, Superchunk is the band that's led by the two people that put out the Arcade Fire records. And that's fine. It's better than nothing.

* * *

Facing Page: Wurster in Mallorca, Spain, 1997.   Next Page: Superchunk at the Experience Music Project in Seattle, August 2001.

Dan Bejar and Fisher Rose of Destroyer backstage at South
By Southwest in Austin, Texas, 2008.

Conor Oberst and M. Ward.

David Kilgour.

Matt Elliott of the Third Eye Foundation at the
Brooklyn Bridge, 1997.

The Magnetic Fields' Sam Davol, Claudia Gonson, and Stephin Merritt on tour in Europe, 2001.

Gonson and Davol at the *69 Love Songs* record release party in New York, 1999.

The Magnetic Fields at the Cat's Cradle during Merge's 10th anniversary fest.

Dudley Klute, Merritt, and LD Beghtol, 1999.

Misspelled marquee, London, November 2000.

Season's Greetings

Merge Christmas card, 1999.

Misspelled dressing room sign.

The Rock*a*Teens.

Video shoot for "Art Class" from *Here's to Shutting Up*, directed by Norwood Cheek (foreground), 2001.

Wurster singing karaoke in Tokyo, 2001.

Backstage at the Paradiso, Amsterdam, 1998.

At the Paradiso.

Mac as Glenn Danzig, Halloween 1998.

Poster by Ron Liberti, 2008.

The Rosebuds.

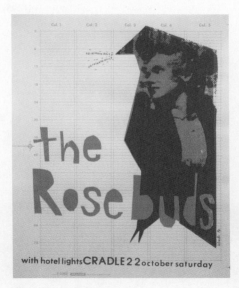

Poster by Ron Liberti, 2005.

Merge coaster.

Wurster on tour.

The "Music Tapes House Capsule," featured on the pop-up album art for *Music Tapes for Clouds and Tornadoes*.

Facing page: Régine Chassagne of the Arcade Fire on the set of the video shoot for "Neighborhood #1 (Tunnels)," July 2005.   Previous page: Win Butler at the same shoot.

Chapter Thirteen

Us Kids Know

The Arcade Fire

In the winter of 1991, Superchunk opened for Mudhoney at a club in Montreal. Howard Bilerman, a twenty-one-year-old student at the time, was in the audience. He'd come to see Mudhoney — he'd never heard of Superchunk before; it was their first foray into Canada — but he was blown away by their set and introduced himself to Mac and Laura after the show. For the next week, he couldn't get the tune to "Slack Motherfucker" out of his head, but he didn't know what the song was called. So he sent away for some Superchunk 7-inches with a note asking, "Can you tell me what the song with the chorus, 'I'm working, but I'm not working for you' is called?" The records came back with a torn piece of scrap paper bearing the answer. Bilerman fell in love with the records. Superchunk played Montreal again, at the same club, a few months later, and Bilerman approached Laura at the merch table to sheepishly ask if he might be able to leave some flyers for his band, which was playing a show there the following week. She said yes, which Bilerman says was "possibly the coolest thing ever." Two years later, when Superchunk came through again, Bilerman

Laura, Mac, and Howard Bilerman in Montreal, 1992.

showed up early during soundcheck to ask if he could tape the show on his four-track. The band agreed, and the next day Bilerman skipped his classes to show them around Montreal during their day off from touring. For the next decade, Bilerman never missed a Superchunk show within 300 miles of wherever he happened to be.

Bilerman kept in touch with Mac and Laura over the years. When Superchunk first played Montreal, it was known mostly for its sluggish economy and the vexing conflict between English-speaking and French-speaking Canadians. But in the late nineties it became the site of a musical renaissance kick-started by the symphonic experimental pop of Godspeed You! Black Emperor, a musical collective that gained a following in the states and instigated a scene in Montreal with their innumerable side projects. Cheap housing, a steady influx of students to the city's six colleges, and the European pace of life made Montreal a suitable place to pursue music. Bilerman founded a recording studio that documented much of the scene — Godspeed, the Nul Set, A Silver Mt. Zion, and many others. He saw Merge as an inspiration, and his preference for analog recording equipment and distrust of major labels earned him a reputation as "the Steve Albini of Canada." Mac frequently tapped Bilerman for advice on how to build and maintain his tiny one-room home studio, looking for guidance on recording techniques and what gear to buy.

In the spring of 2003, Portastatic played Montreal while on tour with Yo La Tengo, and Mac e-mailed Bilerman to see if he could crash at his place. Just two weeks later, a band called the Arcade Fire approached Bilerman about making a record at the studio he runs with members of Godspeed.

* * *

Win Butler, Arcade Fire's tall and somber frontman, was eleven years old on the night that Bilerman saw Superchunk for the first time. He was ten when Nirvana signed to Geffen, and thirteen when Atlantic bought half of Matador. He was six when Hüsker Dü and the Replacements raised cries of "sellout!"

by signing to major labels. Growing up in Woodlands, Texas, a far northern suburb of Houston, he had no local record store with all the latest 7-inches lined up on the racks. Music was whatever you could see on MTV, hear on the radio, or buy at Wal-Mart, or Target, or Sam Goody. Butler, who came from a musical family — his mother is a harpist and songwriter, and his grandfather, Alvino Rey, was a swing bandleader who was known as "the Wizard of the Pedal Steel Guitar" — came of age in an era when labels were hungrily seeking out bands that didn't sound or look mainstream. His early touchstones were the Cure (Geffen, Elektra), Radiohead (EMI, Capitol), and Depeche Mode (Sire, Reprise).

Butler learned to play music out of fear of boredom: The summer before he was to ship off for boarding school at Phillips Exeter Academy, when he was fifteen, he decided to take a few lessons on the guitar his grandfather had given him so he could entertain himself and maybe impress a few kids on his dorm.

Win Butler   **I learned a few chords just because it would give me something to do. I pretty much went from barely being able to play "Free Fallin'" by Tom Petty to just writing songs all the time.**

At Exeter, Butler started playing with his friend Jesson Alexander as a "survival mechanism" in the school's demanding environment. They recorded their songs at first on two boom boxes — bouncing back and forth between them to achieve a crude multitrack recording system — and later on four-tracks. His first public performance was a cover of the Cure's "Just Like Heaven" at the Exeter talent show.

Butler graduated in 1998 and spent an unhappy year at Sarah Lawrence.

Win Butler   **It was the opposite extreme from Exeter. Write your own major; take whatever classes you want. And basically all I was doing was making four-track recordings all day. After a year of that, it was hard to justify spending the money on tuition.**

He impulsively decided one day at school that he, Alexander, and Alexander's friend

Josh Deu would start a band, and spend that summer rehearsing at a farmhouse his parents owned in rural Maine. He called Alexander from a campus pay phone: "Hey man, come live with me in my house in Maine this summer, and let's just write songs and get a stupid job and be in a band."

Win Butler   **We set up a bunch of instruments in one of the bedrooms. From that summer through the next couple years was probably the most intensive period of writing I ever did. I pretty much just ate food, played music, and wrote songs. We got a job together taking pictures of tourists before they got on whale watches. And the rest of the time we were just playing music.**

The band that began that summer, in 1999, would eventually become the Arcade Fire, though it would be years before they were an actual, working band.

Win Butler   **For a while there it seemed like we had one gig a year. We'd do all this preparation, and put this insane amount of work into learning all these songs, and we never had a drummer. So we'd get some temporary**

Sarah Neufeld of the Arcade Fire on the set of the video shoot for "Neighborhood #1 (Tunnels)," July 2005.

drummer, teach him all the songs, and play a show. And it would be a disaster, and we'd keep working for another year.

Alexander quit abruptly at the end of the summer in Maine, and Butler and Deu forged ahead, spending a miserable year in Boston — they chose to make a go of it there almost at random — looking to no avail for a steady bass player and drummer to play with. Shows were rare, and rarely any good. The only upside was the plethora of college radio stations in the area, which exposed Butler for the first time to all that music you couldn't buy in the record stores of Woodlands, Texas.

Win Butler   **That's where I heard the Magnetic Fields for the first time. It totally blew me away. I'd only heard one or two songs, and I went to see them at the Middle East, and I left being able to sing like ten songs from having heard them just once. I also heard Neutral Milk Hotel on the radio up there, and Superchunk. That was my first experience of hearing totally independent stuff that was as good as anything else. I had kind of associated indie music with having an excuse to be crappy. Like, "Oh, we didn't spend that much money. That's why it sucks." Whereas this music was like, "We didn't spend that much money because — who cares? We write really good songs."**

Deu decided to return to art school in Montreal in 2000, and Butler followed him. The music scene there was a little introspective for Butler's tastes, but there were plenty of places to play and people to play with.

Win Butler   **A lot of people move to Montreal because they want to make art, rather than make it making art. I didn't meet many people who were careerists, which was pretty inspiring.**

In their perpetual search for a drummer, Deu and Butler would loiter around the rehearsal rooms at the music school of McGill University, eavesdropping on people practicing and striking up conversations. One day in the McGill cafeteria after an afternoon of making the rounds, he approached the diminutive, curly-haired Régine Chassagne, the bubbly daughter of Haitian parents who fled the "Papa Doc" Duvalier regime for Canada before she was born. Chassagne, who taught herself to play piano by ear, was playing the recorder at the time in a medieval-music band. Butler asked her if she knew any good drummers. She gave him her number and said to give her a call; she might have some suggestions. A few days later, Butler saw Chassagne singing jazz standards at an art opening, and he was taken by her crystalline, childlike voice.

Win Butler   **After seeing that, I was really insistent. I was like, "We have to play together." So she came over to my place a couple days later, and I played her some of my songs. She brought all these weird medieval instruments. There's a song called "Headlights Look Like Diamonds" on our first EP, and we wrote a bunch of lyrics to that song together that day. Pretty much from that day on, we haven't really been apart.**

Chassagne and Butler quickly became the heart of the Arcade Fire (they would get married in 2003). Deu left the band. The lineup

would shift dramatically over the next few years, but Butler and Chassagne recruited Montreal music-scene regulars Dane Mills, Brendan Reed, and Myles Broscoe to start playing afternoon loft shows where you could get in for $3 if you brought a can of food to contribute to a potluck. The Arcade Fire was too big for those rooms, literally and figuratively. From the beginning, their live shows were ecstatic, confrontational, and guided by what Butler calls "aggressive joy." Butler, playing an acoustic guitar, would wander the room and sing directly to the audience while Chassagne, Mills, Reed, and Broscoe would trade a vast array of archaic and folk instruments — banjo, hurdy-gurdy, mandolin — mid-song, bang on whatever surfaces happened to be available, shout out sing-along choruses, and generally lose themselves in an all-out bid to win over the audience, one person at a time. They began wearing uniforms — the men in brown vests, suspenders, and buttoned-up shirts that made them look like extras from *The Grapes of Wrath*, and Chassagne in elaborate, lacy evening wear; *The Guardian* would later describe them as "celestial buskers" — and made clear that they were there to *perform*.

Sleeve of the CDR master that the Arcade Fire sent to Merge for "Neighborhood #1 (Tunnels)" 7-inch, 2004.

Chassagne and Butler, Phoenix, Ariz., December 2004.

Win Butler   There was a lot of shoe-gazing music happening in Montreal at the time, and we didn't relate to it. Our attitude and the look of the band was in response to the stuff we were surrounded by. Nearly every show I'd go to would be someone playing a cymbal with a bow, pretty much. And that was cool, but I wanted to write *songs*. We were definitely into messing with the audience, and connecting, and getting in people's faces a bit. We'd be playing these rooms for like thirty kids, and there would be seven of us playing, so we're like a quarter of the people in the room, and we're just playing so loud, and screaming our heads off, and people were just kind of backed up against the wall like, What the hell is happening? And that was our goal. Some of those loft shows were really amazing. People would be dancing, and it was kind of like we had these hit songs.

The songs had a grandeur worthy of the spectacle. The Arcade Fire marries soaring, joyous, full-throated choral melodies to downbeat-heavy, danceable tunes that owe as much to the Supremes as to New Order. Ragged electric guitars clash with rustic folk instruments, and songs veer from German beer-hall chants to French torch songs to American punk rock with urgency. "As the members of the Arcade Fire emerged from the crowd in their standard Russian military garb," wrote a reviewer for McGill's college paper of an early show, "the eager crowd was immediately captured. For the next 45 minutes, the band played the musical equivalent of a Chinese fire drill. An upright bass was exchanged for a tambourine and a steel drum, and again for an accordion, as keyboards and guitars were switched among the band members with impressive inconsistency."

Richard Reed Parry, who played stand-up bass in a Montreal instrumental band called Belle Orchestre, caught one of those loft shows, and couldn't sleep that night, he was so excited. In August 2002, the band went with Parry to Butler's farmhouse in Maine, cleaned out the barn, set it up as an impromptu studio, and recorded an EP, with Parry acting as producer. They made it just as much to document the rapidly disintegrating lineup as to make a record.

Win Butler   That lineup of the band was on its last legs, personally. It was just a real struggle to get people to rehearse. Régine and I were restless and not really satisfied. We really felt like we had done nothing at all, and people in the band felt like, "OK, this is good." We were like, "We haven't done anything yet."

They self-released the EP, ordering 500 copies from a local CD manufacturer and selling them at shows and online. The inserts were printed on restaurant placemats, which the band had to individually copy and fold. They sold extremely well, and the band pressed more and eventually sold 3,000 or so on their own.

The lineup that played on the EP barely made it to the release party before falling apart. Broscoe, Mills, and Reed left, and Parry came on board, as did Tim Kingsbury, who had previously been in the New International Standards, and Butler's younger brother, Will, who took a semester off from Northwestern University to live in Montreal. There were a few months of what Butler describes as pandemonium during and after the breakup and reconstitution of the Arcade Fire. They were once again without a drummer; Chassagne took over temporarily but wasn't interested in staying behind the kit permanently. The new version of the band was bent on being louder and even more insistent than before, and they marked the occasion with a new composition called "Wake Up," a driving, dyspeptic youth anthem — "Children wake up / hold your mistake up / before they turn the summer into dust" — that would become a signature song.

In August of 2003, still drummer-less but writing material furiously, the band decided to make a 7-inch to document "Wake Up" and another new song called "Neighborhood #3 (Power Out)," the idea being that they could get away with a fill-in drummer for a few songs and worry about a full-length when they found a permanent replacement. A friend referred them to Bilerman. Though Bilerman hadn't been too impressed by the EP, he saw promise when Butler and Chassagne played "Wake Up" for him in their kitchen during a meeting to discuss what they were going to record. When Butler asked Bilerman to recommend a drummer, he offered up himself. After "Wake

Arcade Fire.

Jeremy Gara and Will Butler on laundry day, Montreal, August 2005.

Up" and "Neighborhood #3 (Power Out)" were recorded, they kept at it for another six months, making the record that would become *Funeral*, so named because the Butler brothers' grandfather, Chassagne's grandfather, and Parry's aunt all died during or near the time of the sessions.

While they were working on *Funeral*, the Arcade Fire's profile in Montreal was beginning to grow, on the strength of the EP and the word-of-mouth about their live shows. They played occasional, ill-fated shows in the states, including a New York show in 2003 in front of 11 people, and traveled around Canada for short tours to Guelph, Ottawa, and Toronto. In Canada, however, people were showing up. In 2003, they were shocked to find that they sold out La Sala Rossa, a 250–capacity club in Montreal.

Win Butler   It was the kind of place we dreamed of playing. And we drove up and there was a line around the block. It was like, "Oh, this is weird." And then we went to Toronto, and it was even more people, just from word-of-mouth from the last time we'd been there. This was all before *Funeral* came out, and everything that's happened to us since then has felt like an extension of that initial surprise and excitement at showing up and seeing a bunch of people there.

Bilerman was a good ten years older than the rest of the band, and wasn't quite as gung ho and eager as the rest of them. He was loathe for his relationship with Mac and Laura to descend into an industry "connection," and he rarely sent bands their way, even though he worked with musicians constantly at his studio. But he knew the Arcade Fire was good. Butler, who was aware that Bilerman knew Mac and Laura, thought of Merge as his ideal label, simply by way of its association with the Magnetic Fields and Neutral Milk Hotel. So Bilerman was at pains to find a way to casually suggest that Merge might want to look at his band. He started by sending Mac a DVD of live footage he'd recorded from his first three shows with the Arcade Fire.

Mac   He sent a note that was full of caveats. "Here's this band, I'm playing drums with them. If you don't like it, I totally understand.

It's not a big deal. It's not me, it's not my songs. I'm just helping them out."

The DVD was formatted improperly, and Mac couldn't get it to work. Meanwhile, even though *Funeral* wasn't finished, Butler began to circulate rough mixes of some of the songs to other labels, including Alien8 Recordings, a Montreal label that had handled the first record by the Unicorns, a Montreal trio that had seen some success.

By early 2004, *Funeral* was close to being done. In February, Bilerman sent Mac an exceedingly bashful, almost tortured e-mail:

> hello hello . . .
> i'm writing this letter to the CEO of merge records . . . so, let's put all friendship aside for a few paragraphs.
> i've been put in a slightly uncomfortable position here by the band i'm drumming in called the arcade fire . . . uncomfortable only 'cause i'm really shy & clumsy about these things. basically we're recording a record right now, and are in the process of figuring out who will put it out. there have been several interested parties . . . some more interesting than others. the list includes alien8 . . . and a few others. the alien8 deal feels the best, if for nothing else than they are friends of ours, and the label is based out of montreal. . . . win (singer/songwriter) has been asking me about merge, partly 'cause he loves so much of the stuff on the label, and partly 'cause he knows i know you. after figuring out how the heck i was going to balance wanting to help him out, with not crossing the boundaries of friendship, i came to the conclusion that the best thing to do would be to ask you if win could contact you directly . . . either by phone or by e-mail, and as a result, get myself off the hook as middleman.
> anyhow, i want you to know that there are no strings attached here. if you are completely uninterested in the music, i will take no offense, and you can still crash at my place the next time you roll into town. ok . . . end the business portion of this e-mail. . . .

Mac   First, Howard sent a homemade DVD that didn't work. It sat around for a while before I actually tried it and realized that it was a dud. So I asked him to please just send a CD that I could throw into the stereo and listen to. He did send one, which sat on my desk for a couple weeks after that. He had downplayed the Arcade Fire, and his involvement in the band, so much that I frankly didn't have high expectations. When I finally got around to listening to it, I was surprised at how immediate the songs were, and at how much they reminded me of some of my favorite music in high school and college — New Order, Echo and the Bunnymen — but with a sort of lo-fi grandeur and scrappy aspect those bands never had.

Howard Bilerman   I ended up sending Mac a CD, and Win called and e-mailed Mac a few times after that. Mac never got back to him. We decided to accept an offer from Alien8, and they took us out for a huge dinner to celebrate the deal. Literally twelve hours after that dinner, Mac e-mailed back saying he loved the CD, and was interested in putting it out.

In Mac's defense, part of the delay was from the time it took to pass the record around the office and make sure that it was as good as he thought it was. Rarely had the staff been so enthusiastically behind a new band.

Mac and Laura, who were now signing bands to contracts after their experience with Trail of Dead, were perfectly willing to do a long-distance deal, but Butler and Chassagne wanted them to come see the Arcade Fire's live show in Montreal first, to make sure they really liked the band. But travel was out of the question: Laura was pregnant, and Mac's wife had recently given birth to their first child. The band was disappointed, but Mac explained to them that Merge was offering to sign them anyway, sight unseen. To which Win replied: "Yeah, but I think you'll be more excited about it if you see us play live."

Mac and Laura wouldn't budge, and Butler and Chassagne couldn't arrange a gig in Chapel Hill on short notice. But they wanted to meet Mac and Laura before doing a deal, so Butler, Chassagne, and Parry drove fourteen hours down the Eastern Seaboard to Chapel Hill. Mac and Laura took them to dinner. Butler was reserved and quiet, but Chassagne was bouncing off the walls.

Laura   She was drumming on things. We were like, "Calm down!" She's very enthusiastic.

Mac   For a band that hadn't put their first record out yet, they were super purposeful. Like, "This is what we're doing — all I plan on doing is touring." It wasn't, "Yeah, I don't know, maybe we can get a few weeks off to tour." It was very much, "This is what we want to do."

Butler, Chassagne, and Parry returned to Montreal to think it over. On April 2, 2004, Butler sent Mac some tracks-in-progress from *Funeral* and e-mailed him: "OK. . . the cd is in the mail. . . . Even if the timing of this is too weird for this release, we are still interested in talking about other recordings in the future future future. . . ." The Arcade Fire was planning a U.S. tour opening for the Unicorns at the time, and Mac and Laura urged them to skip a date in South Carolina and play Chapel Hill instead. On April 21, Win e-mailed Mac:

> Hey Mac . . .
> could you help us set up a show in chapel hill on Monday the 7th of June . . . we are trying to avoid playing SC as per your advice . . .
>
> Also if you get the chance could you send me an attachment with the proposed contract . . . for 2 records in north America . . .
>
> If we do do this whole putting out a record with Merge thing, which I am pulling for, but the whole band isn't there yet, in your learned opinion would it be possible to rush the manifacture of a 7 inch and cd single (maybe 1000 each). . . .
>
> Also another hypothetical . . . would it be possible help with local press for this june tour with the unicorns as well . . .
>
> We have set april 30th as the last possible day by which we will have made a decision . . . and questions can cease being hypothetical.
>
> life is insanity right now . . .
> — win.

By April 30, as promised, the Arcade Fire had made a decision. On that day, Chassagne e-mailed Mac:

> Hey Mac.
> We just talked to Alien 8 and told them we were going with you guys. It went pretty well. They knew all along what the situation was, so it wasn't too much of a shock.
> You can make an announcement.
> (I am sitting in the studio and we are mixing neighborhood RIGHT NOW!)
> :)
> — Régine

Win Butler   Once we met everyone, it was a very, very easy decision to make. It felt very comfortable. There was no, "We're going to make you big; we know what to do." It was, "We like the record, we want to put it out." It was kind of a bummer to tell the Alien8 guys that we weren't going with them. But they later told me that if they had put our record out, it would have killed them.

The June 2004 Chapel Hill show that Win had asked for help setting up was Mac and Laura's first chance to see the Arcade Fire live. It was at the Cave, Chapel Hill's oldest bar. The Cave lives up to its name. It fits about forty people, has fake papier-mâché cave walls, and no stage — the bands set up on the floor. Butler's head was scraping the low ceiling. But the cramped environs could barely contain the energy; they played like they were in a stadium.

Mac   It was amazing. There are a lot more people who claim to have been at that show than actually were there.

Laura   I was amazed at how many people were there. The show was booked at the very last minute, and not heavily promoted. But somehow, word had gotten out that this must-see band was playing. At the Cave, the bands set up right near the door, and I wanted to minimize my cigarette-smoke exposure because I was pregnant, so I stayed by the door the whole time and got to watch them from five feet away. I could look out at the crowd and see the faces of people watch-

They were shaking the whole place. I asked Mac, 'Where have you been keeping this band?'

— Jim Romeo

ing them play, and everyone had these huge grins. I was trembling by the end of the show.

Jim Romeo   They were shaking the whole place. I asked Mac, "Where have you been keeping this band?" He said, "I don't know, we got this record from these people in Montreal, it sounded pretty good, we said we'd put it out." They didn't even know.

A few months after that, in July 2004, Mac and Laura asked them to come back to Chapel Hill to play Merge's fifteenth anniversary show at the Cat's Cradle.

Bill Mooney   Everyone was like, "Oh my god, that was just the greatest show I've ever seen." There was a cookout the next day, and everyone was talking about it. Everyone felt like that record was going to be really big. There was a buzz.

No one thought it was going to be *that* big. Merge released *Funeral* in September of 2004. They pressed 10,000 copies, which was an ambitious number for a debut record by a band nobody had heard of. On September 13, *Pitchfork* published what has become a legendary review:

> *How did we get here?*
> Ours is a generation overwhelmed by frustration, unrest, dread, and tragedy. Fear is wholly pervasive in American society, but we manage nonetheless to build our defenses in subtle ways — we scoff at arbitrary, color-coded "threat" levels; we receive our information from comedians and laugh at politicians. Upon the turn of the 21st century, we have come to know our isolation

well. Our self-imposed solitude renders us politically and spiritually inert, but rather than take steps to heal our emotional and existential wounds, we have chosen to revel in them. We consume the affected martyrdom of our purported idols and spit it back in mocking defiance. We forget that "emo" was once derived from emotion, and that in our buying and selling of personal pain, or the cynical approximation of it, we feel nothing.

We are not the first, or the last, to be confronted with this dilemma. David Byrne famously asked a variation on the question that opens this review, and in doing so suggested a type of universal disaffection synonymous with drowning. And so The Arcade Fire asks the question again, but with a crucial distinction: The pain of Win Butler and Régine Chassagne, the enigmatic husband-and-wife songwriting force behind the band, is not merely metaphorical, nor is it defeatist. They tread water in Byrne's ambivalence because they have known real, blinding pain, and they have overcome it in a way that is both tangible and accessible. Their search for salvation in the midst of real chaos is ours; their eventual catharsis is part of our continual enlightenment.

The years leading up to the recording of *Funeral* were marked with death. Chassagne's grandmother passed away in June of 2003, Butler's grandfather in March of 2004, and bandmate Richard Parry's aunt the following month. These songs demonstrate a collective subliminal recognition of the powerful but oddly distanced pain that follows the death of an aging loved one. *Funeral* evokes sickness and death, but also understanding and renewal; childlike mystification, but also the impending coldness of maturity. The recurring motif of a non-specific "neighborhood" suggests the supportive bonds of family and community, but most of its lyrical imagery is overpoweringly desolate.

"Neighborhood #1 (Tunnels)" is a sumptuously theatrical opener — the gentle hum of an organ, undulating strings, and repetition of a simple piano figure suggest the discreet unveiling of an epic. Butler, in a bold voice that wavers with the force of raw, unspoken emotion, introduces his neighborhood. The scene is tragic: As a young man's

parents weep in the next room, he secretly escapes to meet his girlfriend in the town square, where they naively plan an "adult" future that, in the haze of adolescence, is barely comprehensible to them. Their only respite from their shared uncertainty and remoteness exists in the memories of friends and parents.

The following songs draw upon the tone and sentiment of "Tunnels" as an abstract mission statement. The conventionally rock-oriented "Neighborhood #2 (Laika)" is a second-hand account of one individual's struggle to overcome an introverted sense of suicidal desperation. The lyrics superficially suggest a theme of middle-class alienation, but avoid literal allusion to a suburban wasteland — one defining characteristic of the album, in fact, is the all-encompassing scope of its conceptual neighborhoods. The urban clatter of Butler's adopted hometown of Montreal can be felt in the foreboding streetlights and shadows of "Une Annee Sans Lumiere," while Chassagne's evocative illustration of her homeland (on "Haiti," the country her parents fled in the 1960s) is both distantly exotic and starkly violent, perfectly evoking a nation in turmoil.

"Neighborhood #3 (Power Out)" is a shimmering, audacious anthem that combines a driving pop beat, ominous guitar assault, and sprightly glockenspiel decoration into a passionate, fist-pumping album manifesto. The fluidity of the song's construction is mesmerizing, and the cohesion of Butler's poignant assertion of exasperation ("I went out into the night / I went out to pick a fight with anyone") and his emotional call to arms ("The power's out in the heart of man / Take it from your heart / Put it in your hand"), distinguishes the song as the album's towering centerpiece.

Even in its darkest moments, *Funeral* exudes an empowering positivity. Slow-burning ballad "Crown of Love" is an expression of lovesick guilt that perpetually crescendos until the track unexpectedly explodes into a dance section, still soaked in the melodrama of weeping strings; the song's psychological despair gives way to a purely physical catharsis. The anthemic momentum of "Rebellion (Lies)" counterbalances Butler's plaintive appeal for survival at death's door, and there is liberation in his admittance of life's inevitable transience. "In the Backseat" explores a common phenomenon — a love of backseat window-gazing, inextricably linked to an intense fear of driving — that ultimately suggests a conclusive optimism through ongoing self-examination. "I've been learning to drive my whole life," Chassagne sings, as the album's acoustic majesty finally recedes and relinquishes.

So long as we're unable or unwilling to fully recognize the healing aspect of embracing honest emotion in popular music, we will always approach the sincerity of an album like *Funeral* from a clinical distance. Still, that it's so easy to embrace this album's operatic proclamation of love and redemption speaks to the scope of The Arcade Fire's vision. It's taken perhaps too long for us to reach this point where an album is at last capable of completely and successfully restoring the tainted phrase "emotional" to its true origin. Dissecting how we got here now seems unimportant. It's simply comforting to know that we finally have arrived.

— David Moore

As soon as it went live, all hell broke loose.

Pitchfork was launched in 1995 by Ryan Schreiber, a soft-spoken and polite former record store clerk from Minneapolis who sought an online outlet for his musical opinions, which could be venomous or hagiographic, depending on whether you're Stone Temple Pilots or the Wrens. Read by 160,000 or so fans and music-industry insiders each day, by 2004 it was rapidly on its way to becoming a tastemaker for independent music. Schreiber got his inspiration from the zines he used to read in the early nineties, and *Pitchfork* is essentially a sprawling zine with global distribution, no postage costs and an inordinate amount of power. A mention in *Maximum Rocknroll* back in the late eighties may have earned you a spike in mail-orders; ecstatic praise in *Pitchfork* could mean hundreds of thousands of records sold. *Funeral* is an undeniable record, and the Arcade Fire's memorable live shows generated an unstoppable buzz — it succeeded on its own merits. But *Pitchfork*'s effect on the music business is to concentrate and accelerate the

sort of word of mouth that used to percolate over the course of months and even years, and serve it up instantly in a bright, flashing online warning that you may be missing out on the Next Big Thing if you don't buy the Arcade Fire record right now.

Funeral was destined to be a hit, but the attention paid by *Pitchfork* and by regular folks' blogs turned the Arcade Fire into a hit before most people had heard it. Overnight success is nothing new in the music business, but it is usually mandated by a deep-pocketed label's publicity team in concert with glossy magazines like *Spin* and *Rolling Stone*. Because *Pitchfork* is independent, as are most of the labels whose bands it reviews, the traditional corporate publicity machinery is completely short-circuited. A decade ago, a review of a Merge band in *Rolling Stone* was a coup; in 2004, no one even noticed when *Rolling Stone* played catch-up and reviewed *Funeral* (giving it four stars) in December, three months after *Pitchfork*.

Ed Roche **We sent out one hundred advance copies to the mom and pop stores prior to that review, and across the board nobody really cared. It was viewed as an**

Tim Kingsbury at the "Neighborhood #1 (Tunnels)" shoot, July 2005.

Eight of us would stay at some fancy hotel, all crammed into one bed.

— Win Butler

okay record, but nobody got really excited. And then, literally, that review hit within a few days of the release date, and within hours, everybody who had thought the record was okay now thought it was the greatest record of all time. And we sold out of everything immediately. There was no magic happening until that review happened and then all of a sudden everybody reevaluated. *Pitchfork* was powerful enough to scare the stores into making sure they had it; it just steamrolled after that.

Funeral would eventually sell more than 400,000 copies in the states. The first pressing was gone in a week, and because the artwork was, as seems to be the case with most of Merge's successes, complicated and more expensive than a traditional CD booklet, there was a two-week turnaround time to get more copies into stores.

Mac   Yes, Touch and Go had warned us! The artwork was foil-stamped, which means sleeves had to be printed, the ink had to dry, they had to be then shipped to a die-cutter to cut them into the right shape, and then the foil stamping had to be applied and also dry, and then they had to be hand-assembled. It was sold out for weeks. In retrospect I can't say this was the worst thing for the word-of-mouth on the record. But I felt like running out made us look like amateurs, and we were worried the band would be really bummed with us, and they may well have been. At the time there was a lot of frustration to go around.

Adding to the frustration was Touch and Go's reluctance to commit to the notion that *Funeral* was a runaway success and print enough copies to meet demand. As with *69 Love Songs*, Rusk and Roche were worried

that if they pressed more than a couple thousand copies at a time, demand would fall off and they'd be left holding the bag. Mac worried that Merge was letting its biggest record yet slip through its hands.

Win Butler   It was, "Oh fuck, how many do we make?" I know Mac spent a lot of energy trying to convince Touch and Go to print like 100,000, and not 5,000. I know it seemed like a risk, but it would have saved a lot more money. There was a lot of back and forth.

Mac   It just kept going and going. And we kept running into this question of, "Now it's another two weeks before we have more sleeves." I couldn't understand why we had to keep having the same conversation — "Should we make 10,000 more or 20,000 more?" — when I felt like, "Can we please just make a *lot* and not run out?" By February we had made over 150,000 of *Funeral* sleeves and the record was scanning 7,000 a week and still going up.

Cory Rusk   They were just a band at the time. They hadn't previously sold many of their self-released EP or anything. So then the record came out, and it was a great record and everyone started talking about it. There was just ever-increasing demand for it, and that's the problem with special packaging.

Tensions ran high enough to put a dent in Merge and Touch and Go's cozy relationship. Roche memorialized one terse e-mail from Mac by posting it on the wall in mockery: "Just get it done."
    While Mac and Laura were struggling to get *Funeral* into stores, the Arcade Fire were in the center of a maelstrom that would take them, in the space of one year, from playing the Highdive in Champaign, Ill., to opening for U2 three nights in a row in Canada. Bilerman left the band to mind his studio just before *Funeral* came out, and they brought on Jeremy Gara, who had been in the New International Standard with Kingsbury, to replace him. They spent a few weeks holed up at the farmhouse in Maine to rehearse and break in Gara in before descending into

the chaos of CMJ, where they played two showcases. Butler doesn't think the *Pitchfork* review made a huge difference, pointing out that not every ecstatic review there results in the kind of attention the Arcade Fire got, but he credits it with sparking the interest of bigger fish like *The New York Times*, which ran a glowing story about the surging Arcade Fire buzz at CMJ.

David Bowie, Byrne, and Lou Reed were turning up to their shows, and Byrne introduced himself backstage, an experience that Butler likens to "meeting a really interesting professor." A&R reps from every label were hounding them, desperate to coddle them with dinners and hotel rooms.

Win Butler   We didn't have any money at that point. We were surviving off of selling CDs. And all these label dudes would come to our shows and offer to put us up in hotels. We were like, "Well, we're not going to sign with you, but if you want to give us a hotel room, go for it." So eight of us would stay at some fancy hotel, all crammed into one bed.

In 2005, Bowie invited them to play *Fashion Rocks* at Radio City Music Hall, a CBS special that Butler describes as "an advertisement for L'Oréal, with Duran Duran playing 'Hungry Like the Wolf' while a bunch of models pout in the background." Bowie joined them onstage to play "Wake Up" for millions of televisions nationwide.

Win Butler   David Bowie's going to sing your song. On TV. In between a really annoying, hilariously bad thing you can tell funny stories about for the rest of your life. Okay. That's a fair enough trade.

For the first year or so of their newfound celebrity, the Arcade Fire had little money and no manager. They took press calls constantly, passing the cell phone around the van like a hot potato.

Win Butler   It was a mom-and-pop operation. During that tour, we stopped staying with people at shows, because it got sketchy. We used to just ask people from the stage if we could stay at their house, but after staying

at one too many frat houses, we decided to get hotels. So we'd leave the club at 11 and drive around until 1 a.m. looking for a $44.99 hotel room.

Jeremy Gara   We were playing to a thousand people a night, and we were still in a van with a trailer. We'd show up and people would go, "Where's your bus?" We'd point to the van and go, "This is the bus."

Win Butler   We didn't have anything. When we played Coachella, we didn't have road cases for any of our stuff. The keyboard was in a box, and the tom-tom that Richie plays was filled with tambourines and patch cables. It looked like a hobo circus. And we're playing for 30,000 people. After that tour was when we decided we really needed a manager. We spent so much energy saying, "No, no, no, no, yes, no," deflecting things that we didn't want to do. We needed to do the things we wanted to do, not *not* do what we didn't want to do.

Mac   We kept trying to convince them to get a tour manager during that tour. We eventually hooked them up with Superchunk and Portastatic tour manager Dan Mapp for the end of it, which included their performance on *Letterman* and their shows in New York.

Funeral even penetrated into commercial radio with the help of Karen Glauber, with KROQ in Los Angeles playing "Wake Up" forty times a week at one point, despite the band's stubborn refusal to play ball with radio stations.

Win Butler   The whole radio thing is a bullshit circuit of favors for favors. Payouts, bribes, and Mafia-style bullshit. "Oh, well, we'd really love you to do this shitty show we're putting on with a million other shitty bands, and we might not play your record if you won't do it." Once you go down that road, it never ends.

Karen Glauber   There's a certain game that gets played with radio. There's a level of expectation that when a radio station decides to play your record, that you're going to do something with them. With Arcade Fire, it's very, very clear that there are things they'll do, and there are things they won't do. And to their credit, they did do one radio show once, and they still count it as the worst show of their entire career. For whatever reason, they still talk to me, and I have no idea why.

The show was the KROQ Inland Invasion 5, in Devore, Calif., with Jet, 311, Garbage, and Oasis.

Win Butler   It was a rotating stage. It was in an amphitheater, and there's maybe ten people in the seats, on their cell phones, and the 5,000 fans who came to see you are a million miles away on a hill. And they forgot to plug in the monitors. It was just this big pantomime thing that had nothing to do with music. It was horrible.

Backstage, the band had their picture taken with a KROQ DJ named Jed the Fish.

Karen Glauber   There's no part of radio promotion that's any fun. Ever. But radio is still, unequivocally, the number one way to expose artists. You sell more records through radio than any other means.

Of course at most labels, whether or not to play the radio game — especially for a band like the Arcade Fire, which is making real money — wouldn't be an option. But while Mac and Laura let the band make its own decisions, they don't necessarily agree with them.

Mac   I think in general, their approach is great. But it's frustrating, especially for the people who are working their record to radio. They're trying to do the best job they can, but that would require the band to come into the station and do an interview or play a radio festival. And even though they're saying, "We don't care if radio plays our records" — What? You really don't care?

Laura   They do care, because they want us to sell a lot of records.

Mac   They want the record to be as big as it can be, but they don't want to do any of the

attendant bullshit stuff that you have to do to make it as big as it can be. And they say they don't care, but if we don't do a great job on their record, are they going to go to another label?

* * *

The Arcade Fire made a point of not brushing off all the major-label entreaties they received when *Funeral* took off. They had a contract with Merge, and owed them one more record, which they fully intended to deliver. But they saw the attention almost as an intelligence-gathering opportunity, a way to take the measure of the people who were running the industry into the ground.

Jeremy Gara   We'd have lunch with anyone who called, just to grill them about what they do and what that world is about. A lot of times, we would dive into it before they would. "What can you do for us? Why did you want to meet with us?" And pretty quickly, it became clear that they couldn't offer anything we didn't already stumble upon ourselves. They'd say, "We can get you playlisted on commercial radio in the

Jeremy Gara and Richard Reed Parry,
July 2005.

U.S." We were already on KROQ. That's the type of thing they'd offer, and we'd say, "We already have that, you can't possibly help us. If anything, you can match what Merge is doing for us, but we don't know you, and Merge is fine."

Seymour Stein, the legendary president of Sire Records, who signed the Ramones, the Talking Heads, and the Pretenders and is credited with coining the phrase "New Wave," tried seducing the Arcade Fire, and when that failed, he went straight to Mac, buying him breakfast in New York at Balthazar.

Mac   His attitude was, "Hey, this record is doing so well, you must not be able to handle it. How can we work together?" And the answer is, "We can't." I'd never pass up a chance to have a meal with a legend like Seymour Stein. But he wants to give us money, and then he wants a percentage, and then he wants the next Arcade Fire record. It was making us sweat a bit. We hadn't known Win and the band very long, and while they seemed like great and principled people, when someone is throwing large sums of money at you — "write a number down on a piece of paper" — it becomes easier to justify bending those principles a bit. We had a contract for two records, but when it comes down to it, if they wanted to get out of that second record, or if someone at a major wanted to make it happen, they could figure out a way to do it. So it was a relief when it became clear that they were just taking in the whole scene, and not shopping themselves around.

Win Butler   We definitely got offered a lot of money. But we never met anyone who made sense for the band. We feel really lucky to be on Merge. A lot of bands in our position end up getting a lot of bullshit thrown at them, and they buy into it. And we were really fortunate to be around people who had heads on their shoulders and didn't get pushed around or panicked.

The Arcade Fire toured practically nonstop from September of 2004 through November of 2005 for *Funeral*. The U.S. leg ended

in Boston, with Butler and Chassagne, exhausted, sitting in a hotel room with a trash bag full of $40,000 in cash. By the time they were done, they were, in Butler's words, "twenty pounds heavier and shells of our former selves." When U2, which had taken to playing "Wake Up" over the loudspeakers before their shows to rile the audience, invited them to cap off the tour by opening for them on two nights in Montreal and one in Ottawa, they demurred, forcing a personal intervention from Bono to get them to say yes.

Flush with money from *Funeral*, and with an eye toward how to make another record without getting lost in a whirlwind of hype and expectations, the band purchased a deconsecrated church about forty-five miles outside Montreal, and set it up as a recording and rehearsal space, with bedrooms in the basement.

The success of *Funeral* had transformed Merge — it was much bigger than *69 Love Songs* and much faster than Spoon's ascent. They had to bulk up to eleven full-time staffers to handle the record, and faced the innumerable thorny questions that quick success brings. They needed to make sure it got into big-box stores, which required increased participation in "retail programs" and "co-ops" — payments or steep discounts — to put CDs in places where people will see them, or stock them at all.

Corey Rusk   They don't put those records in the racks above because they're cool and they like them. You pay for that because you sell more records, and it will be worth it to you.

In 2006, Best Buy steeply discounted a handful of indie rock CDs, including *Funeral*, for a week, selling them for $7.99, far below the wholesale price — meaning that independent record stores, with employees and rent to pay, were spending more to buy *Funeral* from Merge than a consumer was paying for it at Best Buy. When it emerged that the sale was part of a co-op program, and that Merge and other labels helped subsidize the discount by paying for an advertising circular, a blogstorm ensued. Patrick Monaghan, the president of indie distributor Carrot Top Distribution, lashed out online at the shortsightedness of indie labels helping big-boxes undercut independent record stores and distributors, which were already in dire straits. Mac responded in a comment on Monaghan's blog:

> Obviously Merge's job is to get our artists' records in as many stores as possible and make them available to as many people as possible who want to buy them. . . . Best Buy purchases the Arcade Fire CD from the distributor . . . at the *same* price any other retailer does. Labels and retail (I learned today) are not even legally allowed to discuss pricing, so Best Buy pricing those CDs at $7.99 was completely their choice to lose money on those CDs in order to get people in to buy a DVD player or whatever. . . . To imply that we've abandoned independent retail and distribution (why would we do that?) is not accurate. But running any kind of business (unless you truly are just out for a buck and yourself alone) is a minefield of dilemmas like this. That's what capitalism creates — tensions between artists, consumers, and businesses that are not always easily squared.

But retail skirmishes were the least of Merge's woes. The way the numbers broke down for *Funeral* made obvious something that Mac and Laura had first noticed when the second Polvo record came out: Of all the parties involved in any Merge release — Merge, Touch and Go, and the artist — Merge made the least share of the profits. They approached Rusk about adjusting the profit split, but he resisted, arguing that Touch and Go covered most of the overhead costs — a warehouse, many employees — and that all the other labels he worked with had the same split and it wouldn't be fair to them to start making individualized side deals. But by the time *Funeral* came out, Merge was spending a lot more money promoting and marketing its records, and to them, the split still seemed lopsided.

Mac Essentially, Touch and Go's share of the profit always made sense, because that was like Merge's overhead. But now we had our own *real* overhead — salaries, health insurance for a growing number of employees, a mortgage, not to mention all the escalating costs of doing business as a record label as the cost of even getting your CDs into stores, specifically larger stores like Tower, Borders, or even Best Buy for some of our titles, had risen rapidly in the past few years.

What's more, Scott Rodger, the Arcade Fire's manager, was encouraging Mac and Laura to adjust the deal so that Merge and the band both got better terms. Mac and Laura knew that the only move that made sense for Merge was to leave the nest, as it were. But they'd been with Touch and Go for more than a decade. They ignored the issue for as long as they could.

Mac We didn't have the guts to do it for multiple reasons. It was an insanely busy time, and we didn't need any upheaval at the label. And we were acutely aware that it would appear that, now that we had "a big hit" — though Merge had been successfully operating for years — we were bailing on Touch and Go at an opportune moment. And mainly we're just people who shy away from conflict and didn't want to have that conversation with Corey, so we put it off.

Bob Lawton I remember Mac asking me for advice, and fretting over the whole thing. It's another one of those decisions like "Do we get rid of the drummer?" Here's a person, and a company, who's helped us grow. And now we've got this band asking for more. And we have to cut out the middleman. I don't think it was pleasant for anyone. What's indie about that? I think it all boiled down just to the Arcade Fire — the nature of that beast, good and bad.

Finally, Mac and Laura decided in September 2005 that it was time to call Rusk and have the conversation they'd been dreading. Merge was going to strike out on its own and pursue its own distribution deal with the Alternative Distribution Alliance, a distributor that services indie labels and is owned by Warner Music.

Corey Rusk We had worked with Merge for more than thirteen years. I started with them when all they were doing was 7-inches, and worked with them all the way up to the Arcade Fire. I helped them become what they had become, and I took a lot of pride in it. But it's their business. At the end of the day I'm sure Mac and Laura thought about it and talked about it amongst themselves and just said, "Screw it. If we're ever going to try it on our own, this is the time to do it." There was no arguing with that. If they really ever were going to try and do it, that was probably the right time to do it.

The other Touch and Go employees who worked with Merge over the years weren't as magnanimous. Mac and Laura didn't initially expect anyone's feelings to be hurt over what was, at bottom, a cut-and-dried business decision, and they refused to feel guilty for doing the right thing for Merge. So they never called Ed Roche or any other Touch and Goers to attempt to smooth things over. Roche and others took their silence as an indication that Mac and Laura were happy to let their friendships slide along with the business relationship. Hard feelings festered for months.

Mac   We thought we'd get some good-natured razzing from the folks we'd been working with for thirteen years. So we kept waiting for the ribbing to come from them — for an e-mail or a phone call from Ed giving us shit for taking Merge from Touch and Go. But that never came, and we never called them to get into it because we assumed they were pissed at us for leaving. But they were really just pissed for us not calling to tell them personally. If we had just called them to explain the decision, I think they would have felt slightly betrayed, but that would have faded quickly. Instead, we didn't do anything. Did I mention that conflict and communication is not our strong suit?

Ed Roche   I felt totally blindsided by the whole thing. It was more than the business relationship. I didn't hear from Mac or Laura for a year and a half after that. That was big, for me personally. On a business level, I don't have a problem with what they did. I understand why they did it.

Mac   Laura and I were talking about it once, and she said, "We dropped the ball on this one." She's right.

Ed Roche   For us, records were serious business. You analyzed things, found all your research, you've got the numbers, the costs, you put it all together, you saw what would make the most sense to give the band and the label a good release. Whereas Merge was just really laid-back, super-nice people and maybe more innocent and sweet than we were. And then for them to take it to that next level, maybe they just had to become more businesslike and a little more cutthroat.

Mac   But whose throat were we cutting? Touch and Go's? Hardly. It's not like we took *Funeral* away from them.

* * *

The Arcade Fire spent 2006 working on and off on their follow-up to *Funeral*. The pressure to match the grandeur of their debut would have undone many bands, but they did everything they could to insulate themselves from noise about sophomore slumps and worked away in the church. It couldn't have been a less hyped environment to work in. The Arcade Fire doesn't work well without deadlines, so they recorded in fits and starts throughout the year as personal deadlines loomed. Kingsbury's wedding, for instance, was preceded by a flurry of activity at the church in anticipation of his being unavailable for weeks on his honeymoon. As the record coalesced, signs of grandiosity emerged: They rented a 500-pipe organ, and flew to Bulgaria to procure the services of a cheap orchestra and military choir. Anxious to finish a record that they knew they could fiddle with for years if left unattended, the band selected a release date of March 2007 for the album that would become *Neon Bible*.

Jeremy Gara   Mac and Laura were just like, "Yeah, whenever you're done. Can't wait to hear it."

In fact, by late 2006, Mac and Laura were becoming increasingly worried that the record might not make its release date. *Neon Bible* was by far the most important record Merge had ever done. It was their first chance to follow up a record that had caught

Coachella, 2005.

lightning in a bottle – an opportunity they didn't have after *Aeroplane* or *69 Love Songs* – and prove that they could plan and launch a record that would be successful in major-label terms. And they had to do it without the help of Touch and Go.

Mac and Laura visited Montreal in May 2006 to see the church and listen to some of the songs, but it was more a social call than a label checking up on its signature act.

Laura **They were in the studio so long, and since they'd gotten a manager, it was starting to feel like they were remote from us.**

But as the release date drew near, there was radio silence from Montreal. Loosed from the constraints of working in a regular studio, the band was obsessively working and reworking songs, then spending weeks mixing them. But they still set a release date and booked a tour around it before the record was finished.

Win Butler **We kind of screwed ourselves over with our impatience. It was like, "We want it to come out now!" But we always**

forget what an insane amount of work it is to make something come out now. We'd be mastering or mixing a song, going to bed at six in the morning and waking up at eight to listen to track listings.

Mac and Laura didn't hear the final mixes until January, just two months before the record was supposed to be in stores. And the Arcade Fire had been so consumed in finishing the recording that they hadn't begun thinking about what the record was going to look like.

Mac **It was a classic case where, with the one album that you would want a long lead time so you could make sure that everything was set up the way it should be, you actually have the least time possible and the highest expectations. It definitely got to the point where we didn't know if it was going to be in stores on the release date.**

It was. *Neon Bible*, a dark, densely layered collection of apocalyptic pop, debuted at No. 2 on the *Billboard* 200, just behind a posthumous release from Notorious B.I.G. It was an astonishing coup for Merge. Aided by a weird, self-generated viral campaign involving YouTube videos the band made on Parry's laptop, a 1-800-NEONBIBLE number that fans could call to hear snippets of the songs and leave messages for the band, and barely intelligible spam sent out to the group's e-mail list, *Neon Bible* sold 92,000 copies in its first week. The band purposely pared down on the press it did for the new record, preferring to let the shows speak for themselves. They were so intent on not letting the publicity interests get in the way of their performances this time around that they almost turned down an invitation to play *Saturday Night Live* in February.

Win Butler **I was really sick. And we'd just played like ten shows in a row. Régine and I had booked a vacation in the Bahamas before we started touring really heavily. And *SNL* said, "You can't do it, you can't do it, you can't do it – you can do it the day after tomorrow, but if you say no, you'll never work in this town again." It was one of those kind of moves. It was a heartwrench-**

ing decision, because I really, truly wanted to go on vacation. But I'm glad we did it. After the show, they wanted us to keep playing, and we did a little mini five-song set afterwards, and kind of turned the *SNL* stage into our own show. And Lorne Michaels was kind of dancing out in the crowd. It was pretty awesome.

* * *

Perhaps the most stark indication of the impact that the Arcade Fire has had on Merge came on February 8, 2006 in Los Angeles, when Mac found himself at the 48th Annual Grammy Awards ceremonies. The Arcade Fire had notched two nominations: Best Alternative Album for *Funeral,* and Best Song Written for Motion Picture, Television or Other Visual Media, for "Cold Wind," a single that was used in the final season of HBO's *Six Feet Under.* Mac came along for the ride.

Laura   I did not go to the Grammys. It's not the sort of thing that I could handle. That kind of thing is just bullshit to me.

Mac and the band went with Glauber.

Karen Glauber   I just have a really, really good time with Mac in these formal situations. I've also taken him to the MTV Music Awards. I always feel somewhat embarrassed by what I make him do. It was hilarious — at the EMI party, everyone from every label was bombarding me, "Get me Arcade Fire! Get me Arcade Fire! If you can help me sign Arcade Fire or Spoon, I'll pay you!"

Mac   The Grammys last forever. The Arcade Fire was nominated for an award given during the daytime ceremony, which happens in the building next door to the Staples Center. That takes hours, and they don't serve any alcohol. And then you go over to the Staples Center for the televised part. It's a basketball arena, and they sell everything that they normally sell at a basketball game for food *except* they still don't sell alcohol. So it's this endless thing with no beer served. When they said, "And next up, Sting," that's when we were like, "Okay, let's go to the parties."

The Arcade Fire didn't win, but they'd heard that Bruce Springsteen, who was making the rounds of the Grammy parties that night, was an Arcade Fire fan. (He was: Butler and Chassagne would eventually join him onstage with the E Street Band in Ontario.) So they traveled the circuit looking for him, and kept arriving at each party they'd heard he was going to be at just minutes after he'd split. They finally caught up with him at the Interscope party, way out in Santa Monica after midnight.

Mac   The first thing I saw when we walked in was Dr. Dre playing pool by himself. Pretty crazy. U2 was holding court there, too. Springsteen came in late, just as we were about to leave. It was a pretty small room, so even that would have been okay. "I was at a party with Springsteen, that was cool." But I did get to meet him, and I shook his hand and said, "Thanks for everything. You're one of the reasons that I'm involved in music at all." And then I just backed away slowly and let him talk to Win and Régine. I felt relieved that I got away without saying anything too stupid. After that I talked to Jimmy Iovine for a while. I didn't tell him that I thought he stole Trail of Dead.

* * *

Lance Bangs' Polaroids documenting Josh Deu's video shoot for "Neighborhood #1 (Tunnels)," July 2005.
Clockwise from top left: Will Butler and Tim Kingsbury; Jeremy Gara and Richard Reed Parry; Chassagne; Sara Neufeld.

Facing Page: Taking the stage at Judson Memorial Church, New York City, February 2007.   Next Page: Chassagne at a Barack Obama rally in Carrboro, N.C., May 2008.

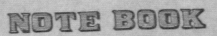

NOTE BOOK

_____

_____

W
80
S

十條製紙物抄中性紙ワールス

Chapter Fourteen

What Goes In Quiet Comes Out Loud

How Merge Got It Right

Facing page: Mac's notebook containing lyrics for Superchunk and Portastatic records from 1993 through 1997.   Previous page: Laura's pencil nub.

In September 2007, Jenny Toomey invited Mac to speak at the Future of Music Coalition's annual policy summit. Toomey cofounded the nonprofit coalition in 2000 as a clearinghouse of information for artists and small labels on how to navigate the massive structural changes underway in the business — the hope was to get independent artists and labels in on the ground floor of the emerging post-CD music world, so musicians would no longer be faced with a choice between signing with a rapacious major label or remaining anonymous and keeping the day job. It was an outgrowth, in spirit at least, of the "Introductory Mechanics Guide to Putting Out Records," which Toomey and Kristin Thomson wrote in 1991 to provide a start-to-finish roadmap for anyone who wanted to make a record, including phone numbers of pressing plants. In 2008, Toomey was named program officer for media and cultural policy at the Ford Foundation, which dispenses more than $500 million in grants each year.

The conference, held in Washington, D.C., drew policy heavyweights. Senators Byron Dorgan (D-N.D.) and Ron Wyden

(D-Ore.) were keynote speakers. Merge was a sponsor, which put it in the company of Microsoft, the National Endowment for the Arts, and XM Radio. Mac was seated on a panel with Bob Mould, Rosemary Carroll, and David Bither, a senior vice president at Nonesuch, the label that had snatched the Magnetic Fields from Merge in 2000.

The future of music, or at least the music business as we know it, was very much an open question at the time, and the introduction to Mac's panel consisted of a bleak recounting of the industry's woes. Record sales were down 14 percent in 2007 from the year before, according to the Recording Industry Association of America; it was the third straight year of declining sales. In 1994, the year *Foolish* was released in the midst of alternative rock hysteria, labels shipped just over 1 billion records into stores; by 2007, that number — including digital sales — was slashed nearly in half, to 555 million. Since 2000, more than 5,000 record-company employees had been laid off. According to *Rolling Stone*, 2,700 record stores had closed up shop in the previous four years (Schoolkids in Chapel Hill made it until 2008 before going under). In 2006, Tower Records went out of business, leaving 89 empty stores, and Musicland, which operated the Sam Goody stores, filed for bankruptcy.

With that apocalyptic scenario in mind, the moderator asked Mac how Merge was weathering the storm. "Business is great for us," Mac said. "The last few years have been our best ever. People may be buying fewer bad records, but I don't see them buying fewer good records."

* * *

Merge's slow and steady two-decade rise from Laura's bedroom to the *Billboard* Top Ten is, in many ways, an object lesson in what went wrong at the major labels. When Mac and Laura started Merge in 1989, the major-label music business was in a slump. Album sales dropped by 6 percent from 1990 to 1991, a decline driven in part by outrageously high prices for compact discs, which the labels had successfully and cynically forced on consumers as a replacement for LPs. Nirvana turned that around — by 1992, sales had shot back up by 11 percent — but the alternative rock boom inaugurated an era of aggressively stupid business practices, as majors paid huge advances to bands based on little more than buzz, and then wrote off the investment the minute the first single failed to get radio play. The record business has always — at least since the dawn of rock'n'roll — been a hit-driven form of glorified gambling, with one big winner covering all the losers. But the "alternative rock" explosion of the mid-nineties intensified that dynamic, because the zero-to-sixty success of Nirvana convinced every executive that a scruffy guy in a cardigan putting pen to paper today could mean bonus-worthy numbers next quarter. Why waste time giving an artist space to grow when The Next Nirvana lurks around every corner?

Most label executives place the blame for the business's current woes squarely at the feet of file-sharers — an excuse that leaves them largely blameless. How can you compete with free, instantly available music? As Danny Goldberg puts it, the concert industry is doing fine these days, largely because if you don't

have a ticket, a beefy guy in a yellow T-shirt that reads STAFF will bodily prevent you from getting in to see a rock show. While the RIAA has been suing people wildly for six years in an effort to frighten the public away from Limewire and other file-sharing services, there's really no one standing in the way of people who want to download a record for free.

But file-sharing is only part of the story. It goes without saying that, had the major labels spent money rationally over the past two decades, they would be better positioned to face leaner years. And the long-term decline in album sales dates to 1995, the zenith of the post-Nirvana frenzy, years before Napster took hold. In all but three of the years that followed — two of which are accounted for by the short-lived ascendancies of Britney Spears and Christina Aguilera — album sales have ticked downward. And it was in the fury of that post-Nirvana frenzy that the major labels threw any credibility as curators of taste, of *cool* — the role of Ahmet Ertegun at Atlantic, and John Hammond when he signed Bruce Springsteen to Columbia, and Seymour Stein when he was shepherding the careers of the Ramones and the Talking Heads at Sire — out the window in pursuit of whatever they thought teenagers wanted to hear. After successive waves of corporate consolidation throughout the nineties, the Sires, Atlantics, and Columbias of the world lived on in name only. Nirvana begat Stone Temple Pilots begat Creed begat Nickelback, and the music that the corporate labels were selling as an authentic revolution from the underground was, with whiplash speed, packaged into a manageable and marketable radio format: Modern Rock.

Glenn Boothe **Literally the number of commercial alternative radio stations went from like 25 to 75 or more after Nirvana. You had the stations flipping formats, so it wasn't like, "Oh, we like your music, let's do this!" It was like, "OK, we're switching tomorrow from country to alternative. What can you do for us?" Overnight, it became a business.**

Little wonder, then, that consumers feel no loyalty to — and show no compunction about "stealing" music from — companies that wear

Merge offices, 1989 to 1991.

Merge offices, 1991 to 1992.

Anybody always likes the idea of an indie label better – dealing with human beings instead of a corporation where you don't know if the person is going to be fired six months after they sign you.

— Danny Goldberg

their cynicism so boldly on their sleeves. And little wonder that Merge — by operating in the margins, and not spending money stupidly, and putting out music that they actually love — could slowly grow to the point where they can compete with the majors for bands, publicity, and consumers, on their own terms.

Mac   We're in the record business, but we're in a different record business than what people think of as "the record business." When we read stories about labels taking people to court for having some MP3s on their computer, or complaining that the industry is going down the tubes because of file-sharing, we don't really relate.

Danny Goldberg   Twenty years ago, a group like Arcade Fire probably would have done what Sonic Youth and Nirvana did, which was leave the indie and go to a major. But now those artists aren't leaving, because there's no advantage to going to the major. Today there's a very even playing field. In fact you can make the argument that a lot of rock artists — having been a manager of artists, most of the people I represent are in this group — want to be on indie labels. Major labels are worse. They fired thousands of people who were in the kind of artist development jobs that were valuable to the development of rock

artists for longer-term planning of a career. Anybody always likes the *idea* of an indie label better — dealing with human beings instead of a corporation where you don't know if the person is going to be fired six months after they sign you. People put up with that corporate culture because there were advantages that the majors had. When they lost those advantages, then the indies were much more attractive. For some artists who wanted to play on a big, mass-appeal stage, there was once really a much better likelihood of getting there on a major. That's not the case today.

Jim Wilbur   I always felt like what Merge was selling was oranges. And the major labels were selling apples. They're just not the same product. There's a lot of blindness, arrogance, apathy — just wrong-headedness. Maybe they don't realize they're selling apples. Maybe they don't even understand what they're trying to sell. Which is why they've done such a shitty job at it lately. Merge managed to do it. And I don't think it's because little elves came out of the woods at night and fixed things for them.

Mac   We've managed to create the business that works for the way we want to do business. Our customers are music fans. Even though we have some records that have sold a lot of copies, we've always seen ourselves as a niche brand. It may be a large niche at times, but at bottom, it's people who love music. And in the record industry, that is a niche. If you ask someone who works for Sony, "Who do you want to sell records to?" they'll say they want to sell them to everyone who has access to a Best Buy. But for us — that's great if those people want what we have. That's awesome and we want them to be able to get it. But we're not swinging for the fences in that way.

Danny Goldberg   There was a time when, for example, Warner Bros. Records, in the seventies and eighties, was incredible. You can go down the list of David Byrne, and Lou Reed, and all sorts of artists that really were nurtured and developed in the major system. You can't say they weren't authentic, sincere artists. They weren't doing schlock hit singles, but there was an economy that provided for that. Out of that, occasionally, an artist like R.E.M. would develop — or U2, or Bob Marley — that didn't make it on their first album. But the money was there to sustain those investments. That's just not there anymore. Merge has done a good job. They still have to deal in a world where it's a lot harder to sell a CD than it used to be. But because they're not part of a huge company, and don't have demand for double-digit profit growth, and never built up these infrastructures, they can survive far better.

Matt Ward (Merge solo artist under the name M. Ward and member of She & Him)   I think it goes back to the amount of trust they put in their artists. They've been, and continue to be, in our shoes. And they just understand that if you need label executives to help you do what you're doing for a living, then maybe you shouldn't be doing it.

Matt Suggs   They don't waste money, trying to impress a band by taking them out to some fancy place in New York. I used to hear about these recording budgets that are just insane. Like $50,000 or $100,000. It used to just blow my mind. Fuck, you know, Merge gives me like $5,000. But that's the reason they lasted. Well, the main reason they've lasted is they've put out good records. But the way that the label has been run, it's a tight ship.

Win Butler   Big labels are so based on a blockbuster model, the Mariah Careys and Jon Bon Jovis of the world end up footing the bill for a lot of stupidly wasteful spending. Like putting Arcade Fire up in hotels and taking them to steak dinners. Thanks Led Zeppelin, for the steak dinner! But when you own your own business, you just can't do it that way. It's like, "Wait a minute, who's paying for this shit? Oh, AC/DC!"

Glenn Boothe   When I worked at Sony, I used to have an $18,000 expense account. And I was expected to spend it. And a lot of times that meant me and my friends went out and ate sushi. Because it's got

to be spent. I used to date this girl who worked for a label, and one day she told me, "Yeah, I needed a Snapple. So I had a friend messenger me one from her office." So instead of going downstairs and buying a Snapple, she spent $20 or whatever to have it messengered.

John Plymale   One group that I was working with that was on a major, the label decided one day, "We've really got to have a meeting. We've got to bring you and Plymale up to New York to come up with a game plan." So we were like, "Great. Just give us a heads up and we'll come up and meet with you." And they said, "Okay let's do it tomorrow morning." And we were like, "Well, we're in North Carolina." And they said, "We'll get you on the first flight in the morning." This was at five in the afternoon. We were both free, but it was going to cost a fortune. Why don't we do it like next week and save six hundred dollars a ticket? So they bought us two $850 plane tickets. We were thinking, "Jesus, that's nuts." We went up, and we get there and basically we hang out with the A&R guy for a couple hours until the big wheel guy that we were going to meet with finally got there. We hung out with him in his office for about half an hour, and talked about everything under the sun *but* the band. And then we had to go catch our flight back. We never really had a meeting! We got phone calls from both of them the next day saying, "Oh, this is awesome. We're so glad you came up. We're really psyched to get going, we're on the same page now." And we were just like, What happened?

Brian McPherson   For a short time, I was an executive at a major label. And a guy would need to come to L.A. for a show from New York, and he'd book himself a $4,000 first-class flight at the last minute. I'd think, "Wow, I could have made three records with that $4,000." Because you had to fly him first class for four and a half hours.

John Plymale   These guys spent about five thousand bucks on one studio day for me to mix one song in New York at Sony Studios. And the A&R guy was there most of that

Laura, Spott, Mac, and John Williams in the Merge office in downtown Carrboro, 1994.

time. Every piece of outboard gear that you would bring in from the storage room there cost like $100 a day to rent. So the A&R guy kept saying, "Is there anything we need to make this mix better?" And I'd say, "I could use another such-and-such." And he'd say, "Well let's see if they got it." And like after about three of those I said, "Are they charging for this?" And he said, "I don't care. We've got the budget for it." And we spent five grand, and we all thought the mix was great. I loved it, the band loved it, the A&R guy loved it. And the crazy thing was, they said, "That is freaking great. This Plymale guy knows what he is doing." So they call me the next week. "So here's what we're going to do: We're going send you and the band to a new studio, and you're going to redo that song from the ground up, because then it will be even better!" So that whole five thousand bucks was just pissed away. They didn't even use it. And the scary thing is that we did rerecord the song, and spent another fortune — and it isn't as good. I really don't speak their language.

Karen Glauber   Because it's not their money. That's why. You don't care. It's all about market share. So you have to spend whatever it's going to take to maintain or grow your market share. So you throw good money after bad and bad money after good. You're just going to chase after whatever you think is going to sell at any given moment. You're not taking a long view. The old equation was you have three CDs to really break a band. Now they need to sell a lot of records out of the box or they're done. Two percent of all major-label records recoup.

Glenn Boothe   Bands might want to be on *a* major label, but they don't want to be on *the* major label. So basically it's, "Who's got the most cash?" So you end up spending all this money to sign the band, and now you've got these huge expectations, which aren't really based on the band's past — they're based on how much you spent to sign them. So the band has all this debt to the label, and all these expectations. It's almost a lose-lose situation before you even make your record.

Karen Glauber   If your record doesn't happen in six weeks, you're done. That would not occur to Mac and Laura. So if it takes me six months to get a record on the radio, it's going to take me six months. We've been working the latest Spoon record for a year now. No one works a record for a year.

Aaron Stauffer   It was kind of funny, because when Merge put out *Actions and Indications*, they gave us $2,000, and we made the record. But we'd already been paid almost $100,000 by Hollywood just for living expenses.

Peter Margasak   I can't think of anything they've done on Merge — even with some of the huge projects — they've never done anything stupid, like any kind of dumb promotional bullshit. They've never wasted money, they always work within their means, and that's the way Touch and Go did it. I think they like that control.

Karen Glauber   Merge has remained very lean. Mac's not driving a Bentley. It's a very frugal label, and they put the money back into the building, or signing bands. It's not flashy. So I think that's why, regardless of whether or not there's an Arcade Fire record next year or the year after, they're going to be fine.

Jenny Toomey   Laura is tremendously concerned with it financially. In the same way that it made Laura nervous to get up and rock on stage, it made her very nervous to overextend herself at all.

Matt Suggs   It's funny talking to Mac and Laura whenever you're planning something. Mac's always like, "Yeah man, let's just do this, let's do that." But then when you talk to Laura about the actual money that it's going to take to bring these ideas to fruition, it's like a whole different tax bracket. Mac might be saying one thing, but then you've got to talk to Laura, because she's going to be like, "I don't know." And that's the reason they never had these bullshit expenses.

Bill Mooney   At one point, Laura was using a pencil at Merge that she had had since high school, that was only like this big. And people would be like, "Do you want a new pencil?" and she'd say, "No, I have had this one forever." I think they're just very conservative in some ways. And very mature beyond their years.

Laura   I use them. Until they're gone. I don't remember that particular pencil nub.

Ron Liberti   They're so open with everything. They were very transparent. And they made it clear, any time you want to come up and look at the books, feel free. If I had a question about anything, they'd say, "Well, here are the numbers." Even though we're the same age, they were almost like my older brother and sister. Not only were they genius musicians, but they had a bit of a business sense about them. It didn't seem like they were ever trying to bite off more than they could chew.

Frank Heath   They've always been very — I wouldn't say frugal — but sensible about finances, and about not wasting money. When they booked Lambchop at the Carolina Theatre for the Merge 15th anniversary festival, they knew Lambchop's not the biggest drawing band. They weren't expecting the place to sell out, and it didn't. But they felt like that was the best way to present that show. And so when it's important to them to do something a certain way, because they feel like it's in the best interest of the artist — or just the best interest of the crowd — they'll do it. They don't say, "Oh, let's just throw Lambchop in this coffeehouse down the street. That'll save us $5,000." They pick their spots.

Matt Ward   One thing that's similar about all major labels is that they're the ones responsible for putting singers' faces in your local weekly newspaper who you've never seen before. And you wish you hadn't, you know? Whereas independent labels don't do that. They rely on the strength of the music, and not the strength of the marketability of somebody's face, or clothes. And I'm really happy to be working with people that have the faith that the public responds well to

Merge offices, 1996 to 2001.

music that sparks their imagination, as opposed to bad publicity photos that spark the darker recesses of your mind.

*   *   *

Rock'n'roll was first harnessed not in the executive suites of RCA or EMI but by independent regional labels such as Vee-Jay Records, the Chicago label founded by husband-and-wife team Vivian Carter and James Bracken that was the first label to release the Beatles in the U.S. (Capitol, the American arm of the Beatles' British label, EMI, refused), and Sam Phillips's Sun Records in Memphis, Tenn. The giant labels failed completely to see rock'n'roll coming, then eventually went on a buying spree when the more nimble and perceptive indies struck gold with acts such as Chuck Berry and the Four Seasons. As soon as the big boys had locked up the majority of the emerging talent, they set about colluding with radio promoters to ensure that DJs around the nation were playing their songs. The payola scandals of the 1950s altered ever-so-slightly the contours of those relationships, but the

fundamentals remain to this day — labels found ways to get stations to play the songs the labels wanted played. They also built massive, nationwide distribution networks to warehouse and move around records that all of a sudden were becoming nationwide hits, and needed to be in record stores in both Scranton and Sacramento at the same time. Those chokeholds — over talent, radio, and distribution — ensured that the dominant forces in American popular music for the past forty years were corporate labels.

Those chokeholds are rapidly disappearing, which is why a band like Sonic Youth, which was one of the first indie bands to go corporate when they signed to Geffen in 1990, decided in 2008 after a nearly two-decade run at the label to jump to Matador. When a label like Merge is able to hold on to bands like Spoon and the Arcade Fire in the face of intense pressure from major labels willing to spend much more money than is rational to sign them, the majors no longer wield the leverage over potential blockbuster acts that they used to. When the number of CDs shipped has fallen by 45 percent over seven years and digital sales have increased nearly ten-fold since 2004, then physical distribution of records has become less crucial to success. And when radio listenership is down 13 percent in the past decade, while the internet radio audience is up 600 percent and nearly a third of American adults and teenagers use MP3 players, then traditional radio isn't the platform for selling records that it used to be. If rock'n'roll had erupted in a world of digital distribution, there would have been no reason for Elektra — once an indie — to sell out to Warner Communications in 1970. For decades, Merge was an outlier and holdout in a corporate-dominated business; as the behemoths fail, it could become a forerunner in the devolution of the music business back to the sort of small, competitive independent labels that made rock'n'roll possible.

Mac and Laura aren't necessarily thrilled at the prospect. They make no bold predictions about the future of the industry, but the notion of a purely digital music world is anathema to them: They started a label with the satisfaction and romance of physically assembling records in Laura's bedroom.

Mac   **Our whole thing has always been that our fans are like us. And a lot of them tend to want the actual item with the artwork, and they tend to like shopping in record stores. And it seems to have worked out so far. I still like shopping in record stores — I download music, too, and I buy music online, but I'd rather be in a record store. We count on the people who buy our records as being like us in that respect.**

But the number of people who like to shop in record stores is falling. Merge's digital sales, both through iTunes and Merge's own digital store, account for roughly 30 percent of their total sales, nearly twice the industry average. To bridge the gap between the old world of musty record bins and the new one of iPods, in 2005 Merge became the first label to sell what they call "LP3s" — every customer who buys a vinyl record of a Merge release (they still sell roughly 3 to 5 percent of each release on vinyl) also gets a free digital download of the same record. It's a way to give vinyl lovers the flexibility of being able to carry

their music around with them, but it's also a way to give digital customers the physicality that used to be so central to the experience of listening to music. A resurgent desire for the old-fashioned rootedness in music that has driven, in part, Merge's success — the almost-disappeared ritual of getting up off the couch and finding the record that you want to hear, then putting it on the turntable to listen to for a full thirty-five minutes — has resulted in a miniboom for vinyl of late. Though it is still a negligible part of the overall record business, shipments of LPs jumped 36 percent in 2007 according to the RIAA, and revenue to labels from vinyl sales was up 10 percent in 2006 and nearly 50 percent in 2007. The only sectors of the business showing significant growth are the outdated technology of LPs and the new technology of digital files. In ten years, there might still be record stores, just not CD stores.

Still, if the CD does fall by the wayside, the vast majority of Merge's customers will want to buy music digitally, a prospect that has Mac and Laura trying to figure out how to instill in that experience some of the sense of surprise and connection that purchasers of *evil i do not* felt when a ripped-up piece of a random photograph fell out of the box.

Mac   **I feel like there's a little bit of a distance there with MP3s and digital music. Something goes in your iPod and just kind of gets lost a little bit. But if people make a decision that this is how they want to get my music, we have to figure out a way to deliver the art, and the liner notes, and the stuff that you get with a CD now. We have to figure out ways to not make it feel distant.**

Whatever the future holds for the music business, Mac and Laura aren't too occupied with trying to figure it out. Merge didn't get where it is by planning for the future, or concocting growth strategies, or trying to get out ahead of its competitors. It simply tried to find music that Mac and Laura loved, and sell it to people who also loved it.

Mac   **We've never had a five-year plan. We never set goals of where we want to be, or how we're going to tackle changes in the business. We just kind of kept our head** down and did what we've always done. And stuff happens, and all of a sudden you're in the middle of it. It seems to have worked okay for us. But it is scary sometimes. Now there are so many people working here, and there's all this overhead. What if, all of a sudden, for three years, we only have records that sell 5,000 copies each?

Laura   At this point, we have artists coming to us that formerly would have only been interested in being on a major label, which really tells me that people are fleeing that model like rats from a sinking ship, and that we somehow represent how a record label should work. At least in their minds. But as Merge becomes more successful, I find myself wary that we may start making some of the same mistakes that the majors have. Because of our track record, when we start to negotiate with bands about putting out a record, their expectations are higher. And their demands are greater. And the more records you sell, the more money you are expected to spend. Sooner or later, that is going to turn around and bite you in the ass. We can't get away with being as conservative as we used to be, and it makes it a lot more difficult to have this same old Merge philosophy and be firm about it: "We're going to give you as little advance as possible, and you're going to like it! And we're not going to pay mechanicals and you're going to like it! And if you want us to put your record out, you just better love Merge!"

* * *

After East River Pipe's short-lived dalliance with EMI, Fred Cornog and Barbara Powers got out of their apartment in Queens and found a nice little house in suburban New Jersey. Cornog cleaned himself up, he and Powers had a baby daughter, and Cornog kept making bedroom masterpieces for Merge. They sold what they sold — certainly not enough to live on — and Cornog got a job in the flooring department of the Home Depot near his house to make up the difference. His most recent dispatch, *Garbageheads on Endless Stun* (2003), a song cycle about addiction, was called "gentle, smart, and unspeakably sad" by *The New York Times*.

The strange and touching discordance of Cornog's life — the guy in the orange smock at Home Depot is also the guy who gets profiled in *New York* magazine and writes exquisitely crafted songs that have touched the lives of thousands and will live on long after he is gone — is, like the regular-guys-can-make-music-too ethic at work in Lambchop, probably the best argument there is for what makes Merge special. The nobility and beauty in making art out of sound is found in the *work*, and in the records, not the imagined lifestyle that our pop culture teaches us ought to accompany it. Cornog may or may not have been able to achieve stardom. But he had the opportunity to try — Kurt Cobain's A&R guy was practically begging him to — and he decided not to. In the prefabricated narrative of how rock works, that would have been the end of it. Cornog would only work at Home Depot, and perhaps still record on that eight-track in his bedroom. But, having turned away the major-label contracts, he would have also forsaken the ability to make records. In the Merge narrative, you can do both.

Not long ago, while Cornog was at work, a gaggle of scruffy kids — "Nigel Tufnel types," Cornog called them — came into the flooring department. They were in a band, and they wanted to hang up carpets in their practice space as soundproofing. They were talking excitedly amongst themselves, as Cornog cut the carpet for them, about a recent record deal they'd struck with Warner Bros., and about how their song would appear on the soundtrack to *Transformers*. They had no idea that the guy sectioning off carpet for them was a masterful pop songwriter, or that — even if they'd never heard of East River Pipe — he was on the record label that put out Spoon and the Arcade Fire. Cornog tried to seem politely impressed at their major-label deal, and sent them on their way.

F.M. Cornog   It's almost as if I had gone out with their girlfriend, and I know what she's really like. It's not going to end up how they think it's going to end up.

* * *

Facing page: The suitcase — called "the Janvii" because it was a jade-colored Anvil case — that served as Bricks' drumkit and Superchunk's cable case. Next page: Merge's Durham office.

Postscript

In February 2009, as this book was going to press, Corey Rusk announced that Touch and Go was discontinuing its production and distribution service to twenty-two labels and laying off some staffers. "It's not coming to an end," he said in a statement, "but it won't be the same company it has been for the last twenty years." Rusk cited the economic downturn as the prime factor behind Touch and Go's retrenchment; as sales of physical CDs decline, distributors are particularly hard-hit because they get the downside of lower sales volume without the upside of increased digital revenue, which goes exclusively to the labels. Rusk says Touch and Go will continue to release records as an ordinary label if not the indie conglomerate that it had been. Touch and Go is one of the most tightly and conscientiously managed independent record labels ever founded, and its setbacks are a blow to anyone who cares about music and a troubling omen for the prospects of other indie labels in the face of a prolonged recession. We hope Touch and Go continues to put out amazing records.

Acknowledgments

We would of course like to thank everyone who patiently spent hours sharing their thoughts and recollections about Merge and took our frantic calls begging them to rifle through their closets for old photographs, but doing so by name would require more space than we have. So to everyone whose words or images appear in this book, as well as to those who were interviewed but not quoted: Thank you.

Additionally, Mac and Laura would like to thank our families, friends, Merge artists, and everyone who has ever worked with Merge or shared a van with Superchunk.

And John Cook would like to thank David Kuhn for introducing him to this project, Allison Benedikt and Harold Cook for putting up with this project, Matt Cook for teaching him how to fall in love with records, and Mac McCaughan, Laura Ballance, Jim Wilbur, and Jon Wurster for Superchunk.

Merge Records
Discography, 1989 to 2009

MRG001   Bricks, *Winterspring* (cassette), June 1, 1989

MRG002   Wwax, *Live / Left* (cassette), July 1, 1989

MRG003   Metal Pitcher, "A Careful Workman Is the Best Safety Device" (7-inch), September 1, 1989

MRG004   Chunk, "What Do I" b/w "My Noise" and "The Train from Kansas City" (7-inch), December 1989

MRG005   Bricks, "Girl with the Carrot Skin" b/w "The Mountain Goes to Mohammed" and "The Sturgeon" (7-inch), 1990

MRG006   Angels of Epistemology, Untitled (7-inch), 1990

MRG007   Superchunk, "Slack Motherfucker" b/w "Night Creatures" (7-inch), April 1990

MRG008   Wwax, "Like It or Not" (double 7-inch), October 1990

MRG009   Erectus Monotone, "Vertigogo" b/w "En Este Momente" and "Bakin' Bread" (7-inch), October 1990

MRG010   Breadwinner, "232 S. Laurel St" (7-inch), October 1990

MRG012   Finger, "Everywhere" b/w "Awful Truth" (7-inch), November 1990

MRG013   Pure, "Ballard" (7-inch), April 1991

MRG014   Superchunk, "Cool" b/w "Fishing" (7-inch), February 1991

MRG015   Coral, "Filling a Hole" b/w "Your Reward" and "Snow" (7-inch), May 1991

MRG016   Erectus Monotone, "Cathode Gumshoe" (7-inch), May 1991

MRG017   Breadwinner, " " b/w "Prescott" and "Mac's Oranges" (7-inch), August 1991

MRG018   Superchunk, "The Freed Seed" (7-inch), August 1991

MRG019   Seam, "Granny 9x" b/w "Look Back in Anger" (7-inch), March 1992

MRG020   Superchunk, *Tossing Seeds: Singles 89–91,* April 1, 1992

MRG021   Polvo / Erectus Monotone, "El Cid" (split 7-inch), March 1992

MRG022   Polvo, *Cor-Crane Secret,* July 13, 1992

MRG023   Drive Like Jehu, "Bullet Train to Vegas" b/w "Hand over Fist" (7-inch), April 1992

MRG024   Fuckers, "Quick Cash" b/w "Coming Home" (7-inch), April 1992

MRG025   Bricks, "The Getting Wet Part" (7-inch), July 1992

MRG026   Honor Role, "Purgatory" b/w "Jank" (7-inch), August 1992

MRG027   Superchunk, "Mower" b/w "On the Mouth" (7-inch), October 19, 1992

MRG028   Erectus Monotone, "Glider" b/w "Soul Taker" (7-inch), October 1992

MRG029   Butterglory, "Alexander Bends" (7-inch), October 1992

MRG030   Bricks, *A Microphone and a Box of Dirt,* November 16, 1992

MRG031 Angels of Epistemology, *Fruit,* November 16, 1992

MRG033 Alf Danielson, "Mary Had a Steamboat" b/w "Glover" (7-inch), October 1992

MRG034 Superchunk, "The Question Is How Fast" b/w "Forged It" and "100,000 Fireflies" (7-inch), January 11, 1993

MRG035 Rocket from the Crypt, "Pigeon Eater" b/w "(The) Paste that You Love" (7-inch), March 1993

MRG036 The Renderers, "A Million Lights" b/w "Primitive Country" (7-inch), February 1993

MRG037 Pipe, "Ashtray" b/w "Warsaw" (7-inch), March 1993

MRG038 Polvo, "Tilebreaker" b/w "The Chameleon" and "Tiara Fetish" (7-inch), February 1993

MRG039 The 6ths, "Heaven in a Black Leather Jacket" b/w "Rot in the Sun" (7-inch), March 1993

MRG040 Polvo, *Today's Active Lifestyles,* April 19, 1993

MRG041 Honor Role, *Album,* April 1, 1997

MRG042 Meanies, "Rhyming Logic" b/w "Operator" and "Darkside of My Mind" (7-inch), August 1993

MRG043 3Ds, "Beautiful Things" b/w "Summer Stone" (7-inch), July 1993

MRG044 Erectus Monotone, *Close Up* EP, August 16, 1993

MRG045 Coral, "Boxtruck" b/w "Half the Time" (7-inch), October 1993

MRG046 Butterglory, "Our Heads" (7-inch), October 1993

MRG047 Superchunk, "Ribbon" b/w "Who Needs Light" (7-inch), February 1994

MRG048 Lambchop, "Nine" b/w "Moody Fucker" (7-inch), February 1994

MRG049 Rocket From the Crypt, "Ufo>Ufo>Ufo" b/w "Birdman" (7-inch), April 1994

MRG050 Superchunk, "Precision Auto Part 2" b/w "Precision Auto Part 3" (7-inch), April 1994

MRG051 Portastatic, *I Hope Your Heart Is Not Brittle,* February 14, 1994

MRG052 Breadwinner, *Burner* EP, March 14, 1994

MRG52.5 Breadwinner, "Supplementary Cig" (7-inch), March 1994

MRG053 Archers of Loaf, "What Did You Expect" b/w "Ethel Merman" (7-inch), January 1994

MRG054 Pipe, "Human Gutterball" b/w "Figure 8" (7-inch), January 1994

MRG055 The Magnetic Fields, *The Charm of the Highway Strip,* April 18, 1994

MRG056 Polvo, *Celebrate the New Dark Age* EP, May 2, 1994

MRG057 Squirrel Nut Zippers, "Roasted Right" (7-inch), May 1994

MRG058 Bats, "Live At WFMU" (7-inch), May 1994

MRG059 Superchunk, "The First Part" (7-inch), March 14, 1994

MRG060 Superchunk, *Foolish,* April 18, 1994

MRG061 Velocity Girl, "Your Silent Face" b/w "You're So Good to Me" (7-inch), May 1994

MRG062 Labradford, "Julius" b/w "Columna De La Independencia" (7-inch), July 25, 1994

MRG063 Odes, "Meltaway" b/w "Honey Gets Hard" (7-inch), June 20, 1994

MRG064 3Ds, "Hey Seuss" b/w "River Burial" (7-inch), March 1994

MRG065 3Ds, *Venus Trail,* May 2, 1994

MRG066 Lambchop, "Soaky in the Pooper" (7-inch), July 25, 1994

MRG067 Various Artists, *Rows of Teeth,* July 25, 1994

MRG068 Cornershop, "Born Disco, Died Heavy Metal" (7-inch), November 15, 1994

MRG069 Superchunk, "Driveway to Driveway" (7-inch), October 24, 1994

MRG070 Lambchop, *I Hope You're Sitting Down,* September 19, 1994

MRG071 Butterglory, *Crumble,* October 3, 1994

MRG072 The Mad Scene, *The Greatest Time* EP, October 1994

MRG073 The Magnetic Fields, "All the Umbrellas in London" b/w "Rats in the Garbage of the Western World" (7-inch), October 1994

MRG074 Cornershop, *Hold On It Hurts,* January 23, 1995

MRG075 The Magnetic Fields, *The Wayward Bus / Distant Plastic Trees,* January 23, 1995

MRG076 East River Pipe, "Bring On the Loser" (7-inch), March 1995

MRG077 The Mad Scene, *Sealight,* May 8, 1995

MRG078 Spent, *Songs of Drinking and Rebellion,* March 6, 1995

MRG079 Cakekitchen, *Stompin' thru the Boneyard,* March 6, 1995

MRG080 Portastatic, *Scrapbook* EP, March 6, 1995

MRG081 East River Pipe, *Poor Fricky,* May 8, 1995

MRG082 Guv'ner, "Knight Moves" (double 7-inch), June 19, 1995

MRG083   Bio Ritmo, "Piraguero" b/w "Asia Minor" (7-inch), August 29, 1995

MRG084   Butterglory, "Wait for Me" (double 7-inch), June 19, 1995

MRG085   Superchunk, *Incidental Music: 1991–1995,* June 20, 1995

MRG086   Portastatic, *Slow Note from a Sinking Ship,* June 20, 1995

MRG087   Butterglory, *Downed,* July 25, 1995

MRG088   Verbena, "I Say So" b/w "Silver Queen" (7-inch), June 20, 1995

MRG089   Superchunk, "Hyper Enough" (7-inch), August 29, 1995

MRG090   Superchunk, *Here's Where the Strings Come In,* September 19, 1995

MRG091   The Magnetic Fields, *Get Lost,* September 19, 1995

MRG092   The Wedding Present , "Sucker" b/w "Waiting on the Guns" (7-inch), October 24, 1995

MRG093   The Karl Hendricks Trio, "What Everyone Else Calls Fun" (7-inch), October 24, 1995

MRG094   The Karl Hendricks Trio, *Some Girls Like Cigarettes,* September 19, 1995

MRG095   Polvo, *This Eclipse* EP, November 14, 1995

MRG096   Verbena, "Everyday Shoes" (7-inch), October 24, 1995

MRG097   Lambchop, *How I Quit Smoking,* January 30, 1996

MRG098   Butterglory, *Are You Building a Temple In Heaven?,* February 20, 1996

MRG099   Odes, *Me and My Big Mouth,* February 20, 1996

MRG100   Various Artists, *Merge 100,* April 22, 1997

MRG101   Cakekitchen, *Bald Old Bear* EP, January 30, 1996

MRG102   Verbena, *Pilot Park,* January 30, 1996

MRG103   Neutral Milk Hotel, *On Avery Island,* March 26, 1996

MRG104   Butterglory, "She's Got the Akshun!" (CD single), January 30, 1996

MRG105   Spent, "Revenging" b/w "Foreign Like a Car" (7-inch) March 26, 1996

MRG106   The Mad Scene, *Chinese Honey* EP, March 26, 1996

MRG107   The Karl Hendricks Trio, *For a While, It Was Funny,* May 21, 1996

MRG108   Lambchop, *Hank* EP, July 9, 1996

MRG109   Guv'ner, *The Hunt,* August 20, 1996

MRG110   East River Pipe, "Kill the Action" (CD single), July 30, 1996

MRG111   East River Pipe, *Mel,* September 10, 1996

MRG112   Guv'ner, "Break a Promise" (CD single), July 30, 1996

MRG113   Cakekitchen, *The Devil and the Deep Blue Sea,* October 1, 1996

MRG114   Spent, *A Seat Beneath the Chairs,* October 1, 1997

MRG115   Verbena, *Souls For Sale,* April 1, 1997

MRG116   Spent, "Umbrella Wars" (CD single), September 10, 1996

MRG117   Portastatic, "Spying on the Spys" b/w "Do You Want To Buy a Bridge?" (7-inch), November 1, 1996

MRG118   Superchunk, *The Laughter Guns* EP, October 22, 1996

MRG119   The Third Eye Foundation, *Ghost,* April 22, 1997

MRG120   Portastatic, *The Nature of Sap,* March 11, 1997

MRG121   The Ladybug Transistor, *Beverley Atonale,* February 11, 1997

MRG122   Beatnik Filmstars, "Off-White Noize" (7-inch), May 27, 1997

MRG123   Pipe, *Slowboy,* July 8, 1997

MRG124   Lambchop, "Cigaretiquette" b/w "Mr. Crabby" (7-inch), May 27, 1997

MRG125   Beatnik Filmstars, *Inhospitable,* September 9, 1997

MRG126   Lambchop, "Whitey" b/w "Playboy, the Shit" (7-inch), July 8, 1997

MRG127   The Gothic Archies, *The New Despair* EP, November 4, 1997

MRG128   Superchunk, "Watery Hands" (7-inch) July 8, 1997

MRG129   Superchunk, *Indoor Living,* September 9, 1997

MRG130   Lambchop, *Thriller,* September 23, 1997

MRG131   Shark Quest, "Blontzo's Revenge" b/w "Pig River Minor" (7-inch) October 14, 1997

MRG132   The Rock*a*Teens, "Turn On the Waterworks" (7-inch), October 14, 1997

MRG133   Butterglory, *Rat Tat Tat,* October 14, 1997

MRG134   The Third Eye Foundation, *The Sound of Violence* EP, November 25, 1997

MRG135 The Karl Hendricks Trio, "The Worst Coffee I've Ever Had Part I" b/w "Out On The Weekend" (7-inch), November 25, 1997

MRG136 Neutral Milk Hotel, *In the Aeroplane Over the Sea,* February 20, 1998

MRG137 The Karl Hendricks Trio, *Declare Your Weapons,* February 20, 1998

MRG138 Dynamic Truths, "You Take It All" b/w "Exit Screaming" (7-inch), April 21, 1998

MRG139 Shark Quest, *Battle of the Loons,* March 10, 1998

MRG140 The Rock*a*Teens, *Baby, A Little Rain Must Fall,* April 21, 1998

MRG141 The Ladybug Transistor, "Today Knows" b/w "Massachusetts" (7-inch), April 21, 1998

MRG142 Guv'ner, *Spectral Worship,* August 11, 1998

MRG143 The Magnetic Fields, "I Don't Believe You" b/w "When I'm Not Looking, You're Not There" (7-inch) July 21, 1998

MRG144 Pram, *The North Pole Radio Station,* July 21, 1998

MRG145 Beatnik Filmstars, *Boss Disque,* August 11, 1998

MRG146 Lambchop, *What Another Man Spills,* September 8, 1998

MRG147 Ganger, *Hammock Style,* September 29, 1998

MRG148 Superchunk, "The Majestic" b/w "Reg" (7-inch), February 9, 1999

MRG149 The Third Eye Foundation, *You Guys Kill Me,* October 20, 1998

MRG150 Seaweed, *Actions And Indications,* January 12, 1999

MRG151 The Magnetic Fields, *Holiday,* January 12, 1999

MRG152 The Magnetic Fields, *House of Tomorrow,* January 12, 1999

MRG153 Ashley Stove, *New Scars,* February 9, 1999

MRG154 The Ladybug Transistor, *The Albemarle Sound,* March 23, 1999

MRG155 The Rock*a*Teens, *Golden Time,* March 23, 1999

MRG156 Versus, *Afterglow* EP, February 16, 1999

MRG157 Spaceheads, *Angel Station,* March 23, 1999

MRG158 The Music Tapes, *First Imaginary Symphony for Nomad,* July 6, 1999

MRG159 Superchunk, "Hello Hawk" (CD single), July 6, 1999

MRG160 Spinanes, *Imp Years* EP, April 4, 2000

MRG161 Various Artists, *Oh, Merge,* July 6, 1999

MRG162 Superchunk, *Superchunk,* August 10, 1999

MRG163 Superchunk, *Come Pick Me Up,* August 10, 1999

MRG164 East River Pipe, *The Gasoline Age,* August 10, 1999

MRG165 Superchunk, *No Pocky For Kitty,* August 10, 1999

MRG166 The Magnetic Fields, *69 Love Songs, Vol. 1,* June 8, 1999

MRG167 The Magnetic Fields, *69 Love Songs, Vol. 2,* June 8, 1999

MRG168 The Magnetic Fields, *69 Love Songs, Vol. 3,* June 8, 1999

MRG169 The Magnetic Fields, *69 Love Songs,* June 8, 1999

MRG170 Superchunk, *On the Mouth,* August 10, 1999

MRG171 . . . And You Will Know Us By the Trail of Dead, *Madonna,* October 19, 1999

MRG172 Ganger, *Canopy* EP, September 14, 1999

MRG173 Superchunk, "1,000 Pounds" (CD single), February 8, 2000

MRG174 The Third Eye Foundation, *Little Lost Soul,* February 8, 2000

MRG175 Lambchop, *Nixon,* February 8, 2000

MRG176 Versus, "Shangri-La" (CD single), April 25, 2000

MRG177 Matt Suggs, *Golden Days Before They End,* June 6, 2000

MRG178 Future Bible Heroes, *I'm Lonely (And I Love It)* EP, July 18, 2000

MRG179 Shark Quest, *Man on Stilts,* August 8, 2000

MRG180 Portastatic, *De Mel, De Melão* EP, May 9, 2000

MRG181 The Rock*a*Teens, *Sweet Bird of Youth,* October 3, 2000

MRG182 Paul Burch and The WPA Ball Club, *Blue Notes,* August 8, 2000

MRG183 Spaceheads, *Pressure,* June 4, 2002

MRG184 Pram, *The Museum of Imaginary Animals,* September 5, 2000

MRG185 The 6ths, *Hyacinths and Thistles,* September 5, 2000

MRG186 Versus, *Hurrah,* October 3, 2000

MRG187 The Clientele, *Suburban Light,* April 24, 2001

MRG188 The Clean, *Getaway,* August 21, 2001

MRG189 The Ladybug Transistor, *Argyle Heir,* May 22, 2001

MRG190 Portastatic, *Looking for Leonard,* May 22, 2001

MRG191 Spoon, *Loveways* EP, October 17, 2000

MRG192 Ashley Stove, *All Summer Long,* March 23, 2001

MRG193 Annie Hayden, *The Rub,* February 20, 2001

MRG194 Pram, *Somniloquy* EP, August 21, 2001

MRG195 Spoon, *Girls Can Tell,* February 20, 2001

MRG196 Paul Burch, *Last of My Kind,* April 24, 2001

MRG197 David Kilgour, *A Feather in the Engine,* January 22, 2002

MRG198 Superchunk, "Late Century Dream" (CD single), August 21, 2001

MRG199 The Third Eye Foundation, *I Poo Poo on Your Juju,* May 22, 2001

MRG200 Lambchop, *Tools in the Dryer,* September 18, 2001

MRG201 Superchunk, *Here's to Shutting Up,* September 18, 2001

MRG202 The Clientele, *A Fading Summer,* October 23, 2001

MRG203 East River Pipe, *Shining Hours in a Can,* March 19, 2002

MRG204 Lambchop, *Is a Woman,* February 19, 2002

MRG205 Stephin Merritt, *Eban and Charley,* January 22, 2002

MRG206 Imperial Teen, *On,* April 9, 2002

MRG207 Superchunk, "Art Class" (CD single), April 9, 2002

MRG208 Crooked Fingers, *Reservoir Songs* EP, May 7, 2002

MRG209 Radar Brothers, *And the Surrounding Mountains,* May 7, 2002

MRG210 Portastatic Featuring Ken Vandermark and Tim Mulvenna, *A Perfect Little Door* EP, October 23, 2001

MRG211 Spoon, *A Series Of Sneaks,* June 4, 2002

MRG212 Eric Bachmann, *Short Careers: Music from the Film Ball of Wax,* August 20, 2002

MRG213 Spoon, "Someone Something" (7-inch), July 23, 2002

MRG214 The Clientele, "Haunted Melody" b/w "Fear Of Falling" (7-inch), November 5, 2002

MRG215 Spoon, *Kill the Moonlight,* August 20, 2002

MRG216 Various Artists, *Survive and Advance, Vol. 1,* July 23, 2002

MRG217 The Clientele, *The Violet Hour,* July 8, 2003

MRG218 Destroyer, *This Night,* October 8, 2002

MRG219 Various Artists, *Survive and Advance, Vol. 2,* February 18, 2003

MRG220 The Clean, *Anthology,* January 21, 2003

MRG221 Superchunk, *Cup of Sand,* August 19, 2003

MRG222 Crooked Fingers, *Red Devil Dawn,* January 21, 2003

MRG223 M. Ward, *Transfiguration of Vincent,* March 18, 2003

MRG224 Pram, *Dark Island,* February 18, 2003

MRG225 Portastatic, *Summer of the Shark,* April 8, 2003

MRG226 Matt Suggs, *Amigo Row,* August 19, 2003

MRG227 The Buzzcocks, *Buzzcocks,* March 18, 2003

MRG228 Essex Green, *The Long Goodbye,* April 8, 2003

MRG229 The Ladybug Transistor, *The Ladybug Transistor,* October 7, 2003

MRG230 Superchunk, *Crowding Up Your Visual Field* (DVD), January 20, 2004

MRG231 Various Artists, *Survive and Advance, Vol. 3,* July 29, 2003

MRG232 Matt Elliott, *The Mess We've Made,* May 6, 2003

MRG233 David Kilgour, *Frozen Orange,* August 24, 2004

MRG234 East River Pipe, *Garbageheads on Endless Stun,* September 9, 2003

MRG235 The Rosebuds, *The Rosebuds Make Out,* October 7, 2003

MRG236 Portastatic, *Autumn Was a Lark* EP, October 7, 2003

MRG237 Karl Hendricks Trio, *The Jerk Wins Again,* July 29, 2003

MRG238 Destroyer, *Your Blues,* March 9, 2004

MRG239   Camera Obscura, *Underachievers Please Try Harder,* January 20, 2004
MRG240   Lambchop, *Aw C'mon,* February 17, 2004
MRG241   Lambchop, *No You C'mon,* February 17, 2004
MRG242   Shark Quest, *Gods And Devils,* August 24, 2004
MRG243   Dinosaur, *Dinosaur,* March 22, 2005
MRG244   Dinosaur Jr., *You're Living All Over Me,* March 22, 2005
MRG245   Dinosaur Jr., *Bug,* March 22, 2005
MRG248   Crooked Fingers, *Dignity and Shame,* February 22, 2005
MRG249   Richard Buckner, *Dents and Shells,* October 12, 2004
MRG250   Various Artists, *Old Enough to Know Better,* July 13, 2004
MRG251   Radar Brothers, *Fallen Leaf Pages,* March 22, 2005
MRG252   American Music Club, *Love Songs for Patriots,* October 12, 2004
MRG253   The Arcade Fire, "Neighborhood #1 (Tunnels)" (7-inch), June 8, 2004
MRG254   Lou Barlow, *Emoh,* January 25, 2005
MRG255   The Arcade Fire, *Funeral,* September 14, 2004
MRG256   Camera Obscura, *Biggest Bluest Hifi,* October 12, 2004
MRG257   Lambchop and Hands Off Cuba, *Colab* EP, October 11, 2005
MRG258   Destroyer, *Notorious Lightning and Other Works* EP, January 25, 2005
MRG259   The Rosebuds, *The Rosebuds Unwind* EP, April 12, 2005
MRG260   M. Ward, *Transistor Radio,* February 22, 2005
MRG261   Tenement Halls, *Knitting Needles and Bicycle Bells,* August 23, 2005
MRG262   Teenage Fanclub, *Man-Made,* June 7, 2005
MRG263   Portastatic, *Bright Ideas,* August 23, 2005
MRG264   The Rosebuds, *Birds Make Good Neighbors,* September 13, 2005
MRG265   Spoon, *Gimme Fiction,* May 10, 2005
MRG266   Annie Hayden, *The Enemy of Love,* September 13, 2005
MRG267   The Clientele, *Strange Geometry,* October 11, 2005
MRG268   Destroyer, *Destroyer's Rubies,* February 20, 2006
MRG269   The Arcade Fire, *The Arcade Fire* EP, July 12, 2005
MRG270   Arcade Fire, *Mirror Noir* (standard DVD), March 10, 2009
MRG271   East River Pipe, *What Are You On?,* January 24, 2006
MRG272   Robert Pollard, *From a Compound Eye,* January 24, 2006
MRG273   Spoon, "Sister Jack," (CD single), November 8, 2005
MRG274   Lambchop, *The Decline of Country and Western Civilization Part II: The Woodwind Years,* April 11, 2006
MRG275   The Arcade Fire, "Cold Wind" (7-inch), August 9, 2005
MRG276   Camera Obscura, *Let's Get Out of This Country,* June 6, 2006
MRG277   Portastatic, *Who Loves the Sun,* June 6, 2006
MRG278   Essex Green, *Cannibal Sea,* March 21, 2006
MRG279   Richard Buckner, *Meadow,* September 12, 2006
MRG280   M. Ward, *Post-War,* August 22, 2006
MRG281   White Whale, *WWI,* July 25, 2006
MRG282   Robert Pollard, *Normal Happiness,* October 10, 2006
MRG283   Portastatic, *Be Still Please,* October 10, 2006
MRG284   Lambchop, *Damaged,* August 22, 2006
MRG285   The Arcade Fire, *Neon Bible,* March 6, 2007
MRG286   Camera Obscura, *Lloyd, I'm Ready to Be Heartbroken,* May 9, 2006
MRG287   David Kilgour, *The Far Now,* January 23, 2007
MRG288   M. Ward, "To Go Home" (CD single), February 20, 2007
MRG289   The Broken West, *I Can't Go On, I'll Go On,* January 23, 2007
MRG290   Spoon, *Telephono / Soft Effects,* July 25, 2006
MRG291   The Ladybug Transistor, *Here Comes the Rain* EP, October 31, 2006
MRG292   The Ladybug Transistor, *Can't Wait Another Day,* June 6, 2007

MRG293   Portastatic, *Sour Shores* EP (digital only), September 12, 2006
MRG294   The Rosebuds, *Night of the Furies,* April 10, 2007
MRG295   Spoon, *Ga Ga Ga Ga Ga,* July 10, 2007
MRG296   Camera Obscura, "If Looks Could Kill" (CD single), January 23, 2007
MRG297   The Clientele, *God Save the Clientele,* May 8, 2007
MRG298   M. Ward, "Early Morning Rain" (digital single), April 10, 2007
MRG299   David Kilgour, *The Before Now: A David Kilgour Retrospective,* January 9, 2007
MRG300   The Arcade Fire, *Neon Bible* (deluxe CD), March 6, 2007
MRG301   M. Ward, *Duet For Guitars #2,* July 10, 2007
MRG302   Superchunk, "Misfits And Mistakes" (7-inch), June 5, 2007
MRG303   Big Dipper, *Supercluster: The Big Dipper Anthology,* March 18, 2008
MRG304   Arcade Fire, "Keep The Car Running" (7-inch), May 8, 2007
MRG305   Oakley Hall, *I'll Follow You,* September 11, 2007
MRG306   Imperial Teen, *The Hair, the TV, the Baby and the Band,* August 21, 2007
MRG307   Robert Pollard, *Coast to Coast Carpet of Love,* October 9, 2007
MRG308   Caribou, *Andorra,* August 21, 2007
MRG309   American Music Club, *The Golden Age,* February 19, 2008
MRG310   Shout Out Louds, *Our Ill Wills,* September 11, 2007
MRG311   Shout Out Louds, "Tonight I Have To Leave It" (CD single), June 5, 2007
MRG312   Caribou, "Melody Day" (CD single), July 10, 2007
MRG313   Arcade Fire / LCD Soundsystem, "Poupee De Cire, Poupee De Son" b/w "No Love Lost" (split 7-inch), September 11, 2007
MRG314   Arcade Fire, "Intervention" (7-inch), July 10, 2007
MRG315   Radar Brothers, *Auditorium,* January 29, 2008
MRG316   Arcade Fire, "No Cars Go" (7-inch), September 11, 2007
MRG317   Robert Pollard, *Standard Gargoyle Decisions,* October 9, 2007
MRG318   The Clientele, "Bookshop Casanova" (digital single), August 28, 2007
MRG319   Destroyer, *Trouble In Dreams,* March 18, 2008
MRG320   Spoon, *Don't You Evah* EP, April 8, 2008
MRG321   Wye Oak, *If Children,* April 8, 2008
MRG322   The Ladybug Transistor, "Always On The Saxophone" (digital single), October 2, 2007
MRG323   M. Ward, *Hold Time,* February 17, 2009
MRG324   She & Him, *Volume One,* March 18, 2008
MRG327   Caribou, *She's the One* EP, March 25, 2008
MRG328   The Rosebuds, *Sweet Beats, Troubled Sleep (Night of the Furies Remixed),* April 15, 2008
MRG329   The Broken West, *Now or Heaven,* September 9, 2008
MRG330   Julian Koster, *The Singing Saw at Christmastime,* October 7, 2008
MRG331   Shout Out Louds, *Impossible* EP, April 8, 2008
MRG333   Portastatic, *Some Small History,* September 9, 2008
MRG334   The Rosebuds, *Life Like,* October 7, 2008
MRG335   Lambchop, *OH (Ohio),* October 7, 2008
MRG336   Volcano Suns, *The Bright Orange Years,* January 27, 2009
MRG337   Volcano Suns, *All Night Lotus Party,* January 27, 2009
MRG338   The Music Tapes, *Music Tapes for Clouds and Tornadoes,* August 19, 2008
MRG340   Conor Oberst, *Conor Oberst,* August 5, 2008
MRG341   Conor Oberst, *Gentleman's Pact* EP, May 5, 2009
MRG343   Arcade Fire, *Mirror Noir* (deluxe DVD), March 10, 2009
MRG344   Telekinesis, *Telekinesis!,* April 7, 2009
MRG349   Conor Oberst and the Mystic Valley Band, *Outer South,* May 5, 2009
MRG355   Richard Buckner, *BloomeD* (digital only), March 3, 2009
MRG356   Richard Buckner, *The Hill* (digital only), March 3. 2009
MRG357   Richard Buckner, *Impasse* (digital only), March 3, 2009
MRG358   Superchunk, *Leaves in the Gutter* EP, April 7, 2009

Photo Credits

p. xv   Top: Allison Miller; Bottom: Bill Mooney
p. xvi   Top: Mac McCaughan; Bottom: Photo courtesy Brian Walsby
p. xvii Top: Photo courtesy the Scott Williams Archives
p. xviii Top Right: Barbara Herring
p. xx   Top: Bill Mooney; Bottom: Matt Gentling
p. xxii Top Left / Center Left: Bill Mooney
p. xxiii Right: Shawn Scallen
p. xxiv Top Right: Pat Graham; Bottom: Jenny Toomey
p. xxv   Dea Bacchetti; Photo courtesy the Scott Williams Archives
p. xxvi Allison Miller
p. 9   Mac McCaughan
p. 13   Bottom: Mac McCaughan
p. 17   Mac McCaughan
p. 18   Aubrey Summers
p. 19   Jenny Toomey
p. 20   Photo courtesy Jenny Toomey
p. 25   Elizabeth Ward
p. 28   Photo courtesy Jenny Toomey
p. 29   Bottom: Jenny Toomey
p. 31   Top: Jennifer Barwick; Bottom: Photo courtesy Jennifer Barwick
p. 33   Jon Wurster
p. 35   Pat Graham
p. 36   Pat Graham
p. 39   Top Right: Jenny Toomey
p. 41   Top Left: Jenny Toomey; Bottom: Photo courtesy Jenny Toomey
p. 43   Bottom: Jennifer Barwick
p. 44   Top Left: Pat Graham; Top Right: Elizabeth Ward; Bottom: David Doernberg
p. 45   Top: Pat Graham
p. 46   Bottom: Elizabeth Ward
p. 47   Photo courtesy Matt Gentling
p. 48   Photo courtesy Matt Suggs
p. 57   Photo courtesy Matt Suggs
p. 58   Maggie Fost
p. 60   Photo courtesy Jon Wurster
p. 65   Jon Wurster
p. 79   David Doernberg
p. 80   Photo courtesy David Doernberg
p. 81   Top Right: Courtesy the Scott Williams Archive;
         Bottom Right: David Doernberg
p. 82   Top: David Doernberg; Bottom: David Doernberg
p. 83   Top: Mac McCaughan
p. 84   Bottom: David Doernberg
p. 85   David Doernberg
p. 86   Top: Gerard O'Brien; Bottom: David Doernberg
p. 87   Top: David Doernberg
p. 88   Right: Claire Ashby
p. 89   Top: Jon Wurster; Bottom Right / Bottom Left: David Doernberg
p. 90   Top Left: Photo courtesy Matt Suggs; Top Right: M. Crews
p. 91   Chris Bilheimer
p. 92   Lance Bangs
p. 96   Lance Bangs
p. 99   Lance Bangs
p. 105   Lance Bangs
p. 106   Lance Bangs
p. 107   Photo courtesy Tom Scharpling
p. 109   Mac McCaughan
p. 110   Matt Steigerwald
p. 111   Phil Morrison
p. 118   Bottom: Angie Carlson
p. 119   Phil Morrison
p. 121   Liz Clayton
p. 122   Liz Clayton
p. 123   John Woo
p. 124   Photo courtesy John Woo
p. 130   Anthony Saffery
p. 135   Top: Mike Yesenosky
p. 137   John Woo
p. 138   John Woo
p. 140   Top: Phil Morrison; Bottom: Dave Fisher
p. 141   Top: Phil Morrison
p. 142   Top: Photo courtesy Jon Wurster; Bottom: Matt Gentling
p. 143   Top: Mac McCaughan; Bottom: Sandra Perez

p. 144   Top: Gail O'Hara
p. 145   Top: Aaron Stauffer
p. 146   Top: Photo courtesy Alasdair MacLean; Bottom: Mac McCaughan
p. 147   Bottom: Mac McCaughan
p. 148   Top Left: Claire Ashby; Bottom: Barbara Powers
p. 149   Spott
p. 150   Spott
p. 151   David Doernberg
p. 154   Dan Mapp
p. 161   Barbara Powers
p. 163   Claire Ashby
p. 164   Claire Ashby
p. 165   Autumn de Wilde
p. 166   Autumn de Wilde
p. 170   Marcelo Krasilcic
p. 175   Left: Laura Ballance; Right: Laura Ballance
p. 179   Brantley Gutierrez
p. 180   Autumn de Wilde
p. 181   Top Left: Mac McCaughan; Bottom: Annie Hayden
p. 182   All: Cesar Viramontes
p. 184   Top: Mac McCaughan; Bottom: Matt Suggs
p. 185   Top Left: Jon Wurster; Top Right: Photo courtesy John Woo; Bottom: Spott
p. 186   Top: Photo courtesy Matt Suggs; Middle: Mac McCaughan; Bottom: Spott
p. 187   Top: Jon Wurster; Bottom Right: Phil Morrison
p. 188   Top Left: Mac McCaughan; Bottom: Mac McCaughan
p. 189   All: Mac McCaughan
p. 190   Top: Mac McCaughan; Bottom Left: Mac McCaughan;
         Bottom Right: John Woo
p. 191   Christian Lantry
p. 192   Phil Morrison
p. 196   Mac McCaughan
p. 198   All: Jon Wurster
p. 201   Phil Morrison
p. 204   Jon Wurster
p. 205   Phil Morrison
p. 206   Phil Morrison
p. 208   Photo courtesy Jonathan Marx
p. 211   Bottom: Laura Matter
p. 214   Mac McCaughan
p. 217   Stephen Dowling
p. 218   Mac McCaughan
p. 219   Mac McCaughan
p. 220   Mac McCaughan
p. 222   All: Jon Wurster
p. 225   All: Matt Gentling
p. 229   Angie Carlson
p. 230   Anna Hovhannessian
p. 231   Top: Mac McCaughan; Bottom: Brantley Gutierrez
p. 232   Top: Stephen Dowling; Bottom: Mac McCaughan
p. 233   Left: Gail O'Hara; Top Right: John Woo; Middle Right: Mac McCaughan;
         Bottom Right: Gail O'Hara
p. 234   John Woo
p. 235   Middle: John Woo; Bottom: Chris Verene
p. 236   Top: Laura Ballance; Bottom: Matt Gentling
p. 237   Top and Bottom Right: Arne Van Peregein; Bottom Left: Laura Ballance
p. 238   Bottom: Tim Lytvinenko
p. 239   Bottom Right: Photo courtesy Spott
p. 240   Julian Koster
p. 241   Lance Bangs
p. 242   Lance Bangs
p. 245   Jeremy Gara
p. 246   Right: Jeremy Gara
p. 248   Top: Brantley Gutierrez; Bottom: Régine Chassagne
p. 253   Jeremy Gara
p. 256   Lance Bangs
p. 260   Mac McCaughan
p. 262   All: Lance Bangs
p. 263   Brantley Gutierrez
p. 264   William Marsh
p. 265   Maggie Fost
p. 272   Lane Wurster
p. 278   Maggie Fost

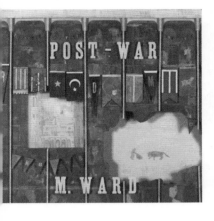

POST-WAR
M. WARD

shark quest
battle of the loons

SUPERCHUNK
"the freed seed" ep.

Pram

DIGNITY
AND
SHAME
CROOKED FINGERS

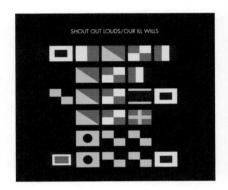

SHOUT OUT LOUDS/OUR ILL WILLS

She &
Him
Volume One

richard buckner   dents and shells

3ds BEAUTIFUL THINGS

LADYBUG TRANSISTOR

Sweet Bird of Youth
*THE*ROCK*A*TEENS*

FIELDS GET LOS

MERGE MRG 052
Breadwinner
Includes both Merge 7" singles plus three bonus tracks
burner

superchunk
foolish

neutral milk hotel
on avery island

East River Pipe
Poor Fricky

Destroyer's Rubies

White Whale
ww1

THE ESSEX GREEN THE LONG GOODBYE

the clientele - suburban light

NIXON

the Third Eye Foundation
LITTLE LOST SOUL

PIPE